RACING HARD

William Fotheringham has been the *Guardian*'s
cycling correspondent since 1994, and since then
has covered 19 Tours de France and four Olympic
Games, launched the magazine *Procycling* in
1998, and has written best-selling biographies of
Tom Simpson, Fausto Coppi and Eddy Merckx.
A racing cyclist for over 30 years, William lives in
Herefordshire with his wife and two children.

To Mick Phil
Happy cycling!
William

WILLIAM FOTHERINGHAM

RACING HARD

20 Tumultuous Years
in Cycling

First published in 2013
by Faber and Faber Limited
Bloomsbury House
74–77 Great Russell Street
London WC1B 3DA

Published with Guardian Books
Guardian Books is an imprint of Guardian Newspapers Ltd

Edited by Richard Nelsson. Typeset by seagulls.net
Printed in England by CPI Group (UK) Ltd, Croydon, CR0 4YY

A CIP record for this book
is available from the British Library

ISBN 978-0-571-30362-5

2 4 6 8 10 9 7 5 3 1

CONTENTS

FOREWORD

My first Tour de France (in 2000) saw me finding my daily pre-start refuge in the *Village Départ* with the British journalists. There were never many, yet William Fotheringham was almost always one of them. I'd head to the *L'Equipe* stand where the daily newspapers would be dished out and join them for a coffee and a welcome chat in English. They were my little bit of home, offering a sense of normality and reality in the bizarre and often lonely world I was inhabiting. They weren't the enemy – they were trusted *compadres*.

Things aren't like that any more. We leave our luxury team buses as late as possible and will often make it through an entire Tour de France without once going to the *Départ*. I no longer feel like I am sharing the journey with anybody outside of my team. There is now a huge chasm between the pro cyclist and the journalist, bridged by a team press officer and media training. This is the modern era of professional cycling and, to be frank, modern professional sport.

But this is not how cycling began. Our biggest event is the Tour de France, and it was created by a journalist, Henri Desgrange, to promote a newspaper. The race was made spectacularly over the top in order to facilitate dramatic story-telling and therefore readership. It was journalists who made heroes out of cyclists and made the Tour de France into the legendary event it has become. Sadly, this is something forgotten by the majority of people involved in the sport these days, and most of the young riders of today will never grasp quite how much they owe to the people – the press – they are advised to tread carefully around.

William and I have known each other since I was a whipper-snapper fresh from Hong Kong. We were equally incongruous members of the cycling world, him more of a rugby chap and me an expat brat. To this day I can't help but refer to him as "WILLIAM-FOTHERING-HAM!" (crisp second world war RAF fighter-pilot tone required, and behind his back of course).

William has put my career into words, from an ambitious teenager to a fallen world champion to a fervent anti-doping campaigner, team owner and father. It was when I sat with William in a London restaurant to tell him how I'd doped and lied that the full scale of how far I'd gone off the rails became apparent. The world I painted to William was a shock to him, and seeing his reaction and disappointment hit home how far removed the world I'd been living in was from reality.

In many ways William has been a barometer for me, a constant through thick and thin. He has become the go-to writer when it comes to anything cycling, and deservedly so. With the confusion that reigns currently in cycling I think it's important for us to have journalists like William to remind us of where we have come from and what we've been through. Our sport was designed to make stories – thankfully there are a few like William to write them.

David Millar

INTRODUCTION

When they named a square in Sean Kelly's native Carrick-on-Suir after the great man himself – well it was actually a bit of the road which happened to be a few feet wider than the next bit – Kelly came up with one of the all-time great Kelly-isms. It was, he said, the sort of thing that normally only happened to you when you were dead. What he meant was that it was the kind of thing that marked the end of a career or a life, rather than happening midway through.

Being asked to put together a selection of your work going back many years has a similar feel about it for the writer. It feels strange to be doing such a thing while you are still in the saddle. The brief, you are asked, is to select your best stuff. However, most journalists, I suspect, believe that their best piece is the next, or the one after that. That's certainly the case with me. In the same vein, what I suspect Kelly would have felt when the plaque went up on Sean Kelly square was that he still had more than a little to give, more races to win.

"Best" in a journalistic context is an adjective that needs qualifying. As a journalist, that "best" is not the "best you can possibly create", in the sense that a writer will craft a great piece of wordsmithery over a period of months, or years if you are Marcel Proust. It's the best within certain limitations: the best you can provide to your paper on a given day, by a given time, in a given amount of words, with a given amount of information to hand. You never have unlimited time and you never have the number of words you want to say what you want. At the back of your mind is the core journalistic principle: the paper needs to get out on time. That deadline has to be met. That "best" is also the best that the sub-editors can make of what you've written, after

1

they've checked your facts, looked at the spellings, and ironed out infelicities, contradictions or sheer stupidities. If it's a piece that has the words Lance and Armstrong in it, it's been picked over by a lawyer who knows that if he or she gets it wrong, the cost could run into millions.

As a result, each of the pieces that follows represents a snapshot of a given story or a race taken at a particular time. There is nothing to apologize for in that, but it has to be kept in mind. Journalism is born of its moment, and part of the challenge in selecting from journalistic work is that it is largely contingent, written on a given day. The pieces you will read here weren't written for posterity. This might surprise, given that we have now come to view much of cycling largely with the benefit of hindsight: how this or that doping story changes and accents the events that preceded it.

Since 1998 and the Festina doping scandal, journalists who write about cycling on a regular basis – as opposed to our colleagues who dip in and out in between covering other sports – have had to do some hard thinking about how to describe what they see in front of them each day and how to convey it to the reader. You simply don't know what the events you are seeing will mean in a week, four weeks, a year, four years, 15 years. That rider who looks so spectacularly at ease on their bike, who talks so persuasively about the unjust nature of accusations of doping, could test positive next week.

The question of how to reflect this in our writing began to occupy the minds of me and many of my peers from 1999 onwards: at times it seemed like the only topic on the table. The method I chose, consciously, was to report what was in front of me as I saw it while making sure I included as complete a back story as I could manage about the individuals involved – in particular whether they had "previous" in terms of police inquiries or positive tests – or about what scandals were ongoing on the race. The concern was not what posterity would read.

As I've said, you don't do daily journalism with that in mind. What mattered was the need to enable the readers to have the same factual information that I possessed so that they too could make up their minds, although more probably I imagined they might retain the same conflicted mix: admiration for the prowess which was on display with concern about what might be hidden. It sounds obvious, but that backstory had to be based on fact: not hunches, not assumptions, not mere connections.

The doping narrative has changed the Tour in another way for me. Over time, cycling's drug stories and their locations – say, the obscure bar where Richard Virenque bade a tearful farewell to the 1998 race – have become part of the Tour's historical fabric for me, and for the way I describe the Tour, as much as, say, the site of the forge where Eugene Christophe had his forks repaired in 1919. I think that's healthy. The history of the Tour should not be a sanitized one. If it includes the grimmer sides of human nature, the brazen lying and bizarre cheating as well as the nerveless mountain descents, battles against injury and bonkers courage in the sprints, that is as it should be: all human life is here in its complexity.

There are common threads that run through the pieces I pulled out of the 2,500-odd I found in front of me: Lance Armstrong, doping, the Tour de France, the Festina scandal, the rise of British cyclists in the Tour, Chris Boardman, Britain and the Olympics. To start with, I separated them into different sections under separate headings; then I realised that, pretty much, the Tour, Armstrong and doping at least were all intertwined like branches of ivy. So apart from an introductory section of pieces that seemed to stand alone, and a final flourish of obituaries, I put the pieces under two umbrellas: Tour de France and Olympics.

Apart from the initial miscellany that stands alone without fitting into any wider context, the bulk of what follows is covered by those two headings. The Tour initially, and latterly the Games, are where the *Guardian*'s attention has been focused in the 16 years since I was asked to become its cycling correspondent. In the 1980s, it was possible for a British writer to travel abroad to report on the feats of Sean Kelly, Stephen Roche, Robert Millar and Greg LeMond as they took on the Europeans. By the 1990s, as Kelly and company retired, that option wasn't there any more. The Tour gradually came to be seen by Fleet Street – with the *Guardian* in the vanguard – as an event worth covering in its own right; the Festina scandal raised its profile still more, while the advent of Armstrong in 1999 made the Tour an event that had to be followed. The irony of that is not lost on me.

But outside the Tour, and the doping saga, cycling has lacked coherent narratives that can be told to a non-specialist British audience, apart from the Armstrong story. The sport itself is not coherent enough in its structure: for years it has not been clear, for example, whether the best rider in the world is the world champion, the Tour winner, or the UCI-ranked No 1, let alone whether they are going to stand the test of time. The rise of the British, of Wiggins, Cavendish, Sir Chris Hoy et al, has been a delightful exception to that rule: a coherent narrative with heroes who, by and large, stuck around over the years, didn't disappear for entire seasons, didn't test positive and lie through their back teeth. It was also one that I could relate to as a cyclist in Britain myself.

The selection that follows was made for a variety of reasons. Some of the pieces seemed important at the time or are now delightfully anachronistic. There are stories I was proud to put out there before anyone else managed to – most notably an interview with David Millar the day after the 2004 Tour ended, in which he gave the first account of his doping – and there are ones that I simply had fun writing at the time. Some have emotional significance – a great comeback, a rider who stirred affection or distaste – some were experiences, good or bad, that you never forget. Some are included because they gave me a chance to tip my hat to cyclists who have never had the recognition they deserve, Jason Queally being the prime example. There are two lengthier magazine pieces, which I put in because they enabled me to go into the kind of detail that is always lacking in daily newspaper work.

There are only a few accounts of individual stages in the Tour, for which I apologize in advance. This is because most of the stage reports form part of a narrative of their own, with the various themes that develop through a particular Tour coming in at times, the next day's stage or the crash two days ago always alluded to; they stand up as a part of that greater whole rather than in isolation. Instead, to show how a Tour develops, I thought it would be more interesting to run an entire Tour diary from the *Observer*, looking sideways at every day of the 2007 race.

There are two things than run through all of the pieces: they rarely include the first person, and they are rarely judgemental. Both are personal preferences: I write about what happens and the people involved, not in order to put me or my personal opinions centre stage. I believe the writer should be discreet, almost invisible where possible. In my view, daily newspaper reporting doesn't lend itself to separating sheep from goats. That is for the columnists. I also feel that casting moral judgement is a nuclear option for a journalist: to be used with extreme caution. I became aware when writing the life of Tom Simpson in 2001 that morality is not black and white. That was reiterated to me when I interviewed Millar after he was busted in 2004: how could you not feel sympathy for the guy's emotional conflict and his resolution to do better, while condemning his deception and cheating? So too with Marco Pantani. Less so with Armstrong, although in his case it's still hard to forget what we saw in the mid-1990s: a likeable, bright young man who was clearly cut to the quick by the death of his team mate Fabio Casartelli in 1995. But that is another story. And with any luck there will be plenty more of those to be read in the next 20 years.

One virtue of a collection of this kind is that it's an opportunity to express thanks to the many who have helped out along the way.

Top of the list is Caroline, at the start of my time in journalism my partner and now my wife, who has put up with me being absent either physically or spiritually through 23 Julys on the trot (bar 2009, which I missed for reasons I explain elsewhere). Without that patience and understanding, I would be in a different profession. Our children, Patrick and Miranda, have been equally forbearing about missed birthdays and my frequent trips elsewhere.

In the 23 years since I first covered the Tour, there have been a select group of hardy souls who have survived long spells driving through France with me, my music collection and my seesawing emotions. For their support and patience over the years, my thanks go to my brother Alasdair, Brendan Gallagher, Richard Moore, Ian Austen, Stephen Farrand, Simon Brotherton and Rupert Guinness. On the Tours between 2000 and 2007 I had the assistance, at various times, of *pilote* supreme and wine supremo John Dowling, without whom those Julys would have been infinitely tougher and less entertaining. In the pressroom, there are too many colleagues to name: all have provided support, encouragement and laughs over the years. You know who you are.

I am in considerable debt to the sports editors who have given me the opportunity to cover cycling, and particularly the Tour, which is a big financial investment for a newspaper. The first was Martin Ayres at Cycling Weekly, who put me on the race in 1990. Mike Averis at the *Guardian* took a gamble and gave me the chance to work for the paper in the first place; I owe him many thanks, as I do to Ben Clissitt, whose support in the Armstrong years was vital, at a time when British success in the Tour was sporadic at best, and more recently Ian Prior for his backing into the Team Sky and Wiggins era. At the *Observer*, Brian Oliver's interest in cycling again bucked the trend in the early 2000s – his prescience over Bradley Wiggins as a future star stands out – while more recently Matthew Hancock has continued in that vein.

Producing any book is a major task, so in getting this one to the page, I would like to thank my agent John Pawsey, Katie Roden at *Guardian* Books, Richard Nelsson, Luke Bird, Kristen and Rebecca at The Curved House, Andy Armitage and Jonathan Baker at Seagulls.

However, none of what follows would be here as it is without the commissioning editors and sub-editors who were on the end of the telephone and in front of computer screens on the *Guardian* and *Observer* sports desk over the last 20 years supporting people like me. They are rarely acknowledged but their contribution is massive both on a given day and in a cumulative way over the years. Step forward Adam Sills, Nick Mason, Neil Robinson, Mark Redding, Oliver Owen, Jeremy Alexander, Ian Malin, Chris Curtain, Chris Cheers, Jon Brodkin, Claire Tolley and Steve McMillan. It is hard to overstate the value for a writer of good editorial support: a bright idea, a correctly checked fact, a supportive word or a kick in the backside at the right time. All the above supplied some or all of these over the years, for which I will be for ever grateful.

1. THE TOUR AND MORE

Where to start? The best place, it seemed to me, is in the middle of the French countryside, in a village waiting to welcome the Tour de France. A scene that is timeless, transcends doping scandals and the rise and fall of cycling within any given nation, and with any luck is one that we will see for a fair while yet. It is also a piece I remember with particular affection, as it gave me a rare chance to step outside the usual box you inhabit as a writer on the Tour – the "start-drive-pressroom-write-drive-dinner-bed" routine that makes up each day. This was also a piece that took me back to my own roots, the first time I'd watched the Tour go by in an obscure bit of la France profonde *as a cycling fan bewitched by the race for the first time.*

State visits that breathe life into struggling country
14 July 2001

Yesterday at about 10am the inhabitants of Mattexey, a hamlet deep in the verdant plains of Meurthe et Moselle, put up a trestle table protected from the elements by a rough shelter of scaffolding poles and plastic sheeting in the Grand Rue. Then they began preparing the *buvette* selling refreshments for their village's biggest day for at least a quarter of a century.

None of the old men in berets, flat caps and serge trousers could remember precisely when the Tour de France last came through the huddle of four farms and about 35 houses, more Austrian in appearance than French, on a crossroads on the D22, but they were unanimous that it was more than 25 years ago. And their fellow villagers were also of one voice: the Tour still has its place in *la France profonde*. "It gives us great pleasure, it brings the village alive, it shows the world we're here, and it brings people here," said the mayor Jean-Marc Fleurance.

"The Tour is still very important in rural France, it's important for people around the world to see Lorraine, and it's an event that brings Lorraine to life. We have been talking about it for ages."

The Tour is unique among major sports events for the way in which it goes out to its public. To paraphrase one writer: apart from war, it is the only form of international conflict that takes place on the doorstep. The welcome varies from region to region: bike-mad Brittany always produces more of a show than yesterday's run east through Alsace-Lorraine, an area which is as German in its identity as it is French. And the towns and villages through which the Tour passes – some 600 of them this year, the organisers say – all find their own ways of welcoming the race.

In one village, Vezelize, the only sign of Tour mania was a sports bike placed incongruously in the window of the undertakers and banners proclaiming "Lorraine" hung around the war memorial. In Vaucouleurs, from where Joan of Arc set out to wage war on the English, there was nothing apart from a small area marked off with tape where the local *pensionnaires* could sit undisturbed. Schirmeck had set up a vast marquee for the locals to compete in their own race using bikes on rollers; in Lutzelhouse the schoolchildren had constructed a vast cyclist from coloured paper, while one enterprising farmer at the entrance to another village had built a huge man on a bike using six-foot-high straw bales.

The only *animation* in Mattexey was a set of loudspeakers on a lawn, and the *buvette*, which the villagers expected to attract about 200 people – three times the usual population. By 11 o'clock a pile of glowing cinders had been tipped from the bucket of one of Mayor Fleurance's tractors into the two oil drums which made up the barbecue, next to the henhouse in front of Mayor Fleurance's straw barn. Sandwiches with *merguez* sausages or beefburgers at 15 francs (£1.44) a shout, beer at 10 francs, said the cardboard sign.

Apart from the Tour, Philippe Leclerc, a farm worker, said, there were few occasions now when villagers could meet, thanks to recent economic pressures and rural depopulation. "Most places this size don't have fetes any more because guys get drunk and beat each other up. They don't have dances either now. Villages can't support a bar. People have no way of socialising. There are few things that unite a village any more apart from things like this." The only other event in the village was their *repas collectif*, two weeks ago.

The locals began gathering at 9am, when the roads were closed "under articles L2213-1 to L2213-6 of the general law of territorial collectivities", but there was little for them to see. "Ah, Coca-Cola," they murmured as an occasional vehicle sped past. There was at least one man on a bike to watch, but he was towing a wheelie bin for the *buvette* and it was not until past one o'clock that the action began, with the arrival of the *caravane publicitaire*, the parade of sponsors' floats created in 1930 to keep the crowds entertained as they waited for *les coureurs*. The 250-vehicle strong *caravane* is itself preceded by a jazz band on a large blue van shaped like a kidney bean, a recent innovation which, one suspects, owes something to the fact that the Tour organiser Jean-Marie Leblanc is known for his love of trad jazz.

[Jean-Marie Leblanc, who had run the Tour since 1989, retired in 2005; the jazz band followed him…]

The lure of its free samples is what draws many of the crowds and is unique to the Tour: no other sports event is synonymous with the daily spectacle of middle-aged ladies battling like rugby forwards for possession of a small plastic key ring with the logo of a telephone bank. For parents of small children, it is a nerve-racking experience.

Bigger and brasher is better is the rule of the *caravane publicitaire*, although at least the freebies are no longer dominated by plastic bags and paper flyers, as was the case 10 years ago. This is not entirely positive, as this brings the risk of being decapitated by a flying washing bag (courtesy of Crédit Lyonnais) or packet of sweets (thank you, Haribo). Tasteless jingles have largely gone, quite possibly because health and safety people took a dim view of their cumulative effect, eight hours per day over three weeks, on the eardrums and the sanity of the *caravane's* drivers.

Through went the firemen spraying water from giant mineral water bottles (Aquarel, *l'eau minerale du Tour de France*), giant orange squares on quad bikes (Orange, obviously), the PMU betting company's pom-pom girls, carefully dressed against the chilly Lorraine winds but strutting their stuff none the less – and most popular of all, Michelin's Bibendum, alongside a precarious motorbike with its driver sitting inside a 10-foot rear wheel.

By about 2.30pm, after more than five hours of waiting, the main act arrived. Heading downhill at almost 40mph, with the wind slightly behind, riding on a wave of cries of "*les voilà*" the 185 riders in the peloton passed in a whirl of shiny spokes and brightly coloured jerseys lasting less than a minute. Mattexey's big day had come to its climax, and, as ever, it was all too brief.

This next piece marked a watershed. For cycling, obviously, because Kelly was the last of the champions who won all kinds of race all through the season. With him went an era when the sport was smaller and its champions more accessible. Also, in a small way, it closed a chapter for me: Kelly had been part of the sport since I began following it as a teenager. Later, as a journalist, I had found him a pleasure to work with as he had become more expansive since his younger days. And as cycling experiences go, this was an unforgettable one.

Sean Kelly retires
17 December 1994

The president of the Irish Cycling Federation called it "the end of an era" but the Sean Kelly years could not have finished more appropriately. His final sprint as a professional, in the Christmas

Hamper race *[in Carrick-on-Suir]* yesterday, took him across the River Suir and up Main Street to lead across the finish line outside Cooney's Bar for the 194th victory of his 18-year career.

The result was hardly surprising. It would have been a tactless outsider who dared to place his wheel in front of the local hero with several thousand of his own people watching. But aspiring amateurs throughout Ireland had been training for weeks for their ride alongside Kelly, and two of them finished close behind.

Carrick's population of 5,000 swelled overnight as every cyclist in Ireland, or so it seemed, came to pay homage to the man who won 12 one-day classics and was ranked No 1 in the world for five years. Initially the organisers expected a maximum of 500 entries but almost 1,200 appeared from as far afield as Galway, Ulster and the west of England.

The idea of combining the annual Hamper race with a mass-participation ride came to Kelly when he guested at the Rominger Classic in the summer and saw 2,000 turn out to ride alongside the current world No 1 and hour record holder. The vast turn-out in Carrick was a tribute to the household status Kelly has acquired in Ireland.

Kelly rang old adversaries and turned the top end of the start sheet into cycling's equivalent of a fantasy football team. Eddy Merckx, the greatest rider the sport has seen, flew in on a private plane between organising a horse race on Saturday and commentating on a football match. Bernard Hinault, five times winner of the Tour de France, directed affairs from a lead car, as he did on the Tour until this year. Laurent Fignon, Stephen Roche and Roger de Vlaeminck, four times a winner of the Paris-Roubaix, all finished a few seconds behind Kelly in a select lead group.

[De Vlaeminck, I seem to recall, spent much of the first two hours ostentatiously rubbing marks on the back bumper of the lead car, with his front tyre, just to pass the time.]

Packing the lanes from hedge to hedge, the vast column of cyclists took six minutes to pass as they rode in tight formation at a steady 15mph for two hours around Carrick. Then they were unleashed for a final 40mph sprint into Carrick down the Clonmel Road on which Kelly achieved one of his finest feats: winning the time-trial in the inaugural Nissan Tour of Ireland in 1985 at almost 35mph.

Perhaps the best expression of how Kelly was seen by his fellow cyclists came from the double Tour de France winner Fignon, never one to mince his words: "Kelly was a pain in the arse. I began racing when he was at his best and it really annoyed me that there were so many races which I wanted to win and couldn't win because of Kelly." The Irishman was, he added, "*un adversaire royal*".

The tone for the whole weekend was set on Saturday evening when the Irish president, Mary Robinson, entered the Sheba Ballroom at the back of the Carraig Hotel, where Kelly was to present her with a racing jersey signed by the weekend's celebrities. As Kelly, a few yards in front, milked the applause, all the Irish head of state could do was to look on in awe-struck admiration like the rest of the fans. The president of Ireland had been upstaged by the king of the classics.

The Linda McCartney team was a brief presence in the European peloton with two distinctive calling cards: its link to Sir Paul's late wife, and its vegetarianism. Plenty of colour there.

Meaty task for British veggies
14 May 2000

"Niente carne, siamo *inglesi*", "No meat, we're English." The headline in *Gazzetta dello Sport* was inevitable when the paper profiled the Linda McCartney foods team, which yesterday became the first English squad to start the Giro, the Italian version of the Tour de France, since it was launched in 1909. And it was the only team of the 20 profiled in *La Gazzetta* with a breakdown of what the riders eat in a day.

As a publicity vehicle for the ready-made veggie meals launched by Sir Paul's late wife, the team is vegetarian, a major talking point in a carnivorous country. It's a quintessentially English mixture, eccentricity plus the Beatles connection, which was irresistible to an anglophile nation where every small town has its "Oxford school" selling English courses.

In Italy, cycling is a national obsession second only to *calcio*. On Friday the team met the Pope, as did the rest of the 180 Giro starters. Yesterday they raced a 6km time-trial in Rome. Today things get serious with 125 km south towards Naples and by the finish on June 4 in Milan, more than 2,300 miles will have been covered, including mountains as big as those scaled in the Tour de France.

This is tough fare even for the giants of cycling, squads such as the mighty Mapei team, with a £5.5m budget put up by a building products company, and 35 riders to select from. McCartney receive well under £1m from parent company Heinz and – since Spencer Smith went back to triathlon and an Italian signing, Emanuele Lupi, simply failed to turn up for his first race two weeks ago – the squad numbers just nine, which is the number needed for the Giro team. Had one of the team fallen by the wayside this week, they would have turned up a man short.

Manager Sean Yates is an iconic figure in British cycling, one of the hard men, who has himself ridden the Giro and has won stages in the Tour de France and Tour of Spain. "We have to get to Milan with as many [riders] as possible, but it's going to be bloody hard for most of the team. Three of the guys have done the race before but for the others, it's going into the unknown."

What is British about McCartney is its name, its staff, its manager and, of course, its character, the plucky underdogs up against the mighty foreigners. After last year's British team failed to live up to Yates's expectations, they were sacked and replaced with a multinational mix: two Britons, an Irishman, two Australians, one Swiss, a Norwegian, a Dane and an Italian.

The better-known Briton, Atlanta bronze-medallist Max Sciandri, has dual nationality and had an Italian racing licence until 1995. He and the Swiss Pascal Richard, who is reigning Olympic champion, are long in the tooth but provide the bulk of the firepower and experience: the pair have won six Giro stages over the years.

The other Briton, the former national champion Matthew Stephens, was stacking shelves in Marks & Spencer in Crewe a year ago; Yates feels that his team's inexperience, rather than its diet, will put them at a disadvantage. "There's no proof that being vegetarian is a handicap or a bonus. I was a vegetarian until I was 20, then I went to France and everyone ate steak so I did. I cut back over the years and had my best Tour de France in 1988, when I ate no meat."

Being vegetarians creates other problems. The team can't haul lorry loads of veggie bangers around Europe – they are frozen and might go off – although there is a vast pile of tofu burgers and lasagne at the headquarters in Toulouse. Instead, they rely upon the cooperation of the hotels where race organisers book them rooms, and – like most of the teams, veggie or not – take protein powder daily.

"We just tell them we're veggie and see what they come up with," says Yates. "But 99.9 per cent of chefs don't have a clue how to make decent vegetarian food. France is the worst, it's supposed to be the culinary capital of the world, but in the chains the food can be dire."

The worst so far, he reckons, "was an egg bake in Northern France. We had it one evening, and the next day they brought it out again. They'd left it all and they'd just filled in the hole we had eaten from the day before." This was countered at a race in Bergamo, where the local vegan society cooked for the team for a week.

For Yates, getting something other than vegetable lasagne over the next few weeks will be a minor concern compared to the worry that his herbivores may get chewed up and spat out. "We've had a lot of write-ups because of the name, but you can't go for ever on novelty value. We have to justify our selection ahead of a couple of good Italian teams. We've taken places from them because of the McCartney name and because we have Pascal and Max."

There is talk of building up the team for a tilt at the Tour de France in a couple of years, but for now the aims are those of any small team in a cycle race this vast: "If we get to Milan and the organiser doesn't regret selecting us we'll have done a reasonable job."

McCartney got several riders to the finish, and more importantly won a stage along the way through David Mackenzie. Unfortunately, that was as good as it got for the team: wages began to go unpaid later in the year, and it was disbanded at the start of the 2001 season leaving its entire line-up – including a young Bradley Wiggins – high and dry. Sean Yates would go on to be a directeur sportif *at Wiggins's Team Sky before retiring in 2012.*

The Tour de France and Olympic cycling take centre stage in this collection, but Paris-Roubaix deserves its place as well. This was one of the muddier editions in recent years, and by sheer good luck there was sufficient space in the paper that Monday for an extended piece.

Riders slip up as mud swamps hell of the north
16 April 2001

A week after the Aintree epic, cycling witnessed its own version of the Grand National yesterday. The bulk of the 200-rider field in the 99th Paris-Roubaix, the third round of this year's World Cup, were eliminated in a series of mass pile-ups after 70 of the 150 miles, and the result was a mud-splattered war of attrition. It was won by a little-known Dutchman, Servais Knaven, but in reality the race was a triumph for an entire team, the Belgian squad Domo, who dominated the final 50 miles and took the first three places.

To the French, this race will always be *L'Enfer du Nord* – the Hell of the North – having earned the nickname when it resumed just after the first world war, and the journey from the French capital to the Belgian border took the cyclists through a devastated landscape of shell craters, trenches and broken trees. Yesterday, all the 55 men who struggled to the finish on the velodrome at Roubaix looked as if they had been to the nether reaches of the earth and back, unrecognisable as each one was under a thick coating of mud from the fields of French Flanders.

These days, the landscape may be more orderly, but Paris-Roubaix remains a cycling version of hell, thanks to the inclusion in the course of about 30 miles of cobbled lanes, some dating back to Napoleonic times, and others boasting evocative names: *Chemin des Abattoirs* and *Chemin des Prières*. The late organiser Jacques Goddet called this race "cycling's last folly"; the 1980 winner Bernard Hinault was more blunt: "A piggery".

Criss-crossing the fields of sugar beet, the cobbled sections double up as drains in wet weather and at the end of the wettest winter since records began they have doubled up so efficiently that they became flooded and some sections had to be pumped out during the week merely so the race could pass. On Saturday night it rained again, there were torrential April showers yesterday and the *pavés* [cobbles] turned into a cyclist's nightmare.

In places it seemed impossible for anyone to keep their bike upright, so thick and slippery was the mud. Vast puddles hid deep potholes, where cobbles were missing, adding the risk of punctures to the ever-present danger of crashes. Any problem, if not terminal, meant at best a strength-sapping chase – assuming a support vehicle had fought its way through the mire to assist – and yesterday there were few who did not either crash or puncture.

A chill wind whipping through the poplars merely added to the agony and among those reduced to a hopeless chase after the early crash were former winners such as Andrei Tchmil of Belgium and the Italians Andrea Tafi and Franco Ballerini, who had postponed retirement solely in order to compete in Hell one more time, plus the Briton Max Sciandri, who was to finish 12th.

"Hell" is geared towards cycling's older men, with knowledge of the cobbled sections vital, as is a cool head when trouble strikes. It was one of the peloton's senior members, the 36-year-old Belgian Wilfried Peeters, who took a grip on the event at its heart, the dank Wallers-Arenberg forest.

The road through the wood is a dead-straight lane just outside Valenciennes with undulations caused by subsidence in the nearby coal mines, where Zola based his novel Germinal, and yesterday it was lined with Belgian fans brandishing the Lion of Flanders as they squelched in the verges.

Here, with over 50 miles and 12 cobbled sections remaining, the leaders had been cut down to a mere 16 when the Frenchman Philippe Gaumont, second in line behind Peeters, fell heavily and broke his right leg. The confusion, as Gaumont's companions tried to avoid him, favoured the Belgian, whose usual role is as chief assistant to cycling's leading one-day specialist, last year's winner in "Hell", Johan Museeuw.

Yesterday, however, it was the turn of Museeuw to play the role of team man, and he marked what remained of the chasing group, led for much of the time by the American George Hincapie, winner on Wednesday of the Ghent-Wevelgem Classic, and a Belgian veteran, Ludo Dierckxsens.

Peeters' valiant effort came to an end in the final section of pavé eight miles from the finish, where Dierckxsens and Hincapie made their final desperate attempts to dislodge Museeuw and his two other team-mates in the Domo squad, the world champion Romans Vainsteins of Latvia and Knaven.

The pair were helped in their task when Museeuw punctured early in the half-flooded lane. He has spent the last eight months recovering from a motorbike accident which left him in a coma, but it was barely noticeable from the way he fought his way back, his bike bucking under him like a pogo stick on two wheels.

Hincapie and Dierckxsens were thus left outnumbered. "What could we do?" asked a despairing Hincapie afterwards. "One of them was on to us whenever we moved." Any of the four Domo men bar the exhausted Peeters could have won but it was Knaven who attacked seven-and-a-half miles from the finish to become the first Dutch victor since 1983, with Museeuw taking second from Vainsteins, who took over the lead in the World Cup. Hell may have been murkier than usual but the result was all too clear-cut.

In its early days, the Étape du Tour was a radical event. It was not the first sportive by a long chalk, but it was the one that brought the concept of riding these events to a worldwide audience. It was the brainchild of Vélo magazine editor Claude Droussent, whose idea of putting it on during the Tour de France was a stroke of genius. It was also a rare chance, again, to get outside the usual journalistic box on the Tour, and write about riding my bike.

King of the mountains for a day
29 June 2002

As well as being the world's longest, toughest and most prestigious cycle race, the Tour de France is also a wannabe's dream. You cannot bowl an over at Lords on the morning of an Ashes Test and fantasise about being Nasser Hussein. But any fan can put on a replica cycling team jersey and shorts, and cycle up one of the Tour's mountain passes.

Indeed, that is just what they do, in their hundreds of thousands, every July. They dream the dream in the morning, wobbling up a mountain or two at walking pace, often baring their backs to the noonday sun to horrific effect, and in the afternoon, they cheer by the roadside as the Tourmen struggle up the same strip of hairpinned Tarmac. The hardest of the hard core can go further. They pay their entry fee, train for months, and get the complete Tour experience in the *Étape du Tour*.

"*Étape*" means stage, and that is what you get: a ride along one of the mountain stages several days before the Tour comes the same way, complete with crowds lining the roadsides yelling encouragement, and *gendarmes* closing the roads to all traffic. Last July, the 7,000 *Étape* riders set off over the passes of the Aspin and Tourmalet in the Pyrenean "circle of death", one of the Tour's great, traditional mountain setpieces, first crossed by the race in 1910 amid fears that the cyclists might be waylaid and eaten by bears. These are roads which are steeped in cycling legend.

Since I began reporting the Tour de France in 1990, at least once a year some bright spark or other has asked me: "Do you follow the race on your bike?" Cycling the *Étape* wouldn't offer me that, but it would be a new way of seeing the mountains I look at every July through the windscreen of a car. It wouldn't show me what it was like being Lance Armstrong, but it would show me how the race looked from the other side of the handlebars. It was a good reason to get fit, too, because the *Étape* is not for the fainthearted – in either sense of the word. The best parallel is with the London marathon: a reasonably fit person can complete it, but it takes several months of training to attempt it with a degree of comfort or safety.

The Tour has been said to resemble a miniature sovereign state as it sweeps across the French countryside with the roads closed for hours beforehand. There was a similarly imperious feel to the start of the *Étape* as we sprinted out of the little town of Tarbes in the early morning, after being sprung from the "pens" used to prevent an unseemly rush for the front of the grid.

The leading 3,000 or so cyclists rode shoulder to shoulder across the road, each front wheel inches from the back wheel in front, seamlessly dividing for traffic islands and roundabouts, and coming back together like a river in flood at a steady 25mph.

Knowing that there is no traffic coming the other way leads to an uncanny feeling of detachment from the normal world; the pistol-packing *gendarmes* standing impassively at every junction to every farm track give the feeling of a state procession.

South of Tarbes in the Pyrenean foothills lies a little known region of fine gastronomy and steep green valleys, the Bigorre. When the clouds parted, I could catch sight of the occasional medieval castle with heraldic flag flapping, vast views across row upon row of foothills that could have been drawn by a child, and, on a 45mph hairpin bend in a wood, one of our number crawling out of a ditch.

The *Étappers* were a disparate bunch. Grizzled Frenchmen in the main, who looked as if they had known their prime back in Eddy Merckx's time, the 1970s. There was a smattering of corporate guests from the Cannondale cycle company wearing zebra-striped jerseys, one of whom I spotted taking a business call from LA halfway up a mountain. And several hundred Britons, easily spotted thanks to cycling club jerseys from Sydenham to Sheffield, their number including the legendary "unluckiest cyclist in the Sydney Olympics", Rob Hayles, for whom this was merely another day's training.

Those who wonder at the millions of spectators drawn to the Tour de France should reflect on this: there were thousands lining the roads of the *Étape*. Some were encouraging their friends – and writing their names on the road in the style of the Tour stars – but the rest had just come out of their houses and campsites, lending weight to the old argument that your average Frenchman will support anyone sitting on a bike with a look of pain on their face.

They did karaoke for us, played the obligatory accordion, sang ribald songs about the suffering in front of them ("who's tired? you, you, you" sang three small boys on one hairpin), wrote graffiti – "no to the Euro", "smash the G8" – and handed up newspapers, designed to keep the cold off our chests on the downhills, rather than to get the latest on Armstrong's progress. And, embarrassingly, they greeted my yellow jersey with cheers, both ironic and affectionate in nature.

After 40 miles with nothing more severe than you would encounter in the Chilterns, the Col d'Aspin was the first "difficulty", as the French euphemistically call mountains. In a car, it is a charming seven miles of hairpins across the high hayfields but it was an hour of hard work for the single file of *Étappers*, spread from one shoulder of the mountainside to the other, trying to steer round giant slugs that slimed over the Tarmac with a shared death wish.

"Suffering" is a facile term to use when writing about the Tour de France, but it is humbling to be reminded of what it actually entails. Instead of the aching legs I had expected, the dull pain spread slowly from my lower back to my shoulders and neck, and down into my backside. I remembered what Robert Millar, the only Briton to lead over these mountains in the Tour, had told me. "The climbers suffer like everyone else, but they go faster." The aching might be the same for a Tourman, then, but he would be travelling twice as quick. This was stage 14 of the Tour: a Tourman would have had a week or two of it before today, and could expect the same or worse tomorrow and for five more days after that until the finish in Paris.

The mental arithmetic in mountain climbing is on another level of reality. Each time you pass one of the boards saying how far it is to the top, you look at the speedometer to work out how long it will take. Disconcertingly, as you slow down there seems to be exactly an hour to the summit each time you look: seven miles a hour, six miles an hour, and so on.

The Tourmalet is even longer, steeper and more mind-bending than the Aspin, rising to 2,100m through a series of concrete tunnels to an amphitheatre of cliffs where the vultures circle past a ski-station of indescribable ugliness, La Mongie. Miguel Indurain and Eddy Merckx made cycling history by flying clear of the field on this mountain; well before the top, some of the *Étappers* were walking.

Going down a mountain, with oblivion waiting a few metres beyond the crash barriers, you are supposed to look for "the flow", which will enable you to sweep through hairpins with a minimal touch of the brakes and the grace of a downhill skier. I did not flow: I froze, with numbed fingers struggling to hold the brakes, my mind deadened by the physical effort of going up and unable to deal with the sudden transition from 5mph to 45mph.

Even in summer, the mountains can turn nasty. Climbing to the *Étape* finish at the Luz Ardiden ski-station, the weather degenerated into a gale, sleet and heavy rain; 1,500 of the 7,000 climbed off en route. Who could blame them: cold rain in the mountains "tetanises" the muscles, turns the descents into skating rinks and makes the eyes burn. But there is no way out in the Tour, if you want to keep honour intact – and that is the difference.

Since the great drug scandals of 1998, cycling has been riven with suspicion over what the participants may, or may not be, taking to help them along the way. As a reminder of the colossal physical and mental demands that the Tour makes on its participants, the *Étape* was a welcome antidote to my cynicism. The difference between the Tourmen, artificially assisted or not, and a reasonably fit mortal is brutally simple. I rode the *Étape's* 90 miles in seven hours and 18 minutes. Two days later, the slowest man in the real thing, Jacky Durand, was almost 2½ hours faster.

The devil has been a presence on the Tour since 1993, and has given colour writers plenty of material over the years. This was the sort of piece we all love to write: just run with the idea for the sheer hell of it (sorry).

Jesus battles devil for a fast buck

22 July 2000

Time was, a man would yank on a devil's outfit and chase alongside the peloton shaking his toasting fork just for the fun of it. Not any more. In a stark reminder of how commercial concerns are taking over sporting ideals, Didi Senff, a 48-year-old German bike inventor and the infamous "Tour devil", is turning his art into a business. Senff's "devilish bike show" will open at a beer museum in Schussenrieder, near Stuttgart, on August 5. His eccentric bikes are the centrepiece, including the eight-footer he brings on the Tour de France.

He has shown up on each Tour since 1993, having first been spotted on a mountain in Andorra when the Italian Claudio Chiappucci, nicknamed *"el diablo"*, was still a Tour challenger. To Germans the "red devil" also refers to the red banner flown at the one-kilometre-to-go point, so Senff dresses in a red catsuit to ululate his variant of the French yell of encouragement *"allez, allez, allez"*.

He drives a battered VW trailer van with limited washing facilities, or so the aroma emanating from the diabolical armpits suggests. Perhaps this is what put off Mrs Devil, who turned up for one Tour in matching red tights but has not been seen again.

A few hundred metres in front of the trailer's parking place, he paints 6ft-long toasting forks on the road to prepare the cyclists, who respond by throwing *bidons* (water bottles) as they pass. Last year an angel joined him on the Tour. Occasionally they stood on opposite sides as the cyclists passed. This year several small devils brandishing inflatable forks have also been prominent and a second angel has put in the odd appearance.

But surely the most bizarre spectacle was the sight of Jesus stirring on a cross in the Dordogne. For a moment it seemed that 3,000 miles of driving in the wake of the Tourmen had finally taken its toll; but no, it was a cycling fan, complete with fake tan, crown of thorns, beard and loincloth, hoping the TV cameras might notice him. Is nothing sacred any more?

Senff was probably the first fan to do the roadside dressing up thing on the Tour – it may well be down to him that we now see everything from mad cows to giant syringes and Borat – and his "career" lasted close on 20 years, although his manic energy appeared to dissipate with age. He was definitely running more slowly alongside the riders in his latter years, and his beard was tinged with grey. The last I heard, his sponsorship had fallen foul of the existential crisis that has hit German cycling due to the sport's doping problems. But he will be back, I'm sure.

2. TOUR DE FRANCE 1994–2003

The Guardian *began following the Chris Boardman story early in 1994, when the then sports editor Mike Averis decided it might be a good idea to chart the Olympic gold medallist's progress towards a possible ride in that year's Tour de France.*

That seemed highly unlikely at the start of the season, given that the Wirral racer was a complete novice in road racing. But Boardman did get that start in the 1994 Tour and he won the prologue time-trial with a ride that stunned the cycling world.

He was the first Briton to wear the yellow jersey since Tom Simpson in 1962; unlike Simpson, he actually defended the jersey. He also avoided one of the worst finish-line crashes in Tour history. This piece, written for the Guardian *on the following Monday, had to include a summary of Saturday's prologue, as the paper was, at that time, still run independently of its Sunday sister, the* Observer *and the assumption was that the readerships were not necessarily the same.*

Boardman escapes police pile-up
4 July 1994

It is an unwritten rule of the Tour de France peloton that riders with serious pretensions for the yellow jersey do not get involved in the 40mph melee of men and machines which traditionally ends a flat stage. These are too risky for all but the fastest sprinters with the steeliest nerves.

Careful inspection of the rule book enabled Britain's Chris Boardman to avoid risking his yellow jersey yesterday when the final metres *[in Armentières]* became a bloodied tangle of bent metal and writhing bodies in the worst sprint pile-up the Tour has seen since Djamolidine Abdoujaparov performed a series of somersaults down the Champs-Élysées in 1991. Ironically Abdoujaparov, who gained notoriety that year with a series of finish-straight scuffles, was in the clear yesterday and stayed that way to take his sixth career stage win.

The stack was caused by a *gendarme* taking advantage of being on the wrong side of the barriers to photograph the sprint that was led out at hellish pace by Wilfried Nelissen, the champion of Belgium, who won a stage last year at Vannes. Unaware of the 189-strong bespoked behemoth bearing down upon him, the *gendarme* stood a good 18 inches in front of the barriers – his fellows stood well back, aware that to a sprinter 18 inches is sufficient space for a double-decker bus.

With his head right down, aiming to take the shortest route to the line, Nelissen hit him full tilt and brought down a dozen other riders. Worst off was the 1992 points winner Laurent Jalabert, who was right behind the Belgian and bounced into a giant cardboard Coca-Cola can before falling from several feet on to his face.

Boardman crossed the line 29th after an untroubled first day in the yellow jersey, which he took in stupefying fashion in Saturday's 4½-mile prologue time-trial in Lille in which he broke the Tour's speed record for any time-trial stage with 34.47mph and beat Miguel Indurain by 15 seconds. Once he descended the starting ramp in Lille's baroque Grand Place, his protestations that he was "not 100 per cent", that he was "worried about his health", were put behind him.

"I realised I was on a great day," he said afterwards, adding that he had not felt as good since he took the hour record last year. That performance was achieved in the full glare of the Tour de France publicity machine, and first proved he has the unique ability to rise to the occasion – he is the first Briton to take the yellow jersey since Tom Simpson in 1962. "Super", said the Tour de France director Jean-Marie Leblanc, five times. "Unheard of" was the verdict of the five-times winner Bernard Hinault. "Incredible", said Laurent Fignon.

The rest of the caravan could only echo their words. "He demolished them," said Sean Yates, the only other British rider to have won a time-trial stage in the race. Indurain can be content with second, given that he gained four seconds on Tony Rominger, billed as his big rival. That sounds very little with about 2,000 miles to go but, given Indurain's troubled attempts to find his best form, and the fact that Rominger has been assumed to have the edge, it is an important psychological boost for the Spaniard.

Until its hellish finish yesterday's 140-mile leg from Euralille, Lille's new business area and TGV station to Armentieres, an outlying suburb, was routine, with the heat deterring the foolhardy souls who usually try to put daylight between themselves and the bunch at this early stage.

The only riders who threatened to prevent Boardman becoming the only Briton to defend the yellow jersey – Simpson waved goodbye to it after one day – were Rob Mulders and Jean-Paul van Poppel of Holland and Herman Frison of Belgium, who gained 90 seconds in the final phases before being reeled in, as is routine, by a phalanx of Nelissen's team-mates in the Novemail team. Little did they know what lay in wait for their leader.

Boardman held the lead for another two days, but relinquished the yellow jersey the day before the Tour visited Britain for two stages in the south of England.

Le Tour en Angleterre
7 July 1994

A quick spin along the route of the first stage of *Le Tour en Angleterre* between Dover and Brighton yesterday would have warmed the cockles of *[the then EU President]* Jacques Delors's heart. The multinational invasion force landed more or less smoothly, took Dover Castle by storm – after a brief traffic jam to remind the assault force that the castle was built to keep the French out – then was given a rapturous welcome along 125 miles of Kent and Sussex lanes, decked out for the occasion with multilingual greetings and flags of every hue.

Demure Tunbridge Wells was anything but disgusted: its citizens lined the High Street three deep. Biddenden, Bethersden and Horsmonden were *en fete*. Cream teas were dished out from village halls. Pubs were clearly open all day. Local farmers were charging up to £5 for parking. There were even T-shirt touts. The police estimate the crowds may have reached one million. Apart from a little road-painting – not something the highways departments approve of – they were a decorous but rapturous guard of honour. The atmosphere was that of a coronation procession in days of yore.

What shocked above all about Le Tour's first visit since 1974 was how unBritish the occasion looked, apart from the inevitable rain shower of course. The 1974 visit had been furtive, with the authorities unwilling to close any roads; yesterday the closure was better in many places than the Tour enjoys in France. And the people came out of their houses in droves, setting up barbecues and picnic tables, Thermos flasks and ice-boxes, waving glasses of wine and warm beer at the caravan. The sight of old ladies sitting outside their cottages in camping chairs waiting for the race to arrive is indelibly French; yesterday it was common from Capel-le-Ferne to North Chailey.

The day's heroes were suitably pan-European. Spain's Francisco Cabello ran out the winner after a 100-mile joint effort with France's Emmanuel Magnien. The Spaniard, who is under a suspended ban after testing positive for the steroid Nandrolone in February, left the Frenchman on the final climb of Elm Grove in Brighton, then held him off to the finishing line on the seafront. Magnien finished just ahead of Italy's Flavio Vanzella, part of Tuesday's team time-trial winning GB-MG team, who took third on the day and whipped the yellow jersey off the back of his own team leader, Johan Museeuw.

Chris Boardman celebrated his fourth place – just ahead of a ravening bunch – with clapping hands and the double-arm salute usually reserved for victory. But it was more than Pyrrhic: after spending most of Tuesday chivvying his team-mates before losing the yellow jersey, he showed his ability to recover from such a setback by holding off the field for a whole lap of the demanding Brighton finishing circuit.

Though Cabello and Vanzella took the glory, the hearts of the crowd – and 90 per cent of the placards and road graffiti – were wholly given to Boardman and Sean Yates. Boardman was overwhelmed by the support, but Yates was typically low-key. He respected to the letter the Tour tradition that the local man is given a little breathing space to say Hello to his family, with a brief attack in the Ashdown Forest and a long hug for his wife Pippa. "Yates the king, Boardman for prime minister" a placard read.

As ever European unity was not totally harmonious. Museeuw and Vanzella's GB-MG team are half-Italian, half-Belgian, and the Italians opted out of helping Museeuw and the Belgians defend the yellow jersey. As a result he was forced to call on his fellow-countrymen in the Lotto team for help in the chase behind Magnien and Cabello. Transfers on the Tour are rarely happy either and the trip through the Eurotunnel was not pleasant, for much of the race cavalcade and the riders faced delays of up to 90 minutes. The press also suffered, which did not bode well for Eurotunnel's write-ups in the French and Italian newspapers.

The 1994 Tour saw two other key events: Sean Yates's brief acquisition of the yellow jersey, and – on the same day – Greg LeMond's abandon in what turned out to be his last Tour. LeMond had given an immense amount to the race, but his exit went almost unnoticed. He has resurfaced in recent years as a strident campaigner against doping, and against Lance Armstrong in particular.

Greg LeMond retires
3 December 1994

There will be no magic comeback this time. Greg LeMond, the first English-speaking cyclist to win the Tour de France, will officially announce his retirement today. Fittingly, he will do so at a gala dinner in Hollywood. After that his only contact with the sport is likely to be in the law courts as he prepares to sue his old team.

LeMond's first Tour win came in 1986, but his dramatic victory in 1989 caught imaginations worldwide. Not only was his 8 second winning margin the closest result in the race's history, captured on the final short time-trial stage of the three-week race, but it came two pain-racked years after a shooting accident in April 1987 left him within 20 minutes of bleeding to death. Many, including the race organisers, were reduced to tears.

LeMond went on to win the world championship a few weeks later. Only a handful of cyclists, notably Eddy Merckx and Stephen Roche, had managed to win both events in the same year, but LeMond still had 30 buckshot pellets in his body, including two in his heart lining. Others had been removed from his liver, kidney and intestines. A few weeks later, to complete the dizzy rise from also-ran to top dog, he signed cycling's biggest ever contract: $5.5 million over three years with the French Z team.

It has been downhill all the way since in a steepening curve of decline: LeMond's third Tour win, in 1990, was overshadowed by criticism that he had failed to win a stage, and that his form had been appalling since the early season. Since then he has fought almost continual ill health and poor fitness: his last two attempts to complete the Tour, this year and in 1992, ended in ignominious withdrawal. LeMond's only explanation is that he has "sub-acute lead poisoning" that has made it impossible for him to perform.

After starting every year since his 1990 Tour victory convinced he could come back and defy his critics again, he is bitterly disappointed at finally being forced to admit defeat. At his home in Minnesota, he said: "I imagined being able to pull off another Tour de France and world championship at least. If you had told me in 1990 I would win only three Tours I would have said you were crazy. I have been constantly hoping to regain form, but I have always been struggling."

LeMond kept faith with the managers who had brought him to Z when the team was taken over by France's nationalised insurance company GAN, but his persistent inability to justify his salary with the necessary results, coupled with the rise this year of England's Chris Boardman, has inevitably embittered relations. Now he is threatening a lawsuit to regain money he says he is owed. "They suck," is his verdict.

"Last year, when I had a year to run of a two-year contract, they dragged me to Paris. I had to take a pay cut or they would go to court. They dropped my salary $400,000. Then they stopped paying me as of September 1." LeMond claims Boardman's victories this year, and his spell in the Tour's yellow jersey in July, have led to the rest of the team being ignored in favour of the Englishman. He said that, with Boardman, the team manager is "like a puppy following his father".

LeMond is no stranger to controversy: last year he fell out with his father over the management of his cycle company. Relations with his former team-mate Bernard Hinault, whom he beat to win his first Tour in 1986, are still strained. When Hinault won the 1985 Tour, with LeMond second, he promised to help the American win the following year. Amid intense speculation, that continues to this day, LeMond did win in 1986, but maintains the Frenchman did everything in his power to make him lose.

Hinault, who attacked persistently during the race on the spurious ground that he was softening up the opposition, denies the charge, but claims he could have won if he had so wished. "That's total bullshit," said LeMond. "Everything he did was to screw me." To keep it quits, he now says that in 1985, when he played the role of the dutiful team-mate behind Hinault, he could have won.

When team leaders quit the Tour they are allowed to climb into their team's official cars, where they are protected from the gaze of the public. When LeMond abandoned the race on the back roads of Brittany this year, he was relegated to the "broom wagon" that patrols behind the riders to sweep up those who drop out. His look of stunned disbelief as he was carted to the finish was as anguished as his grin had been ecstatic on the Champs-Élysées only five years previously.

The following year, Boardman returned to the Tour after a promising performance in the Dauphiné Libéré where he finished second to Indurain. But his Tour ended almost as it began when he crashed in the prologue time-trial. Again, this piece from the Guardian *the following Monday is written on the assumption that the readership may not have read the previous day's* Observer.

"I was going from the gun. I'd ride the same again"
3 July 1995

Stephen Roche, the 1987 *maillot jaune*, always liked to say that whereas the Tour could not be won in a single day, it could easily be lost in one. Chris Boardman, who came in search of experience, learned that lesson in the hardest possible manner after crashing in Saturday evening's prologue time-trial [*in Saint-Brieuc*]. He was picked up off the tarmac by his team manager like a stricken child and taken to hospital, his Tour over, after breaking two bones in his ankle and one in his wrist.

As he was carried on to one of the Tour organisation's private jets in pouring rain at Dinard airport yesterday morning, to be taken to Manchester and on to Arrowe Park hospital in the Wirral for an ankle operation, Boardman said: "I was going from the gun. I wanted to win. In retrospect you can say it was my fault for racing hard. It was my responsibility to decide, that's what I'm paid for."

It was a decision which, had it paid off, would have won him both a second spell in the yellow jersey and fulsome praise for his courage. He reckoned he was only 600 metres from the end of the most dangerous section of the gloomy, rain-soaked 4½-mile course, little more than 90sec into a target time of 9min, when he fell. "There was one more corner, then it was uphill all the way to the finish."

When his prologue came to its sudden end Boardman was only 2sec down on the eventual stage winner, Jacky Durand, who had ridden in earlier dry conditions. The Englishman had already raised eyebrows as he courted disaster on the course's toughest three turns, his back wheel skidding on the drenched white traffic markings.

To fit in with the growing demands of television and attract holidaymakers from the nearby beaches, the Tour organisers had scheduled the last riders to start in twilight. Nocturne races are popular in Brittany and Normandy, and are highly atmospheric – until it rains. Saturday's downpour turned the event into a 45mph Russian roulette with the *maillot jaune* as jackpot and a tarmac scraping as booby prize.

Boardman explained: "In the dim light you couldn't see which bits of the road had grip and which were smooth. It was a matter of luck which line you took because it was so dark. It was like riding on ice. Once you had chosen a course you had to stay with it."

On a shallow left-hander where riders were being radar-timed at 48mph, rider and bike parted company. Boardman slid down the tarmac on his hip and elbow, stopped only by the kerb, as behind him his GAN team car aquaplaned out of control and came within inches of running him over.

With blood dripping from a deep cut in his elbow, Boardman leant against the barriers before limping to his bike in a vain attempt to start moving again. It took just a couple of pedal strokes for him to accept the inevitable. As he tried to regain his composure he was almost hit by the next rider on the road, Maurizio Fondriest of Italy.

"You race so many times that you will fall off in one race," he said. "I'd ride the same way again. It's the Tour de France, everyone is on the edge, everyone skidded."

The 1995 Tour de France was won by Miguel Indurain, who took victory for the fifth successive year. The race was marred by a fatal accident when the Italian Olympic champion Fabio Casartelli fell on the descent from the Col du Portet d'Aspet in the Pyrenees. As a tribute, the following day's mountain stage was "neutralised" by mutual agreement among the riders.

A procession in memory of Casartelli
20 July 1995

Fabio Casartelli's six remaining team-mates crossed the line together in an emotional finish to the 16th stage of the Tour de France here *[in Pau]* yesterday. Riders were credited with some eight hours' road time, but no stage placings were announced. This is unprecedented.

The Motorola riders finished side by side, a few hundred metres clear of the bunch, a gesture not seen since the death of Britain's Tommy Simpson in 1967. It was the Tour's way of paying tribute to Casartelli, the Italian Olympic champion who died after crashing in the Pyrenees on Tuesday.

After speaking briefly to some of the team leaders all six Motorola riders came to the front with 10 kilometres to go. With expressionless faces they led the field into town and, when one of them – the New Zealander Stephen Swart – punctured, the whole field waited for him and a rider from a rival team dropped back to pace him back to the bunch.

[In 2001, Swart was to be the first rider to give a witness statement to the Irish writer David Walsh that pointed at Lance Armstrong's use of banned substances.]

Two kilometres from the line someone behind the rear Motorola rider put on the brakes and the six were permitted to cross the line together. "It was a unanimous decision," said Italy's Eros Poli, a stage winner last year. "We're all married and we can imagine our wives and children being bereaved like Fabio's."

Casartelli's death had stunned this close-knit community, men who like coal-miners and fishermen earn their livelihood by ignoring danger on a day-to-day basis. Laurent Jalabert and Alex Zulle's ONCE team wore black ribbons. "Everyone was very emotional," said Jalabert, the points leader.

Led by Swart the six Motorola riders rode to the start together amid respectful applause, climbed the podium in line to sign the riders' register, then retreated to their team cars to await the minute's silence. For some of their fellows this proved too much. Max Sciandri was among those in tears and the double world champion Gianni Bugno offered him a comforting arm.

The Col du Soulor, first mountain of the day, is one of the Tour's most magnificent playgrounds, a vast circus of peaks dotted with old snowdrifts above the dazzling green of the high meadows. The road performs a vast horseshoe turn across the gentler slopes on one side, clinging impossibly to the cliffs on the other. It was climbed with the pace and mood of a funeral cortege, with the prime at the top awarded to Motorola's former world champion Lance Armstrong. The first intermediate sprint of the day was given to Swart.

The Col de Marie-Blanque and Col de Soudet, intended to be the final obstacles in Miguel Indurain's magisterial progress to his fifth Tour win, were climbed some 45 minutes behind schedule, with the favourites controlling the pace at the front. Their feelings were summed up by Jalabert: "No one wanted to race."

Two days later, Armstrong won the stage into Limoges, turning that stage into a further tribute to Casartelli. The emotional resonance of this victory is important for what followed in the next 17 years: Armstrong's raw emotion captured the mood of the moment. Already a likeable champion, it made him all the more likeable. And when Armstrong finished first in the 1999 Tour, this day was still fresh in many minds.

Armstrong makes his fast, moving point
22 July 1995

As befits the only Texan in the Tour de France, Lance Armstrong is one of its larger-than-life characters. Miguel Indurain never says he is going to "kick ass" on a particular stage, whereas the 25-year-old from Austin leaves nobody in any doubt as to his emotions at a given moment.

So it was yesterday, when Armstrong approached the line at Limoges to take the second Tour de France stage win of his career. It followed a 25-kilometre solo break reminiscent of the escape which won him the 1993 world championship in Oslo, the same year he won the Verdun stage of the Tour. First he pointed to the sky with an index finger above his head, then with both index fingers. Then he blew a two-handed kiss and pointed again.

It was as moving a tribute to Armstrong's former Motorola team-mate Fabio Casartelli, who died after crashing on a descent in the Pyrenees, as Wednesday's collective show of emotion by the peloton, who let Armstrong and his five remaining team-mates cross the line together, a little way in front, after riding the whole stage in slow-moving cortege formation.

After the finish Armstrong was in tears, as he had been on Wednesday. "I did it for one person. I started suffering in the last few kilometres but I had Fabio in my mind the whole time. He motivated me the whole way. I felt very bad at the end but I kept thinking about him. I did it for him. In the past I have won bike races and I tried to make a little show because I think the show is good for the people. Today was no show. I was only trying to recognise Fabio."

As well as a tribute to the late Olympic champion, Armstrong's victory was a personal triumph at the end of a stage completed at an average of 27mph through the woods of the Dordogne. Having lost what looked like an assured victory last Saturday, when he was out-sprinted by Russia's Sergei Outschakov at Revel, Armstrong was taking no risks in what was his team's last chance for a stage win this year.

Armstrong broke away from a 12-man group, which never looked as if it was going to find the collective willpower necessary to catch him. "I didn't like my chances in a sprint," he added. "I had a feeling nobody would react. There were too many of them." Bales of hay lined the back lanes of the Dordogne and Haute Vienne regions as the holiday crowds waved the riders through. Indurain's 1995 harvest is almost complete as well: nothing short of an act of God will prevent him winning today's 30-mile time-trial around the Vassivière Lake, where Greg LeMond clinched his 1990 victory.

With that in the bag, all that will remain is tomorrow's traditional promenade to the Champs-Élysées, where victory number five should be completed, and he equals the record of Belgium's Eddy Merckx and the Frenchmen Jacques Anquetil and Bernard Hinault.

Miguel Indurain did indeed go on to win that Tour, meaning that since Armstrong's disqualification from the results, he is the only man with five consecutive Tour victories to his name. The Spaniard is renowned as a "boring" Tour champion. This is unfair. He was a rider who could attack when he needed to. In hindsight, I think I am a little unfair to Indurain in the following piece in describing him as a rider who only took the Tour seriously; he was always prominent in the world championships, for example. However, I would stand by the point that he was the first rider to specialise in the Tour, to the detriment of cycling as a whole.

Spain's colossus of roads
23 July 1995

Unless the unthinkable happens in the shape of yet another of the crashes which have marred this Tour de France, Miguel Indurain will today become the first man to win the greatest bike race on earth five years in succession. This feat eluded the three other five-times champions: Jacques Anquetil of France (who took from 1957 to 1963), Eddy Merckx of Belgium (1969–74), and another Frenchman, Bernard Hinault (1978–85).

Indurain's is a unique record of domination in an event as testing as the Tour. It reflects his absolute dedication to one task. The idea of Indurain missing the Tour in order to ride the Tour of Spain, as Merckx did in 1973 after winning four Tours on the trot, is ludicrous. Indeed, Indurain has missed his home event three times in order to prepare for the Tour. He has faced huge criticism in Spain each time, although once the Tour has been won the critics have shut up.

Just as Anquetil, Merckx and Hinault dominated their respective eras, so Indurain bestrides his, a genial, tanned colossus, who has grown in confidence and stature since his first Tour win in 1991. So tough and specialised is the Tour that no rider has finished second to Indurain more than once, and the men who were runners-up in 1992, 1993 and 1994 all failed either to start or finish the next year. The Spaniard stands alone.

Like Merckx, Hinault and Anquetil before him, Indurain has become the point of reference for all cycling's major stage races. When another rider wins the Tour of Spain or Italy the debate begins about whether he can take on Indurain in the Tour. Indurain's hegemony through his time-trialling ability has sparked debate about whether the route should be more mountainous, and whether time bonuses (seconds deducted from a rider's overall time) might be awarded on the major mountains to encourage the climbers, who spend each Tour trying to claw back the time Indurain gains in the time-trials.

For all his domination of the Tour, Indurain has never achieved the status of *patron*, cycling's equivalent of senior mobster, who controls the day-to-day activities of the rest with an iron hand. Hinault, the "badger", was the most extreme example of a "patron" – if the field began riding aggressively when he was not feeling good, they would be reminded that at some point he would be in a position to make them suffer, and often they would stop. The "badger" used to protest that it was for their own good, but that had all the veracity of a gangster extolling the virtues of protection. Merckx and Anquetil would rarely step in directly, but resorted to displays of team strength to make the point.

Indurain carries no such clout. Getting heavy is not his style. Whereas on occasion Hinault was seen punching demonstrators who blocked race routes, the number of times Indurain has been seen to lose his temper can be counted on the fingers of one hand. He only races seriously in the Tour and the events leading up to it. The rest of the year he is relatively anonymous, if unmissable due to his size and perfect style.

The difference is also in his attitude to racing. Pierre Chany, a journalist who has followed 49 Tours de France, says: "Indurain is best compared to Anquetil in the way he races. Like Anquetil, he is calculating, saves energy and bases his Tour de France around the time-trials. The other two were more unpredictable: they could come to the fore at any moment when you weren't expecting it."

Of the four, Indurain is by far the most conservative. Merckx holds the record for stage wins in the Tour, 34 in seven appearances, and he is followed by Hinault with 28. Indurain has won just 10, and during his four previous Tour wins, and the fifth which is expected today, he has restricted himself to taking victories in the time-trials, which is where it really matters. For Hinault, taking a Tour without winning a stage was an affront, to avoid which in 1982 he risked losing the Tour itself in order to fight the sprinters on the final stage to Paris.

While he never reached the extremes of Merckx, who won one Tour with a lone break of over 100 kilometres through the mountains, even the calculating Anquetil won stages in the Pyrenees and the Alps on the way to his victory in 1963. Indurain would view such a success as a distraction from the job in hand, which is winning the race when it ends in Paris.

No one doubts that he is capable of winning mountain stages – in 1989 and 1990, before he reached the height of his powers, Indurain took convincing victories in the Pyrenees. He says of his reliance on the tactically vital but emotionally unappealing time-trial: "I would be stupid not to use my strongest weapon, but I can understand people not liking it."

Indurain's conservatism extends beyond his style in the Tour to his approach to the whole season. Whereas Merckx, Hinault and Anquetil all notched up victories in one-day classics on a regular basis Indurain has never even started some of the greatest one-day events as he might fall off and wreck his preparation for the Tour. It has worked for him, but it has only contributed to the Tour's disproportionate importance. Merckx, known for his insatiable desire for victory anywhere, says, with some frustration at Indurain's incredible strength: "He's too limited in what he does to satisfy me totally."

It is a question of priorities. Indurain lacks the overweening pride of a Merckx or Hinault, although when unleashed as he was this year on the stages to Liège and La Plagne, he is equally awe-inspiring. A practical man, who was happier on the family farm than at school, he does not deal in abstracts: "Nothing concrete comes out of victory," he once said. "A man who makes furniture makes something concrete." His horizons may not be broad, but the result of his total focus is utterly impressive. His manager José Miguel Echavarri, who raced with Anquetil, says: "Of the four, Indurain is the best all-rounder." After a moment's reflection he adds, tellingly, "For the Tour."

The 1996 race saw the end of the Indurain era, at the end of one of the most dramatic stages in the race's history: this leg to Les Arcs. Johan Bruyneel, who made such a spectacular exit from the road, is now notorious as Lance Armstrong's former directeur sportif, *but was just another journeyman bike racer at this point.*

The rain and pain of the long-distance cyclists
8 July 1996

It was the first of many sobering sights over the weekend: on Saturday morning most of the field scrambled for shelter from a torrential rain shower five minutes before the start of the 200-kilometre stage from Chambery to Les Arcs. They ran for trees, cars, the podium where they sign on each day: any port in this storm.

It must have struck each man that, if they thought the last week of crashes, torrential rain and stress had been hell, they had been kidding themselves. The road south from Hertogenbosch was merely purgatory: hell lay in the next 125 miles.

There had been stress and danger aplenty since the race left Holland six days earlier. Headwinds meant that stages scheduled to finish during television prime time ended when riders would normally be receiving massage or eating dinner. The wind led to fears of crashes as the rain battered down every day. "It has rained more in five days than in the last five Tours," said Miguel Indurain's manager José Miguel Echavarri.

Alex Zulle summed up the feelings: "I am getting to sleep at three in the morning, we are eating like pigs, as quick as we can every night, and just go to our rooms. I'm taking pills to sleep. There are rumours that the stages will finish later next year: if they do, I won't be here."

The stress mounted as the pile-ups happened, and fights broke out among the riders: the American Lance Armstrong had a close encounter with the Frenchman Gilles Bouvard, which he put down to "the nerves of the race", while Andrei Tchmil of Russia and Peter Luttenberger of Austria – who could be this year's surprise climber – came to blows over dangerous riding.

But all this was as nothing compared to Saturday's epic. On Alpine climbs such as the Col de la Madeleine and Cormet de Roselend, suffering is prolonged in cold rain, while 60-miles-per-hour descents in blinding spray have taken on a new resonance since the death last year – on a fine dry day – of Fabio Casartelli.

It was no surprise then to see Zulle – one of the Tour's more accident-prone riders – finish covered in grazes after two slips, one of which took him into a ditch. It was Zulle's third smash in three days. Johan Bruyneel's crash was heart-stopping: the Belgian went straight on at a left-hand bend, rode between a large rock and a crash barrier and flew into a ravine, followed by his bike. His fall was broken by a tree, and he clambered back up to finish 20th and in a state of shock.

There had been speculation over the long-term effects of the rain and stress, and they began to be seen on Saturday. Stéphane Heulot, the *maillot jaune*, was just one of many riders suffering from tendinitis caused by the wet and cold. In such weather the tiny tears in the musculature do not heal as quickly. In addition, when riders crash – and there are few who have not – the bruises and strains make them sit awkwardly on the bike, causing compensatory injuries.

Heulot's tendinitis made itself felt as he climbed the Madeleine but his true *calvaire* came on the Cormet de Roselend, where the pain became so intense that he was forced to quit in tears. The last time a *maillot jaune* withdrew during a stage was in 1983, when Pascal Simon of France rode for several days with a fractured shoulder.

Chris Boardman and Laurent Jalabert also waved goodbye to their chances on the Roselend, as Boardman finished 29 minutes off the pace. "I have never been close to tears on the bike before," he said, "but, when I saw the group go, that was it, all my chances of glory disappeared up the road."

Jalabert suffered a similar fate, losing 12 minutes, but the biggest shock was Indurain's demise just two miles from the top of the climb to the finish in Les Arcs. Indurain failed to eat or drink enough during the stage – an elementary mistake and a sign that he was probably in trouble from early on – and was reduced to begging for a bottle. That he was eventually fined and had 20 seconds added to his time for taking water from a rival team was entirely in the spirit of a thoroughly nasty opening week. Forty riders have left the Tour in seven days and more will follow if the heat arrives this week.

The 1996 Tour was a race of transition. Bjarne Riis and Telekom's dominance raised eyebrows, as did the sudden emergence of the Festina team as a dominant force. In the absence of any evidence other than an uneasy feeling, they had to be taken at face value; it would only become apparent two years later that in that Tour they were doped up to the eyeballs. As the next chapter shows, this warning from Jean-Marie Leblanc was incredibly prescient.

Tour call for drugs clean-up
26 October 1996

The organiser of the Tour de France yesterday made an unprecedented call on cyclists and their team managers to combat doping.

Speaking at the presentation of the 1997 Tour de France route here yesterday, in the presence of the leading four finishers in this year's race, Jean-Marie Leblanc called on leading cyclists to maintain "moral probity in the face of temptation", to remember the example they set to children and warned that failure to do so could be "suicidal". Only if the problem was solved, he said, could cycling champions remain "the giants of the road".

The appeal, unprecedented in a gathering of this nature, follows the publication on Thursday of an open letter signed by Leblanc, Daniel Baal, the president of the French Cycling Federation, and Roger Legeay, Chris Boardman's team manager at GAN. The letter called on the governing body, the International Cycling Union, the IOC and the French ministry of sport to take swift action in improving drug control.

"We must do it for the future of the sport and the credibility and image of our champions," Legeay said. Two of Legeay's riders this year tested positive for steroids. "We must have a credible sport; we must give credibility to dope control."

The latter is a reference to the bizarre situation whereby urine samples taken from riders after all major cycling events may be tested for steroids and amphetamines, but may not be used to find the synthetic performance-boosters erithropoetin and human-growth hormone. That has given rise to persistent warnings from riders and drug experts that both substances may be widely used in the sport.

The tour will be one of the most mountainous for years, with three stage finishes at high-altitude ski stations in the Pyrenees and Alps: Andorra, l'Alpe de Huez and Courchevel. The mountains are packed into the tour's second half after a long run down France's western side from the start at Rouen.

Lance Armstrong is mentioned briefly in the 1996 Tour piece [The rain and pain of the long-distance cyclists]; he made no impression on that Tour apart from that fight and quit before the race reached the Alps, complaining of poor form. Unbeknown to him, he was suffering from testicular cancer, which was announced to the world that October. The initial stage of his comeback to racing – his attempt to get a contract at the end of 1997 – was fraught. My belief is that the bitterness this engendered him coloured the rest of his career. His

feelings can be measured simply: the interview which follows was
written after Armstrong called me from the US – at his expense –
and ranted about the iniquities of European teams for the best part of
an hour. It is rare for any sportsman to call a journalist long distance
and pay for the call.

Armstrong's uphill ride at prejudice
27 September 1997

Lance Armstrong, America's leading road rider, is out of work and angry. A double stage winner in the Tour de France and the 1993 world champion, he seems to have won a year-long battle against cancer but none of Europe's professional team managers is willing to take a chance on him or pay him what he feels he is worth.

Armstrong, who turned professional after the Barcelona Olympics, plans to race again next season. He is negotiating with the American professional team sponsored by US Postal Service and has received offers from several European teams, but he describes their offers as "insulting" and "completely disrespectful". He feels "very bitter" towards the continental cycling establishment.

His comeback would be certain to generate immense publicity for the team he joined, so Armstrong infers that managers are not prepared to gamble on a rider who could fall victim to cancer again. "People are unwilling to take the risk. I think the impression is that I am still sick and bald and weak. But I am nothing like a sick person."

Early in October 1996 the Texan was diagnosed with testicular cancer, which looked life-threatening when it spread to his lungs and abdomen, but since he finished chemotherapy at the end of January he has been cancer-free and puts his chances of being permanently cured at "95 per cent". He also believes that he can return to the level of fitness which gave him two one-day Classic wins in 1995 and 1996.

"Just getting rid of the cancer and all its effects on my body means that there is no reason why I couldn't be better than before. I would have raced this year but the doctors felt strongly that I should take a year out."

When Armstrong did not come back this year it was rumoured that he had fallen out with his team, sponsored by France's biggest telephone credit company, Cofidis. They signed him last September, before cancer was diagnosed.

"Initially they were very supportive," he said. "When I announced the cancer they said they would honour their commitment to me 100 per cent but two or three weeks later, when I began the fight against it, they began to waver on that and a couple of weeks later, when I was at the hardest stage, they tried to get out of all of it."

Shortly before Armstrong announced that he was open to offers for next year he was released by the French team, who reportedly then offered to rehire him at less than one-tenth of his previous salary. The annual income of a fully fit rider of Armstrong's quality and record would usually be in the half-a-million pound bracket.

Somewhat ingenuously, Armstrong insists that he is not in the sport for a few dollars more. "I don't need to race a bike again for a lot of reasons," he said. "I don't need the money, the results or to be away all the time. But it means a lot to prove what I can do after what I went through, mentally and physically, with the chemotherapy. It was just so awful. To be competitive again would say a lot for chemotherapy and the cancer community."

His reasoning is that he has a certain price which he feels he is worth, if only out of regard for his past results. "It's not like I have to earn the money. I feel I am worth a certain amount out of respect for everything I've done in the sport, the fact I was world champion and had the results I had."

To some extent Armstrong's experience mirrors that of America's last cycling hero Greg LeMond, who won two Tours de France. He came close to death after losing a lot of blood in a shotgun accident in 1987, and ended his career embittered by contractual wrangles when he was diagnosed as suffering from lead poisoning. He has not visited the Tour de France since his retirement in 1994.

"I will never forget the experience of the last three or four weeks," says Armstrong. "It's very unfortunate and very sad that sport can treat one of its champions like I have been treated. I never understood why LeMond was so bitter but now I completely understand. To be forgotten about and pushed out without any support is an amazing feeling and it says a lot about cycling. It is a sport where you can replace anyone."

His threat never to ride another race in Europe will evaporate if this weekend's negotiations with US Postal go to plan but his bitterness against the European cycling world is certain to add frisson to what should in any case be an emotionally charged comeback.

Jan Ullrich is now mainly known as Lance Armstrong's biggest rival and as one of the many riders implicated in the Operación Puerto blood doping scandal [see Chapter Five]. In 1997, however, he was feted as a possible winner of five Tours, thanks to the effervescent – and presumably drug-fuelled – form he had shown that year and in 1996. By the following spring there was incredulity at how much weight he'd put on during the winter after his Tour win.

Tour winner who carries a heavy burden
9 May 1998

It is make or break time for the Tour de France winner Jan Ullrich. After a disastrous spring, during which he was mocked by the media and took a pasting in virtually every race he rode, the German has gone into hiding at his home in the Black Forest in a desperate attempt to find form.

Ullrich will cover 1,100km next week under the supervision of Peter Becker, his trainer since childhood and the man who built the East German cycling system. It is, say his team, a crucial phase of his build-up. With just over two months until this year's Tour de France starts in Dublin, the 24-year-old is overweight, under-raced, and his chances of winning the event for a second year running are in jeopardy.

The Tour winner's most recent outing, in the Grand Prix of Frankfurt on May 1, gave grounds for cautious optimism as, at last, he was able to hold on to the front runners. Crucially, given the spotlight the German media have placed on him, he did not make a spectacle of himself in front of his home crowd in his country's biggest race.

The days when a Tour winner was expected to win all year round ended with the retirement of the five-times champion Bernard Hinault in 1986. Tour contenders race selectively, building their fitness through the spring to peak in late June, and aim to hold their form for six weeks at most. This is what Ullrich did last year.

This spring, however, his build-up has been appalling. He has failed to start races which he rode last year, failed to finish the toughest events on his schedule and has spent much of those races which he has finished as last man on the road. In March he reached rock bottom in the Tirreno-Adriatico stage race in Italy, when he stopped after 22 miles before even reaching the first hill.

After finishing last year's Tour weighing 73 kilograms (11st 6 1/2 lb), he did too little, ate too much and ballooned to 85kg at Christmas. Now he is a more respectable 78kg but he needs to lose about a kilogram per fortnight to start the Tour on July 11 at the correct weight. "It's possible, but only just," says his team manager Rudy Pevenage.

Ullrich's weight gain meant that when he began racing in February he was forcing his body to work too hard, simply in order to haul himself over the hills. This meant he had difficulty recovering between races and became tired and vulnerable to illness: a bout of flu put him out for a fortnight in March.

Embonpoint is only one of Ullrich's problems. A rider's performance in the Tour depends on the number of kilometres he has spent in the saddle, how much racing he has in his legs, as the jargon has it. Ullrich has missed so many races – he has completed two-thirds of the kilometres he did last spring – that he may not have the basic endurance to perform in the Tour. Last year, after a perfect spring, he struggled in the final few hilly stages.

Ullrich's team agree with his critics that he cannot afford to be troubled by another problem which will cause him to miss any more races. "If he has just a cold, or anything which puts him out for a couple of weeks, we'll be really worried," said Pevenage.

The German media, so quick to rush to the Tour last year to hype up their new hero, have fallen on Ullrich as they fell on Boris Becker in his lean years. A radio show commented that the German people wanted to know about two pairs of buttocks: those of Ullrich, and Claudia Schiffer. "They are bastards," said Pevenage.

In France, where they like their Tour winners at least to race respectably, there has been undisguised fury in the cycling establishment. The newspaper *L'Equipe* – which sponsors the race – ran a picture of Ullrich, flab and all, on its front page with the comment "unworthy of his stature".

The Tour organiser Jean-Marie Leblanc said: "His conduct is unworthy of a Tour winner. It's unforgivable." The world No 1 Laurent Jalabert said it was "pitiful" to see Ullrich struggling and the double Tour winner Laurent Fignon accused him of "professional misconduct".

"He has only himself to blame if he put on so much weight," said last year's runner-up Richard Virenque, presumably trying hard not to smile. Ullrich has apparently worked that out as well. "He will be more careful in future: he has learned his lesson,"

Pevenage says grimly. If he fails to win a second Tour, the lesson will be expensive indeed.

The 1998 Tour de France was billed as a showdown between the little Italian climber Marco Pantani – of whom more later – and Ullrich, who had lost weight by hook or by crook and was in decent shape by the start. That year marked the most ambitious "international" start the race had ever seen: the Grand Départ *and three days racing in Ireland.*

Riding on Eire
6 July 1998

Pat McQuaid, one of the organisers of the Tour de France's Irish stages, finally realised the scale of what he had achieved last week when he walked down the main street of his home town, Bray, on the route of stage one just south of Dublin. "That's been a rickety old road for as long as I can remember but last Monday they shut it down for two days and now it's perfect, brand-new lovely tarmac." Similar sprucing-up operations have been taking place the length of south-east Ireland since the Tour de France route was announced last October; virtually all the 240 miles the Tour will spend on Irish roads have been resurfaced. The build-up gained new intensity in recent weeks as the towns along the route published plans for a fete lasting far longer than the few minutes the riders will take to pass through small communities such as Sean Kelly's Carrick-on-Suir and Stephen Roche's Dundrum.

Tallaght, close to the start of Sunday's loop through the Wicklow Hills, is, according to its publicity, *"en Tour"* for a full week before its few seconds of glory. Cork, where the riders finish a week today before flying to France, is "in gear for its biggest festival ever", lasting three days, with entertainment including a vast street parade of French history. Carrick-on-Suir has become "Carrick-on-Tour", holding seminars, literary evenings, amateur cycle races and a timed race to the next town up the river Suir, Clonmel, with the prize of a car for anyone who can beat the record set, of course, by Kelly.

The campaign to bring the Tour to Ireland has lasted several years, led by McQuaid, currently president of the Federation of Irish Cyclists, and his English business partner Alan Rushton, the man who ran the Tour's 1994 stages from Dover to Brighton and Portsmouth. Kelly, one of cycling's most respected figures, and Roche, Tour winner in 1987, have both done their share of discreet lobbying.

Two factors clinched Dublin's bid to host the start: one was the support of the Stena ferry line, which is taking three vast vessels off its scheduled routes to transport the Tour back to France next Monday. The other was France 98. The clash between the Tour start and the World Cup finals meant the Tour had to go far from its homeland, to a nation which had little chance of reaching the final. The Tour organisers looked at recent soccer form, added in the fact that Jack Charlton was not in charge any more, and the Irish bid was on.

The Tour has never been so far from home, yet it is starting in a nation with a tradition in the race which goes back 35 years, to the day when a stocky, dark-haired young man named Shay Elliott broke away from the peloton in northern France to win the stage at Roubaix, taking the yellow jersey. He was to hang on to it for three days.

Jean-Marie Leblanc, a former professional who has organised the last 10 Tours, remembers asking the Irishman for his autograph in the Pas de Calais back in the 1960s. Elliott met a tragic death a few years later but Leblanc's fondness for English-speaking cyclists and things anglophone has blossomed.

Elliott was a bulldog of a man, with what the Tour loves to call the Irish temperament. Leblanc recalls that he had the reputation of being *"un attaquant, un gentleman"*. On Friday the Tour organisers will lay a wreath at his grave in the little churchyard at

Kilmacanogue, just south of Dublin, where the Tour riders will pass on Sunday en route to the Wicklow Hills, which rise in their green magnificence behind the graveyard.

The other Irish Tour stars will be recognised as well. After Saturday's prologue time-trial in the heart of Dublin the first proper stage of the Tour will have a ceremonial start in O'Connell Street, but the flag will be dropped to denote the start of racing in front of a sculpture in Dundrum commemorating Roche's achievements. Stage two will have a ceremonial sprint outside the Sean Kelly Sports Centre in Carrick, en route to the Cork finish.

Kelly won his first stage 25 years after Elliott, Roche arrived at the Tour in 1983 and for a decade the Irish could boast a redoubtable presence in the world's greatest bike race, with Kelly's dependable, bespectacled sidekick Martin Earley, a stage winner in 1989, to back up the two stars.

The Kelly-Roche effect led to a Tour of Ireland, sponsored by Nissan, where the pair took on all-comers from the top of the European game. Leblanc, then in his early days as Tour de France organiser, was invited to the race as a guest and, so rumour has it, he was plied liberally with Guinness and introduced to "the *craic*".

Kelly's lengthy reign as No 1 in cycling's computer rankings and Roche's magic year of 1987, when he won the Tour, the Giro d'Italia and the world championships, a feat only Eddy Merckx had managed, brought everything to Irish cycling except another Roche or Kelly. There will be no Irish starters in this year's Tour and there are no amateur hopefuls displaying signs even of matching Earley's solid yet modest career, let alone reclaiming the heights scaled by Roche and Kelly.

McQuaid, as president of the Federation of Irish Cyclists, hopes *Le Tour en Irelande* will leave some tangible benefit, in terms of an influx of new membership, once the ferries have pulled out for France and the hangovers have subsided. But increasingly there is a feeling that the era of Kelly and Roche was a one-off event in Ireland's relatively obscure cycling history.

Unlike the stages in Britain four years ago, when the local councils hosting the stages complained of a lack of government support, the Irish government has stumped up two million punts for the Tour start. The President, Mary McAleese, will host a dinner for team managers; the Prime Minister, Bertie Aherne, will present the first yellow jersey after the prologue time-trial; and Dr Jim McDaid, Minister for Sport and Tourism, looks set to be a ubiquitous presence.

Gaining government support, and the necessary finance, was the biggest challenge but others have arisen. The Irish police, the Gardaí, have been involved in a pay dispute and there were strong signs that they would take industrial action – which is known in Ireland as the "blue flu" as it involves calling in sick en masse – on the days the Tour was due. With 3,000 Gardaí operating a road closure which will effectively pedestrianise Dublin for this weekend, and operating security to prevent what one organiser called "a Grand National-type episode", their absence could have been catastrophic.

Ironically, given that the Tour's Irish trip is intended partly as a homage to Roche and Kelly, there was a little local difficulty involving the 1987 winner and the four-times points victor. The dispute between Roche and l'Evenement, Rushton and McQuaid's company, was over the level of the 1987 winner's fee for working on the Tour and culminated in a lengthy Sunday newspaper interview in which Roche claimed he had been responsible for the Tour's decision to come to Dublin, and he would leave Ireland in disgust at the way McQuaid had treated him.

That seems to have been resolved, as has the question of whether the Tour should pass through Sean Kelly Square in Carrick, initially considered too dangerous by the Tour organisers, who have become safety conscious after a spate of pile-ups in the opening week of recent Tours. The locals were outraged but some discreet lobbying by Kelly ended in a compromise.

All that remains now is to get the Tour infrastructure and caravan to Dublin – this week's job – and then to get the 3,500 Tour personnel, 1,200 international media and 1,500 vehicles to Brittany in time to start next Tuesday's stage in the port of Roscoff. This is the greatest logistical challenge the Tour has faced in its 95-year history; the plans for future Tours depend on it being carried out with the minimum of disruption to the riders and caravan.

Rushton and McQuaid hope the British government will be inspired by the Irish experience to back a London bid for the start in 2004, a date already pencilled in provisionally by Leblanc. The Tour organiser's intention is that a successful Irish start will strengthen his case for a spectacular depart to the first Tour of the new millennium – from one of the French West Indies. Today Ireland, tomorrow the New World.

It was indeed a case of today Ireland, tomorrow the New World, but not quite the New World any of the Tour caravan had envisaged, including journalists like me. As for the dramatis personae *of the Irish start, Pat McQuaid went on to head the Union Cycliste Internationale from 2005 onwards, while Alan Rushton continued to organise bike races, going on to run the PruTour of Britain in 1998 and 1999. He now works mainly in the Far East.*

3. FESTINA LEAVE, ARMSTRONG RETURNS

When the 1998 Tour caravan arrived in Dublin, it did so minus one key member: Willy Voet, a soigneur – a helper responsible for massage, race food and basic medical care – at the Festina team. Voet had been arrested by French customs while driving to the race with a car-load of drugs, mainly EPO. It took a while for the crisis to break. The Festina scandal and its aftermath was a watershed for the sport, although not, as many of us hoped at the time, a point that marked the end of a drug-riddled past and a doping-free future.

A week into the Tour, Festina were thrown off the race, although they did not go willingly. The fact that the Tour organisers were willing to countenance them being anywhere near the start of the stage, having barred them from the race, indicates just how hard it was for the men who ran cycling to come to terms with the shocking facts that were emerging on a daily basis. When compared with today's zero-tolerance policies, it is also an illustration of how attitudes have hardened – and rightly so – over the last 10 years.

New chapter in saga of the pedallers and the peddlers
19 July 1998

After a week of crisis as its biggest ever drugs scandal unfolded, the Tour de France avoided becoming a farce yesterday only at the last minute, when the cyclists of the Festina Watches team went back on their decision to start the stage, even though their director and masseur have been suspended as a formal investigation has begun. As French President Jacques Chirac watched from his holiday home on the route, his country's greatest summer institution was in a state of crisis.

Festina's team at the Tour included the darling of the French public, Richard Virenque, and the current world champion, Laurent Brochard, as well as the double Tour of Spain winner Alex Zulle. They were banned on Friday night after team *directeur sportif* Bruno Roussel was charged by magistrates in Lille with supplying banned drugs for use at sports events.

Roussel's lawyer told the press his client had admitted that riders, team doctors, masseurs and team management were all involved in administering performance-enhancing drugs under medical supervision. This was felt to be necessary in order to prevent a situation in which the riders risked their health by obtaining the drugs for themselves.

Since police sources in Lille had revealed a team masseur had been arrested and that his car contained a large quantity of two undetectable drugs – the blood booster erythropoietin and human growth hormone – there had been little doubt the drugs were destined for the Tour.

However, Roussel's confirmation that the drugs were intended to be used by his riders to improve their performance in the race meant the Tour's management had no choice but to ban the team. "Doping took place on an organised basis in the Festina team," said the director-general of the Tour, Jean-Marie Leblanc.

But yesterday morning, several of Festina's riders, led by Virenque and Brochard, were adamant that they would turn up at the start of the seventh stage, a 58-kilometre time-trial. "I do not accept the decision," said Virenque. "A press release is not enough for us to leave the Tour. We will start." The response of the Tour organisers was that the riders could start, but that their times would not count.

Then Virenque and his team-mates bowed out of the Tour at a brief press conference in a bar near the stage finish. "Legally we could continue, because we are only witnesses in this case, we

58

have not committed any offence. We are leaving for the sake of cycling and the Tour de France," said Virenque, before dissolving into tears.

[This "press conference" in the Chez Guillou bar tabac is now the stuff of legend among senior Tour hacks; one I know stumbled on it while in search of cigarettes after after working late the night before, as the announcement the team were being thrown off the race came at about 11pm.]

The Festina case may be only the tip of the iceberg. "You cannot deny that a quantity of other riders are doing the same thing, that is certain," said Frenchman Cyrille Guimard, who won seven Tours as a team manager between 1976 and 1984. He added: "The riders are victims of the doctors and the sponsors who pay the doctors."

There have been persistent allegations in recent years that there is a vast trade in undetectable drugs taking place in professional cycling and, due to the amounts seized, the Festina affair lends weight to this. So does the revelation yesterday that in April, mechanics from another team taking part in the Tour de France, Dutch squad TVM, were stopped by customs near Rheims and found to be transporting 104 syringes containing erythropoietin.

There is no test for erythropoietin but the Union Cycliste Internationale carried out blood checks on 53 of the Tour field yesterday. The tests ensure that riders do not have a red cell count so high that it might lead to heart failure; in other words, they ensure that if erithropoetin is being used, it is being done under medical supervision. All the riders passed, as they usually do.

Virenque and his colleagues did not ride yesterday's time-trial but, like Banquo at the feast in Macbeth, they were there in spirit. The stage, like all the Tour's time-trials, was sponsored by Festina, official timekeepers to the race. "Free Festina", "We want Festina" and "No tour without Festina" said the placards on the backroads through the exquisite Correze countryside.

As expected, the 1997 winner Jan Ullrich opened his campaign for a second, successive victory by finishing 1min 10sec ahead of American unknown Tyler Hamilton, taking over the race leader's yellow jersey from young Australian Stuart O'Grady. The German's main challenger is now set to be French national champion Laurent Jalabert, who finished only 1min 24sec behind. The race now heads for the Pyrenees, but the riders probably have other matters on their minds.

This piece pretty much sets the tone for how I and other journalists would write about the Tour in the post-Festina years when a major scandal unfolded; drug revelations and their implications first, bare facts about the race second. The fact that this time-trial marked Tyler Hamilton's emergence is an exquisite little irony in itself. The Tour continued, with daily revelations from the police inquiry – which set the tone for the leaks that would be the hallmark of all French and Italian drugs investigations – and an increasing sense of unrest among the riders.

Jalabert the reluctant leader as the big family breaks up
25 July 1998

The Tour de France likes to consider itself as one large international family, which has united for three weeks each July for the last 95 years to celebrate the country's greatest annual fete. Yesterday *la grande famille du Tour* seemed riven after two weeks of unfolding scandal, its members united only in acrimony.

The scandal could not run deeper. The Tour's biggest star Richard Virenque spent Thursday night in police cells; he and his nine team-mates were strip searched and interrogated by police investigating the traffic in banned drugs. Virenque's Festina Watches team, the stars of last year's race, have spent the last fortnight shopping each other to the police over who provided whom with drugs and on what basis.

60

Yesterday, a week after it was revealed the TVM team were the subject of another police investigation, the Tour organisers issued a communique on the matter. It ended: "The dignity, the profound values of sport and morals which the Tour de France bears, and its exemplarity deserve to be respected by everyone."

Dignity was in short supply when the riders went on strike yesterday morning *[at the start in Tarascon-sur-Ariège]*. They were clearly arguing among themselves over whether to race or not. One party, led by the French champion Laurent Jalabert and including Britain's Olympic bronze medallist Max Sciandri, wanted the stage to be abandoned; Jan Ullrich's Telekom wanted to race and they were backed by other team managers and the race officials.

If further evidence of the breakdown of the *grande famille* were needed, it came when Jalabert's team manager Manolo Saiz was involved in a scuffle with one of the race officials as the palavering reached deadlock and when police ordered team mechanics to get back in their cars. Later Saiz and Jalabert accused the race organisers of using moral blackmail to make the riders race. *[Saiz went on trial in a Spanish court in January 2013 for his alleged role in the Operación Puerto blood doping affair.]*

The *paterfamilias* of the Tour is the former professional cyclist and journalist Jean-Marie Leblanc, who has aged visibly since the Tour left Dublin. His authority has diminished equally rapidly; yesterday, as he attempted to persuade the riders to move on, he got in his red Fiat and started driving away four times. Eventually he was forced to issue an ultimatum: if they did not start within 10 minutes the stage would be cancelled. These were not the acts of a man who is in control.

The daily drip-drip of revelations about Festina has shown the "profound sporting and moral values" of the Tour – or parts of it – in stark relief. The team's manager admits supplying banned drugs on a systematic basis; the riders are said to have been forced to pay a percentage of their bonuses into a secret fund to finance the purchase of the drugs; one rider has been linked to robberies of erythropoietin from a hospital in Poitiers in February. The moral values seem to be those of the jungle.

There is a terrible inevitability about all this. Two years ago revelations by the former cyclists Gilles Delion and Nicolas Aubier in the newspaper *L'Equipe* and in a report prepared for the Italian Olympic Committee by Dr Sandro Donati pointed to a vast underground trade in erythropoietin to fuel the needs of professional cyclists. The response of the men who run the sport was to hide their heads in the sand.

Hein Verbruggen, head of the Union Cycliste Internationale, dismissed the testimony of Delion and Aubier as that of embittered men and effectively called Donati a crank. The Canadian Guy Brisson, who was working to perfect a blood test for erythropoietin received little support and gave up for lack of funding.

What shocks about the Tour's drug seizures is the sense of impunity in the milieu. The TVM team had known for a week that they were the subject of an inquiry by French customs, yet banned drugs and masking agents were found in their team hotel as recently as Thursday. Voet, the Festina masseur, clearly felt few inhibitions about transporting his team's drugs to the Tour in an official car.

The impression of a world where normal rules do not apply is reinforced by the UCI's system of blood thickness tests, brought in as their response to the Donati report. The tests, said the UCI, could not stamp out erythropoietin use but would prevent riders dying from its abuse. The clear implication was that the UCI felt powerless to stop the drug being used.

The prime mover behind yesterday's protest was the world No 1 and French national champion Laurent Jalabert. The UCI was his main target: "The UCI have turned up at the race 10 days after they should have done and they have brought a whole load of new rules which mean nothing, which are meant only to make them look good in the eyes of the world." The word he should have used is window-dressing.

Appropriately yesterday's protest took place at the location the Tour calls kilometre zero, marked by a 6ft high, phallic inflatable tower next to which a *gendarme* waves the start flag. After the scandal and the strike the Tour will have to look for a fresh start: "*repartir à zero*" as the French put it.

Only the two world wars have stopped the Tour, which General De Gaulle insisted should go ahead after the "events" of 1968 to signal to the world that the country was in a state of normality. Whether it continues this year, and in years to come, seems to lie yet again in the lap of the French government; their police and their inquiries hold the key.

There were moments in 1998 when it seemed impossible that the Tour would go on, most notably when police swooped at Aix-les-Bains in the final week and the Spanish teams walked out en masse. But it did so and was marked by one of the better wins of the 1990s. Marco Pantani had returned from a horrific injury in 1995 to harass Ullrich mercilessly all the way for a victory which sealed the Italian's place in the pantheon... for about 10 months.

Tour de France: Legal eagle's swoops eclipse superb Pantani
2 August 1998

Two personalities have dominated the 1998 Tour de France: the little climber Marco Pantani, who yesterday became the first Italian to win the world's greatest bike race for 33 years; and the Lille prosecutor Patrick Keil, leader of the investigation into the supply of banned drugs which has dominated the Tour, completely eclipsing Pantani's remarkable performance.

Pantani is now one of just seven men who have won the Giro d'Italia and the Tour de France in the same year but Keil and his team have achieved a first in prosecuting a Tour cyclist for trafficking in banned drugs. On Friday charges were laid against the Italian Rodolfo Massi, King of the Mountains until the police took him from the race on Wednesday, and winner of a spectacular stage in the Pyrenees. Banned drugs and cash were found in his hotel room. The 32-year-old, in his 12th season as a professional, was released on bail. *[The charges were subsequently dropped against the Italian.]*

In three and a half weeks, Keil has produced sensation after sensation. Three cyclists in the world's leading team, Festina Watches, have admitted publicly that they used the banned blood-boosting hormone erythropoietin. The Festina manager, Bruno Roussel, has admitted that the team were systematically supplied with banned drugs and has been charged. The team's secret fund to finance drug purchases has been uncovered. The doctor at ONCE, the Spanish squad who include French champion Laurent Jalabert, ranked No 1 in the world, has also been charged with supplying banned drugs.

Simultaneously Keil's opposite number in Rheims has charged the manager and doctor of the Dutch TVM team with supplying banned substances. Both investigations began with seizures of banned drugs in team vehicles, from TVM's lorry in March, and a Festina team car on 8 July. The timing of the Festina seizure can hardly have been coincidental, coming as it did immediately before the Tour, when the investigation would receive maximum media exposure.

Professional cycling is a small, tight-knit world which has developed its own grey morality in the last 100 years. This is the first time that its values have come up against the black-and-white of any legal system; the impact as the two have collided, with riders detained and stripsearched, team hotels and vehicles searched, has almost ripped this Tour apart.

Twice the riders have gone on strike, seemingly because they could think of no other response and they have squabbled among themselves as they have struggled to find a common position. The race organisers have looked on in impotence. The show has struggled on, but one team, Festina, have been thrown off and another five teams have quit, including the entire Spanish entry.

Already, there are signs of change. The organiser, Jean-Marie Leblanc, who vets entries to the race, yesterday stated: "We will look more closely at the morality of the teams. For example, we will not take a team who have had a rider test positive in May. No more teams who have been raided by the police."

These steps sound basic; for cycling they are radical advances – this year Festina were allowed to include in their team a rider who was on appeal over a positive test for steroids; last year the organisers permitted the Italian MG–Technogym team to ride in spite of the fact that Italian drug police had seized drugs from their hotel.

Yesterday, it was raining in the lush fields of Charolais, backdrop to the 52-kilometre time-trial, last act before today's grand finale on the Champs-Élysées. The finale will not be as grand as usual – only 96 cyclists will make it to the French capital, just over half the number who left Dublin three weeks ago.

Thanks to an epic win on Monday at Les Deux Alpes, and a fine defensive operation against last year's winner, Jan Ullrich, the following day at Albertville, Pantani gained so much time in the two Alpine stages that yesterday he really did not have to worry about his closest challengers, Ullrich and the American Bobby Julich. His main concern was a freak crash or puncture.

As expected, Ullrich was the winner yesterday, taking his tally of stages to three. He was unable to dislodge Pantani but jumped to second overall, cutting the Italian's victory margin to 3min 31sec and pushing Julich into third place. The Colorado man has the consolation of being the first American to finish on the podium since Greg LeMond won in 1990.

[Julich later became a directeur sportif *at Britain's Team Sky, but left having admitted the use of banned drugs.]*

The pattern of this Tour has been that the racing has tended to take first place only at weekends, when the French police go off

65

duty. So today Pantani's lap of honour on the Champs-Élysées will be a joyous affair; the little Italian is universally liked by fans and media for his spectacular attacks in the mountains.

Tomorrow, however, six TVM riders and their masseur will face questioning in Rheims; more cyclists from the Française des Jeux and Casino squads will be questioned in the near future. The Tour has stuttered to its end; the drug investigations will run and run.

A year later, the Tour caravan assembled again, reeling from a series of further scandals, most notably Pantani's ejection from the Giro d'Italia after failing the haematocrit test. That pretty much dispelled the notion that he might have won the 1998 Tour "clean".

Last chance to banish the drug pedallers
28 June 1999

When it starts on Saturday in the Vendée, this will be the Tour de France of crossed fingers, murmured prayers and nervous glances over Lycra-clad shoulders. For there was no precedent for last year's disastrous, scandal-stricken Tour – either in the closed world of cycling or the broader world of sport.

This year's race has been billed as "the Tour of reconstruction", but events took on a momentum of their own last year after Willy Voet, the masseur with the Festina team, was stopped by customs police on a quiet back road where France meets Belgium in the suburbs of Lille, on his way to the Tour. This year's race cannot afford further scandal, but the revelations, police inquiries and confessions have not let up in the intervening 11 months and show no sign of doing so.

The only shred of credibility left to last year's Tour came from the victory of the little climber Marco Pantani, the most charismatic cyclist in the peloton. This disappeared when Pantani was expelled from the Tour of Italy earlier this month, for failing a blood test intended to restrict use of the red blood cell boosting hormone erythropoietin (EPO).

His reputation is now in tatters, after last week's publication of a report by the Italian Olympic Committee, the CONI. Its findings were gloriously Byzantine and couched in official language. The conclusion was that the available evidence indicated "with extreme probability" that Pantani had taken banned drugs to increase his red cell level. However, it added that there was no hard evidence from a positive drug test, so there should be no further proceedings.

The report merely interpreted Pantani's blood test readings during the Giro and other races. It concluded that his readings of haematocrit – the percentage of solid matter, mainly oxygen-carrying red cells, in the blood – were so consistently high, they could not have been achieved without the administration of EPO. It also touched on his habit of measuring his haematocrit level with his own personal centrifuge, and pointed out that his iron level – another indicator of EPO administration – was between five and 50 times the norm for a healthy athlete.

A new inquiry has since been set up into allegations that Pantani and a team-mate switched blood samples so that he could avoid being caught by a similar blood test at the end of the 1998 Tour of Italy, which he also won. Pantani strenuously denies any involvement with banned substances. "I am a clean rider, my conscience is clear," he said after his Tour of Italy expulsion. "I have nothing to do with doping and I do not need drugs to win." Pantani, however, will not start the Tour and, due to inconvenient injuries, neither will the two men who preceded him down the Champs-Élysées in the yellow jersey.

Jan Ullrich, the winner in 1997 and runner-up in 1996 and 1998, is taking legal action against *Der Spiegel* after the German news magazine accused him, together with the rest of his Deutsche Telekom team, of the same systematic drug use as that practised at the Festina team. Ullrich, who has not failed any drugs test, has also insisted that he is drug-free. "I have not taken drugs, I do not take drugs and I will not take drugs," he said recently.

The 1996 Tour de France winner, Bjarne Riis, was accused of drug taking by a former team masseur in a Danish television programme, and also had his high blood readings revealed in an Italian newspaper. He was questioned for a full day by a magistrate leading one of the eight current inquiries in Italy into drug use in the sport.

As the man who provided much of their drugs for 20 years, Voet is perhaps the man who understands best what drives cyclists to use banned substances. His view is that cyclists are addicted to the effects of EPO in particular, because its performance-enhancing properties are so dramatic, and that they cannot kick the habit. "A whole generation of cyclists is shafted," is his conclusion in his best-selling autobiography, *Breaking the Chain*.

As last year's Tour collapsed into chaos, there were many observers who hoped the participants would realise that their sport and their livelihoods would be in grave danger if they did not change their ways, and quickly. For the past 15 years, the Tour has been the hub of the professional cycling season and if it is damaged beyond repair, the sport will wither.

The major sponsors of the Tour – Coca-Cola, Crédit Lyonnais, Fiat – have served notice that they will review their backing if this year's race is hit by further scandal. Team sponsors – notably La Française des Jeux, the French national lottery, and the chemical company Mapei – have let it be known that, for them, the next drug scandal will be the last.

But evidence of a change of heart in the peloton is patchy at best and limited to France. French team doctors are confident their charges are approaching the sport in a new way, and there are signs that teams in the peloton who are now clean are putting pressure on those of their peers who are clearly not, to change their ways. Younger riders have suddenly begun to appear in the results: older men who were ruling the roost until 1998 have, curiously, slipped away.

The cyclists have been slow to react, but in France, sponsors, race organisers and the French Cycling Federation have realised they are facing economic oblivion and acted accordingly. Riders now undergo in-depth health checks which alert them to the effects banned drugs have on their long-term well-being: all too predictably, the results of the first checks showed the bulk of French cyclists to be suffering the side effects of erythropoietin and corticosteroids.

Ethical conduct charters have been drawn up by teams in an attempt to set definite parameters, removing the ambiguities which in the past meant drug taking was tolerated or swept under the carpet. Cyclists who test positive or who are involved in police inquiries are now suspended from competing until the issue has been settled. A confirmed positive test now results in the sack, whereas in the past it would have been met with sympathy similar to that given to someone caught speeding.

There are those who say there is now an atmosphere of paranoia over what medicine a cyclist can or cannot take, and there is clearly doubt about where sports medicine ends and doping begins. "We have got to the point where prescribing vitamin C is a problem," said one cyclist. "My team doctor doesn't like doing prescriptions for me any more, and, for example, will tell me to go and buy a diarrhoea medicine in the chemists."

Some French cyclists are talking about *"cyclisme a deux vitesses"* – two-speed cycling – by which they mean they are no longer competing on a level playing field because some riders in Spanish, Italian and Dutch teams are artificially assisted and they are not. "We will know at the end of the Tour and perhaps, if the French riders have come nowhere, that will be the time to call it a scandal," said the former yellow jersey holder Cedric Vasseur, when asked how the phenomenon might affect this year's Tour.

[There was not a single French stage win in the 1999 Tour – the first time this had happened for many years.]

Last week, as the CONI committee was pondering Pantani's plasma levels, there were uncanny echoes of Voet's arrest when another Festina team car, driven by a masseur and conveying banned drugs, was stopped by police on the Franco-Belgian border. Compared to the cocktail of heavy-duty hormones – EPO, growth hormone, testosterone – which Voet had been conveying 11 months earlier, the soigneur was carrying a lightweight mix of creatine, which is not banned, and medicines which included cortisone, which is banned. The team promptly sacked him for transporting substances which had not been provided by the team doctor.

The greatest change can be seen in the Tour's attitude to its biggest hero of the mid-1990s, Richard Virenque. When Virenque was thrown off last year's race, together with the rest of Festina, following confirmation from the team manager that he had run a system of drug administration, the race organiser Jean-Marie Leblanc revealed he had met the four-times King of the Mountains, and shared a hug and a tear as "Rico" left the race. Virenque is among the riders who have been excluded from this year's Tour by the organisers.

[This article was written a week before the Tour started – Virenque was admitted to the race at the very last moment after the intervention of the Union Cycliste Internationale which ruled the Tour organisers had no legal right to stop him riding.]

They are taking other measures. All team personnel will be given a general warning about use of drugs by the organisers on Friday, at which they will be reminded that the race's rules provide for the exclusion of any rider or team who might damage the race's image – the grounds on which Festina were disqualified last year.

And on Saturday, before the Tour's prologue time-trial begins at Le Puy du Fou, every starter will undergo a blood test – and no doubt they will all have Pantani's fate at the back of their minds.

70

A similar mass test at the Giro put two riders out of the race before it had even begun. The Tour organisers' attitude is that only world wars have stopped the race, so the fete will go on. At best, it will be three weeks of paranoia. In a worst-case scenario, further police action will result in irreparable damage.

The 1999 Tour was, of course, Lance Armstrong's first "victory"; it was also marked by the departure of one of the few riders in cycling at the time who was openly riding "clean" – Christophe Bassons.

Drug-free Bassons is sent packing
17 July 1999

This is a Tour of mixed messages, summed up perfectly by a vignette on the final hill of yesterday's sumptuous stage through the Massif Central. On one side of the road stood a mad German dressed as the devil, on the other a lunatic Frenchman got up as an angel. The peloton passed between the two: it is impossible to tell which of the riders are on which side in this race.

It is exactly a month since the Tour organisers announced which cyclists would not be welcome at the race for "ethical reasons". Yesterday the stage started without the one man who should have been welcomed here, the young Frenchman Christophe Bassons, who is the one rider in the peloton to have taken a high-profile stand against doping.

Bassons, who rides for the La Française des Jeux team, was, according to a team-mate, made to leave the race on Thursday night by his manager Marc Madiot after the two had an argument when the rider was late for dinner because of media interviews. Madiot appears to have felt that Bassons was not focused on the race and was spending too much time with journalists, which for some people on this Tour is a crime in itself.

The media attention probably was affecting Bassons' race but it seems shortsighted not to support him. La Française des

Jeux are in danger of losing their sponsor, the French national lottery, which is worried that the team are presenting the wrong image. Madiot has spent a total of five days being questioned by police over drugs; a former member of the team's management company, Bertrand Lavelot, is under formal investigation by the authorities over the alleged running of a drug-supply ring. Bassons was perhaps the team's best chance for survival.

"For a Tour without doping, come back Bassons" read a plaintive placard at the roadside. It was, of course, outnumbered by posters in support of Richard Virenque, the cyclist who was said by the Tour organiser Jean-Marie Leblanc to "crystallise the doping problem"; the organisers did not want him in the race but he was awarded entry by the Union Cycliste Internationale, the world governing body.

Bassons went to ground yesterday, Virenque was prominent on the podium, putting on the King of the Mountains jersey which he is likely to wear to the finish in Paris. It seems a strange way for cycling to leave its doping problem behind.

In hindsight, the following piece acclaiming Lance Armstrong's Tour victory seems bizarre, but the backstory is everything. All those of us who reported on the Armstrong Tour of 1999 had also covered his comeback from cancer; it was impossible to separate the two. Many of us had also known the Texan before his cancer and respected his charisma and openness. This was one of sport's greatest comebacks. It was also proven, six years later, to be one of the great sporting frauds.

Armstrong's giant leap
24 July 1999

When Lance Armstrong won his first Tour de France stage at Verdun in 1993 a journalist asked him where he was aiming for, given that his namesake Neil had made it to the moon. The young Texan, already turning heads with his cocksure personality and utterly focused racing style, modestly replied: "Mars". Two and a half years ago, when Armstrong was diagnosed with testicular cancer which required immediate surgery, France, its Tour, the Champs-Élysées and the yellow jersey might as well all have been on another planet. Yet tomorrow, in a sporting and medical miracle, he is set to ride into Paris as winner of the Tour de France.

By any standards, even compared with men who have not had cancer, it will be one of the biggest Tour wins in recent years. Armstrong has defeated the time-trial and mountain specialists on their home terrain in crushing style and has exuded confidence, which has extended to his mainly American US Postal Service team. There is every chance that today he will extend his lead to the greatest margin since Bernard Hinault's 14min 34sec in 1981. He already leads Fernando Escartin by a bigger margin than Miguel Indurain achieved in any of his five Tour wins.

The journey has been remarkable. No endurance athlete has ever recovered from cancer as advanced as Armstrong's, including surgery and chemotherapy, and returned to dominate an event as lengthy and demanding as the Tour. Once he left the Saint David hospital in Indianapolis, determined to continue his career as a cyclist, he was in uncharted waters.

"I'm totally confused. I'm going completely into the unknown. A comeback like this has never been attempted. I don't know, my oncologists don't know and obviously the sport doesn't know," he said when he set up his base in Nice at the end of 1997. Tellingly, he had no idea how much furniture to buy: he had no idea how long he would last in professional cycling. He had announced his cancer to the world in a telephone press conference at the start of October 1996; by the end of the month he was weak from chemotherapy, had lost his hair and bore the scars of surgery to remove lesions from his brain, abdomen and lungs.

"Initially, in the first two weeks, I thought I might die, but at the point where they discovered the lesions on my brain I was prepared to die."

Armstrong's comeback has always begged one question: why should anyone want to attempt to return to the most demanding endurance sport in the world when they have just cheated death? He has recalled the time he was diagnosed. "I was scared that I was going to die, and I was scared that I would lose my career. I'm not sure what I thought first: "I'll never race again" or "I'm going to die". That's why it makes sense."

There were other motivations: the fact that a successful comeback would prove to the cancer community that it was possible to combat the disease has been crucial to Armstrong. In addition, once he was healthy again he was seized with the desire to prove to a sceptical European cycling establishment that he could return to his previous level.

He is still bitter at the way he was treated by European teams during his illness. The Cofidis squad, who hired him just before his diagnosis, attempted to renegotiate his contract downwards as he lay in hospital. Other teams simply did not want to pay him anything like the salary he earned before he became an invalid.

"I was talking to Roger Legeay, the manager of Chris Boardman's team," Armstrong has recalled. "He told me what I was expecting was "the money of a big rider". Teams think if I get sick again it will be bad publicity. There is no precedent for what I went through, maybe I'm naive or stupid, but I would have thought that people would want to be part of the story."

He is still bitter about the lack of belief in what he has achieved. On Wednesday, replying to the newspaper *Le Monde*'s story on the fact that minute traces of a corticosteroid had been found in his urine, he said: "This is the story of someone who was not given any chance, everyone said I could not come back. I saw the same mentality when I wanted to find a team, and no one wanted me because they said it was not possible."

[With hindsight, the corticosteroid positive was a pointer to the fact that Armstrong was not clean. However, compared to the Festina drugs seizure with its industrial quantities of EPO, or the massive

fluctuations in blood levels revealed during the Pantani saga, it felt like relatively small beer at the time.]

There have been false starts in the past two years as Armstrong became "completely terrified that the illness was coming back". In March he left the Paris-Nice stage race and was on the point of quitting. Several weeks of monastic seclusion in North Carolina prompted another rethink, and that marked the start of the upward trajectory which has taken him to the verge of victory in this Tour.

The principal pointer towards his current performance was Armstrong's fourth place in the Tour of Spain in September last year, after which he reflected that even racing in the Madrid sierra in hail and snow was nothing like as bad as being treated for cancer. He had never climbed mountains with the ease he showed then, but during his illness his physique had changed, with the loss of the broad swimmer's shoulders which were the product of triathlons he raced in his youth.

He has another explanation: "I was half dead and was put back together by the best doctors in the world. Perhaps the illness was there for a while and I was training and living with it. Perhaps when I got rid of it, that helped me. You can imagine if you have an advanced form of cancer what it does to your body."

He has also pointed out: "To race and suffer, that's hard. But that's not being laid out in a hospital bed in Indianapolis with a catheter hanging out of my chest, with platinum pumping into my veins, throwing up for 24 hours straight for five days, taking a two-week break and doing it again. We've all heard the expression "what doesn't kill you makes you stronger" and that's exactly it."

Perhaps the same will be true of the world's greatest bike race. Even after the drug scandals, police inquiries and revelations of the past year, the Tour de France still inspires awe at the physical and mental efforts it demands of its participants, from the yellow jersey to the *lanterne rouge.*

Its attraction for its international crowds which, on the evidence of this year's roadsides, are still as warm as ever in their affections, has always been founded on the fact that most people ride a bike and can have some idea of the physical effort involved. One thing sets this year's race apart from the 85 that have preceded it: only Armstrong and the rest of the cancer community truly know what it has taken to win.

As for the bigger picture, the best that can be said is that it was confusing, as it has remained since then. This summary attempts to make a little sense of it all.

Tour of transition riddled with doubt
26 July 1999

There were no strikes, no police raids, no arrests, no positive drug tests and no riders prevented from "working" because of "ill health". The Tour de France lives off drama, crisis and controversy, but the event billed as "the race of renewal" arrived in Paris relieved that the only drama over the three weeks and 3,250 miles was the Lance Armstrong miracle.

After last year's Tour de Farce, this was the Tour of doubt. The contradictions were perfectly illustrated when Richard Virenque rode on to the Champs-Élysées in the wake of Armstrong's US Postal Service team – tradition demands that the winner's team-mates lead the race into the heart of Paris – and promptly attacked.

Virenque won the polka-dot jersey of best climber for the fifth time in six years and is now only one King of the Mountains win away from equalling the joint record-holders, Lucien van Impe and Federico Bahamontes. But the organisers had not wanted him to ride, and he only made it to the start when the Union Cycliste Internationale took fright at the arguments of his lawyers.

Appropriately the organisation's vice-president handed him his bouquet at the finish, after which Virenque said he would like to come back and win the race next year. It was hardly the outcome the organisers were expecting; nor would they have wished to see three of the Festina cyclists they threw off the race last year, Virenque, Laurent Dufaux and Alex Zulle, finish in the top eight.

Zulle and Dufaux were suspended until June 1 this year after admitting the use of erythropoietin in the wake of last year's Festina scandal. The UCI reduced their bans by one month in the expectation that they would not have sufficient racing to be fit for the start of the Tour. But they finished runner-up and fourth respectively and should thank the governing body for its leniency.

The Spaniards Fernando Escartin, pushed from second to third overall by Zulle during Saturday's time-trial, and Angel Casero, fifth, have reason to feel aggrieved but, given the peloton's unwillingness to discuss drug issues, they are unlikely to comment.

The doubts in this Tour revolved around the willingness and ability of the UCI to combat the drugs problem, and the extent to which last year's scandals have encouraged riders to stop taking drugs.

The race organisers and some of the riders insist they can see changes in the way the racing is done. Others, such as the French Cycling Federation's medical officer, consider that the peloton is divided into those taking fewer or no drugs – largely French, in the aftermath of last year's police inquiries – and those set in the old ways.

The answer to the first question lies in the confused little episodes which did not destroy the credibility of the race as a whole but made one wonder about the coherence of the men who run the sport. The only cyclist to leave the race over doping, the Belgian Ludo Dierckxsens, winner of the stage to Saint Etienne, did not actually fail a drug test but merely admitted using a banned substance for therapeutic purposes. Apparently he did not have a prescription, but there was confusion over this.

There was also confusion over a new test for corticosteroids, which have been widely used in cycling and are now detectable; no one knew whether it was experimental or whether positive tests would carry sanctions. One rider tested positive for a corticosteroid in the first week but apparently he had a medical certificate; questions are now being asked about the large number of cyclists who suffer from asthma and pollen allergies.

The mix of confusion and paranoia meant that Armstrong's use of a cream for saddle sores was blown up into a minor scandal. The one rider in the bunch who spoke up about his desire to race without drugs, the young Frenchman Christophe Bassons, received no support from his peers or the race organisers, felt ostracised and quit.

"Light at the end of the tunnel" was the verdict of the race organiser Jean-Marie Leblanc, who did not specify how bright the light was or how long the tunnel. The French sports minister Marie-George Buffet put it differently: "A Tour of transition." Renewal will take longer than expected.

The day after the 1999 Tour ended I drove north with Guardian *photographer Tom Jenkins to chart the next step in Armstrong's triumphant progress through Europe; the idea that the Tour winner would be racing the next day raised eyebrows, but it was firmly in the old tradition.*

Armstrong hits the money trail
27 July 1999

On Sunday the Champs-Élysées, on Monday Spoor-straat in [Boxmeer] this little Dutch village just inside the border with Germany. The end of the Tour de France did not mark the start of a period of well-earned rest for its stars, including the winner Lance Armstrong; for the Texan and many of his fellow finishers, it is the beginning of a series of lucrative appearances such as last night's 25th "Day after the Tour" race.

Armstrong's asking fee last night was said to be about $12,000 for a two-and-a-half-hour race and a five-hour drive from Paris. This morning at nine o'clock he flies south from Brussels to Switzerland for the Across Lausanne race. Tomorrow he is back in Holland, at the Acht van Chaam, near Breda. Meanwhile, many of the Frenchmen who rubbed shoulders with Armstrong for the last three weeks were racing last night at Lisieux in Normandy. Tomorrow they are in Brittany, at Callac.

August is a demanding but lucrative month, when villages around Europe go *en fete* to welcome the stars of the Tour in a more intimate, family environment. Last night Armstrong and his fellows rode 100 kilometres on the brick setts that make up most of Boxmeer's streets, in between the Amstel Beer bus and the candyfloss stands, past the bouncy castle and the jerry-built grandstands, finishing at 11pm.

The whole show was put on the road by the "King" of the Dutch criterium circuit, Gerry Van Gerwen, with each rider receiving a start fee in proportion to his racing record.

The speed was high, but not too high. Criteriums are as much exhibition as competition, and the small peloton knows it should ride in a strung-out line so that fans can see the heroes of the Tour de France in front of them. The riders are well aware of what the public expects to see, so it is not uncommon for a Tour star to win, with a local hero putting up a plucky fight in second place.

More than 35,000 people were expected here last night, swelling the population several times over. High wire barriers were erected at every street where there was access to the circuit, channelling fans into turnstiles where old men took 15 guilders (£5) and stamped their hands as if welcoming them to a rock festival. To match the mood, Marillion blared from the sound system in the evening sun.

Old ladies sat eating their dinner in picnic chairs outside their front doors on the trim, narrow streets while the oompah band thumped and parped. The warm-up acts included a women's race, a cavalcade of vehicles of every kind from the local fire engine to a dustcart, and a parade of well-kept dogs walked on leads by well-kept local ladies. Girlfriends, who are usually not welcome at major races, checked tyre pressures.

Cyclists' trainers do not approve of their riding too many criteriums. The hectic mix of travelling and racing and the irregular hours wreak havoc with their systems and means that for many French professionals, the season ends in August. Not surprisingly given the mix of driving and competition, there have been many accounts of drugs, principally amphetamines, being used in the criteriums, where tests are a rarity.

While Armstrong marched on to a second Tour victory in 2000, that year's Tour was marked by Pantani's comeback to win two stages after he had taken almost a year out of the sport. Whatever the background, it was impossible to ignore his sheer guts as he took on Armstrong on Mont Ventoux that year.

Bald mountain falls to Pantani
14 July 2000

Among Mont Ventoux's many nicknames is *la montagne chauve* (the bald mountain) and yesterday, fittingly, it was conquered by the Tour's bald man, Marco Pantani, who has made a shaven scalp one of his trademarks. His bronzed bonce glistened with sweat, the veins above his skinny neck pulsated with the effort, and the 1998 Tour winner rode what was perhaps the most courageous race of his career.

Yet the little Italian was not the strongest man on the mountain. Lance Armstrong, as outrageously dominant as he was on Monday at the Hautacam finish, might as well have waved him across the line with a regal hand for all the effort he made to win. But courage and bloody-minded persistence made Pantani a worthy addition to those who have conquered this fearsome summit, other great climbers such as Charly Gaul and Julio Jimenez, nonpareils such as Eddy Merckx and Raymond Poulidor, and, farcically, the non-climber Eros Poli who led over the top when the route crossed the Ventoux in 1994.

In *Mythologies*, the writer Roland Barthes described the 6,000ft summit, which looms in a single white-topped ridge above the Vaucluse vineyards, as "a god of evil to whom sacrifice must be made". Pantani's offering was painful to watch, and it will be seen in the cycling world as a form of atonement for what he calls his "vicissitudes": the past year's drug scandals and black depression. It remains to be seen, though, whether this view will be taken by the Italian judge who will try him in October on charges of sporting fraud – falsifying results by the use of banned drugs.

This was, in any event, an epic fightback. Three times Pantani could not hold the pace on the steep initial ramps, as Armstrong's team-mate Kevin Livingston set a searing rhythm through a rock cutting lined with cedar and fir trees. Three times he fought grimly back to the tail of the little group, finally sprinting up to the leaders as they took the steep hairpin at Chalet Renard, four miles from the top, where fans perched high on the bouldered slopes.

Then, as the road kicked up steeply into the rocky wasteland leading to the summit, the little man in the Mercatone Uno pink attacked. He admits he is not in top form, and it took four attempts before there was daylight behind him. Inevitably, Armstrong was the only one able to get on terms, conscious that the only rider he now fears, Jan Ullrich, was floundering.

Equally inevitably, the American closed the gap with almost contemptuous ease. With only the blue sky above, and the whole of Provence below, the chilly wind was only blowing with half the ferocity of Wednesday, when 80mph was registered, but the gusts still made standing up difficult.

With the gale in their faces the pair slogged past the pile of tyres, feeding bottles, photographs and saddles left by fans at the memorial to Tommy Simpson, who paid the ultimate price for taking on the Ventoux 33 years before to the day.

It was a muted finish, redolent of a bygone, more straightforward era. The inflatable banners and podium that mark the finish line had been left at the bottom – they would have been blown into oblivion – and Armstrong simply let Pantani ride across a white line on the tarmac for the seventh Tour stage win of his career.

As the American saw it, the bargain was straightforward: Pantani did his share of the pacemaking and he himself increased his lead over Ullrich. "Victory in Paris is what counts," he said simply. That is now a step closer: Armstrong leads Ullrich, who kept in contact until two miles from the top, by 4min 55sec. Given that no one is climbing more strongly than the Texan, this is a solid lead with two alpine stages over the weekend.

No one quit on the mountain but Marcel Wust, the Vitre stage winner, did not take the start because of illness and eight stopped before the first slopes. They included Tom Steels, so imperious in the first two stage finishes but now stricken with stomach trouble.

Thus the malignant mountain again took its toll of blood, sweat and pain. At least today is flat. Well, flattish.

The Festina saga came to an end that autumn with the trial of Virenque, Voet and others in Lille. As legal theatre, the moment when the presiding judge, Daniel Delegove, coaxed a confession out of Virenque was unforgettable, although it simply confirmed what had been blindingly obvious to most people for over two years.

Virenque confesses to using drugs
25 October 2000

The unthinkable has finally happened. Millions of ordinary French people who watch the Tour de France each summer now have to digest the fact that their idol Richard Virenque took banned drugs.

Having remained in denial for two years and three months since he and his Festina team were thrown off the Tour, Virenque, France's most popular cyclist and biggest Tour star of the 90s, created a sensation here yesterday morning when he finally admitted that he had used the blood-boosting hormone erythropoietin (EPO).

At 9.15, immediately after the session opened, Virenque was called for questioning by the presiding magistrate Daniel Delegove, who had been advised by the rider's lawyer that he wished to speak. "Do you accept this reality, that you took doping products?" asked Delegove. "Yes," replied Virenque.

Under further questioning, his voice, with its brittle *meridional* accent, cracked and he seemed close to tears as he described why he used drugs. "It was a like a train going away from me and, if I didn't get on it, I would be left behind. It was not cheating. I wanted to remain in the family."

His admission led to what will remain an enduring image of the trial, at the end of the morning session, when Virenque was reconciled with his former masseur Willy Voet, with whom he had had a "father-son" relationship that ended when Voet was caught by police. Both men were in tears as Voet clutched Virenque and told him that he had done the right thing; but almost simultaneously Voet's wife Sylvie harangued the cyclist over his allegation that Voet was a drug dealer.

For Virenque it is a bitter volte-face. During the 1998 scandal, as his team-mates confessed one by one to police that they had taken drugs, especially EPO, Virenque denied point blank that he had taken drugs, both to the police and, most memorably, in the face of a Paxmanesque interrogation live on French television.

In the opening session here on Monday Virenque maintained his denial. But Delegove pointedly asked the other two men at the centre of the case – Voet and the former Festina manager Bruno Roussel – if Virenque could have been doped without his knowledge. Both were adamant that it was impossible.

Faced with this reality, Virenque decided to change his tactics on Monday evening. It is a decision that may well mean he is not found guilty of the charge he faces here, that of inciting his teammates to take drugs, as he is now essentially in the same position as the rest of the team.

However, his career may have ended with his 19th place in Saturday's Tour of Lombardy. Although he won a stage of this year's Tour, he is currently without a team – no sponsor wants to hire him until the outcome of the trial is known – and he faces a ban of between six months and a year, as a confession of drug use is regarded in the same light as a positive test. He said to Voet yesterday: "I'm unemployed now and I'm glad."

Adding to the impression that an entire sport is in the spotlight here, Lance Armstrong, who has won the last two Tours de France after coming back from testicular cancer, also came under fire. The former Festina trainer Antoine Vayer said: "Armstrong rides at an average speed of 54kph. I find this scandalous. It's a nonsense. Indirectly, it proves he is on dope," said Vayer.

Vayer's protege, Christophe Bassons, who quit the Tour de France in 1999 after riders ostracised him for his assertions that he would not use drugs, spoke under oath about how Armstrong told him to leave the race. "Armstrong said that I was very bad for cycling. He said I had better go home and that I had nothing to do on a bike." Voet, who knows Bassons well, said that he did not consider Armstrong to have behaved well. "Bassons is a small rider and, when you have Armstrong's class, you don't need to say those things to a small rider. Armstrong is a classy guy but that is not a classy thing to do."

Vayer remains a prominent anti-doping campaigner, an erstwhile member of the group Change Cycling Now which met first in London in early December 2012 in the aftermath of the Lance Armstrong scandal and issued a manifesto for clean cycling.

4. THE ARMSTRONG SAGA

By 2001, Lance Armstrong was heading seamlessly for his Tour de France hat-trick; his dominance would last until July 2005 and would result in the entire event becoming increasingly centered on the Texan and his entourage. There was a 1ittle local difficulty, however, as his partnership with the notorious trainer Michele Ferrari was exposed in the Sunday Times *by David Walsh. That was the first step in a gradual process which saw Armstrong steadily become more controversial, with increasing questions about his ethics, even as he became more and more successful. The Ferrari revelation was the first step in the 11-year process of exposure that would culminate in the explosive USADA report of October 2012.*

On a less serious note, my Tour de France diaries were begun in homage to the Observer's *late cycling correspondent and my personal role model, Geoffrey Nicholson, who used this as a model for his coverage of the race in the early 1990s. The diary format offers the writer the chance to look at the race obliquely, to pick up the many strands that unite Tours over the years and to poke a little fun at the obvious targets: Richard Virenque, the French on Bastille Day, Armstrong, the gifts that stage towns give the press.*

The diary also gives a sense of the Tour's unique quality for a journalist: the fact that pretty much every day you end up somewhere different and see different things. Most importantly, for a Sunday paper, the whole week's events could be encapsulated without it being too laborious. This one had to be included, running as it does the full gamut of experience you can have in just six days on the race.

Tour 2001: week 4

Luz Ardiden, Sunday 22 July

Disaster: the bell rung by the Tour organisers to alert the non-cycling part of the caravan to the impending depart each morning is stolen at the start town of Tarbes. There is consternation about how to rouse the *suiveurs* from their morning coffee in the start village and make them take to their cars before the riders get going. A *cloche* is lent by the organisers of the Dauphiné Libéré, another French race; it is too puny. A town close to the finish, Argèles-Gazost, finds a bell, paints it in its colours and presents it to the organisers. It is no louder, and the Tour remains bell-less until Paris.

If it does not look slippy the bell will toll for the *autobus*, the group of non-climbers who fight their way to the finish together inside the day's set limit, a percentage of the winner's time; short mountain stages such as today's, where the limit is tighter, are particularly feared. "We had 30 minutes to play with, and we were 18 behind at the bottom of Luz Ardiden, so we knew we could afford to lose another 12," recalls the first-timer from New Zealand, Chris Jenner. "There was no celebration when we got there, we were too tired."

Pau, Monday 23 July

For the first time, Lance Armstrong talks publicly about his relations with the controversial Doctor Ferrari. *[The story broke on the first weekend of the Tour, over two weeks earlier.]* As theatre, his prickly press conference is hard to match. David Walsh, who broke the Ferrari story, is greeted with a sarcastic, "Well David, I'm glad you showed up finally." Armstrong pleads his good faith and that of the doctor's.

Later, Armstrong is said to have complained that the press kept looking at each other and making signs, as if in collusion. The press mutter the same about him and his advisers. His

86

lawyer, Bill Stapleton, casts icy glares at Walsh, who asks a final question about a performance-enhancing device called a molecular sieve, which increases red-cell levels. "I guess I'll have to check it out if you think it's so important," comes Armstrong's implacable drawl.

Once, stage towns vied with each other to produce gifts for the press, from the surreal – a tennis ball on a plinth from Montlucon in 1992 – to the prosaic: a penknife from Superbesse in 1996. The Cathar stopping point, an intimate little jumble of half-timbers and sunbaked brick, outdoes its richer brethren with a goodie bag that shows a deep understanding of life on the Tour for the majority who travel on four wheels: suncream, smelly foot lotion and two bottles of wine.

The Tour's political affiliations are not hard to read: the organiser, Jean-Marie Leblanc, likes to quote De Gaulle – visited by the entire peloton at his home in Colombey-les-Deux-Eglises in 1960 – and the current President Jacques Chirac has visited the Tour seven times with great fanfare. Francois Mitterrand came just once, anonymously, to the roadside like any old fan. Today's finish is next to the Chirac museum in his home village, where his wife Bernadette is the deputy mayor. Like all French women of a certain age, she cannot resist the lure of the polka dot climber's jersey, and declares Laurent Jalabert her favourite.

Eight miles from the finish the peloton passes the *bar-tabac* Chez Guillou. It looks anonymous, but has a minor place in cycling history. Three years ago, this is where the Festina team made a last-ditch attempt to start the race after being thrown out at the height of the drug scandal.

Montlucon, Thursday 26 July

The farmers put in their annual appearance, protesting about factory farming early on and protesting about life in general on the run in to the finish. Probably to prevent them putting tractors in the way of the race, the organisers invite the *agriculteurs* to kill and roast a very large fatted calf for the caravan the following day. There is no mention of steak's traditional use on the Tour: raw, interposed between bottom and shorts, as a cure for saddle sores.

St-Amand-Montrond, Friday 27 July

The Tour's historian, Jacques Augendre, has described the intimacy between riders and press in the 1940s and 1950s, before the Tour turned into the mammoth event it is now, how he would pass riders bottles and pace them back to the bunch with his press car after punctures. Such complicity is a thing of the past, he says. Not quite. In the 38-mile time-trial, we follow Jacky Durand, a pugnacious French veteran popularly known as "Dudu". For him this is merely a day to be got through before the last two days into Paris, when he will make the last of the hammed-up, do-or-die attacks that have won him the "combativity" award twice.

He is not acting when his aerodynamic handlebars come loose soon after the start. He fiddles with the fixing, consults his support car, wobbles and stops, then starts again; cursing. We ask his car what is wrong: shamefacedly they confess they do not have the necessary allen key. A boy scout among us has a Swiss Army knife which is duly handed over, and passed to "Dudu", who completes the repair by the roadside. Rescued by the British press, he finishes ninety-second and his mechanic at the Française des Jeux team can expect an earbashing that evening.

The drugs question had not gone away since the Festina trial at the end of 2000, with Italian drugs police staging the biggest ever raid

on a race at the 2001 Giro, the notorious San Remo "blitz". At the
Tour, Armstrong's exposure as a Ferrari client and his crude attempts
to news-manage the story meant that doping remained centre stage.
As in every Tour since 1998, the reporting job was twofold: the
doping story and in parallel, the bike race.

Ferrari links keep the drugs issue simmering
30 July 2001

In a neat twist in the tail of this year's Tour, the organisers placed
yesterday's final intermediate sprint of the race at Chatenay-
Malabry, the little town in the south-west suburbs of Paris where
France's anti-doping laboratory developed the test for the banned
blood booster erythropoietin (EPO) and where urine samples
taken during the Tour are tested.

It was a small reminder that the EPO test is being used for
the first time in the Tour this year, and by happy coincidence
the International Cycling Union revealed yesterday that of the
122 of the 170 drug samples taken on the Tour tested there
so far, only one – from Txema Del Olmo – had been positive.
They concluded: "We think that the problem of EPO no longer
influences cycling at the highest level."

[They were right. Armstrong and company had moved on to blood
doping. EPO was used by the smaller fry without the resources to
remove and store blood or who were squeamish about the whole
removal-reinjection process, or for training outside "windows" when
it could be detected.]

Though progress in combating EPO is undeniable, the signals
from the Tour remain mixed three years after the Festina drugs
scandal blew the sport apart. On Saturday, French campaigners
against doping in all sports held a conference only 50 yards from
the start in Orleans, where the French "Association for Fighting
Doping" is based. You would not have known it if you were a
spectator enjoying the show as the riders signed on.

The campaigners, who included grass-roots groups, the former Festina trainer Antoine Vayer and the former Tour stage winner Gilles Delion, and who had ridden on their bikes from Friday's finish 100 miles to the south, clearly felt marginalised. Indeed Vayer went so far as say they were "treated like the devil".

The rumblings about Lance Armstrong's work with the controversial Italian trainer Michele Ferrari continued yesterday, when Greg LeMond, a triple winner of the Tour, summed up the feelings of many on this Tour in saying: "When Lance won the prologue to the 1999 Tour I was close to tears, but when I heard he was working with Michele Ferrari I was devastated. In the light of Lance's relationship with Ferrari, I just don't want to comment on this year's Tour. This is not sour grapes. I'm disappointed in Lance, that's all it is."

Even the Tour organiser Jean-Marie Leblanc concedes the name of Ferrari is a dubious one. "I am not happy the two names are mixed, but as long as there is no decision in court we have to wait," he said. Leblanc feels the Tour is cleaner this year, but says "the questioning of Armstrong lacks dignity, as the presumption of innocence is fundamental. For Armstrong it is the presumption of guilt. The world is turned upside down."

Armstrong himself says of the relationship with Ferrari: "Is it questionable? Perhaps." But he adds, referring to himself in the third person: "Has Lance Armstrong ever tested positive? No. Has Lance Armstrong been tested? A lot."

Vayer, who has watched the Festina riders dope themselves in the past with undetectable products, and has attacked Armstrong before, spoke of why the Tour organisers have kept at a distance from the campaigners. "They are afraid of us," he said. "They think we are about polemic."

Squaring the circle of Armstrong, who shouts his cleanness from the rooftops, and Ferrari, who is to go on trial on drugs charges, has proved impossible for many, for all the Texan's protestations. Their work is about altitude training and low-oxygen chambers and diet, but surely there are other specialists in these areas who are not facing charges of recommending banned, and possibly dangerous, hormones? Not so, says the man who manages Armstrong's training, Chris Carmichael. "It's about putting together the best people with the best athlete, searching high and low."

Armstrong's agent and lawyer Bill Stapleton describes Ferrari as a brilliant scientist with an awful public reputation who has made very, very irresponsible comments. With complete confidence, he concludes: "I'm not worried, because he [Armstrong] will never, ever test positive."

Armstrong did actually test positive, when samples from the 1999 Tour were re-tested for EPO in 2004, but the results were not a conventional anti-doping test and no sanction was issued. So Stapleton was both right, and wrong.

The Armstrong Tours followed a pattern: an undercurrent of doping stories making it clear that the problem had not gone away, but rarely ever offering any concrete insight into its extent. Simultaneously, Armstrong dominated the event while rebutting rumours that he might be doping. The 2002 Tour was typical: a fourth triumph for the Texan, and a massive scandal involving the third-placed rider, Raimondas Rumsas. As with the San Remo blitz in 2001, the Rumsas affair gave some insight into how many different kinds of drugs were in circulation. As for the mother-in-law story, no one believed it.

Police reveal extent of drug haul
13 September 2002

The curious case of Raimondas Rumsas's mother-in-law took a further twist yesterday with the publication of a list of 37 drugs found by customs men in the boot of the car driven by the cyclist's wife, Edita, on the day her husband finished third in this year's Tour de France.

The drugs were, according to Edita Rumsas, destined for her sick mother. But the list of substances leaked by French legal sources to the daily newspaper *L'Equipe* includes two different varieties of the male hormone testosterone and a cortisone product widely used in cycling over the past 20 years, Delayed Action Kenacort, plus insulin and two different types of growth hormone.

Rumsas has maintained since his wife's arrest that the drugs found in her car are nothing to do with him. He was tested several times during the Tour de France and came up negative each time. The only anomaly to attract the interest of drug testers was a rise in his blood thickness level – haematocrit – during the race when, according to the laws of physiology, it should have diminished.

The only item in the car that has been directly linked to the Lithuanian cyclist is an envelope bearing his name which contained six syringes ready for use. They contained a colourless liquid which is still being analysed, as are several foil packages of powders and pills with no name on them.

[The syringes were subsequently found to contain EPO.]

Several of the drugs are on the IOC's list of banned substances. Among these are the growth hormone norditropin and a dwarfism cure, Geref, which stimulates the body's natural production of growth hormone. Neither is detectable by current drug tests. The suitcase in the car contained eight Androderm patches, which release the male hormone testosterone slowly into the body, enabling the level to be maintained without breaching limits considered "natural".

As well as "natural" aids to maintaining health, such as large vitamin B and E tablets, there were also items similar to those found when police raided the Giro d'Italia last year: three different kinds of caffeine tablets and a preloaded syringe of insulin, which is banned for all but diabetics as it can enhance sugar uptake after exercise and counter the diabetic effect of growth hormone.

Some of the products are readily available through US internet sites. Some are apparently homeopathic, such as Spascupreel, a stomach remedy containing the poisonous herb belladonna, and *testis compositum*, available on the internet from an English company and supposed to stimulate testosterone production.

Edita Rumsas has been detained in Bonneville, in the French Alps, for six weeks, despite three appeals, diplomatic protests and demonstrations in front of the French embassy in the Lithuanian capital Riga. The investigating team will remain in Tuscany this week to interview Rumsas and members of his Lampre-Daikin team.

Armstrong was not the only star with image problems at that time. Mario Cipollini's issues were not drug-related, but came down to his unhappy relationship with the Tour de France organisers. The annual question of his inclusion, or not in the race, was an amusing sideshow, as indeed was Mario himself. The saga went centre stage in the run-up to the centenary Tour of 2003.

Pin-up star left down and out
25 May 2003

This should have been a triumphant week for the world champion Mario Cipollini, but injury was piled on top of insult and Italy's most charismatic cyclist has been left with road rash on his bottom, aching ribs and anger in his heart, while his country is just plain outraged.

On Wednesday afternoon, Cipollini slid across the road at 30mph on his backside, decked out in rainbow-striped shorts matching his rainbow-striped world champion's jersey, just 160 metres from the finish line in the little Veneto town of San Dona di Piave. He had the demeanour of a man who had thought things could get no worse, only to suddenly realise he had been mistaken. With bruising to his ribs and back, Cipollini was unable to continue the race and returned home on Thursday morning.

In recent years, the Giro d'Italia has left most followers of cycling shaking their heads, but that has been because of doping scandals. This week's *polemica* has been a different matter. Since Monday, cyclists, press, officials and fans have been united in their condemnation of the organisers of the Tour de France, who refused Cipollini a place in their race for the third year in succession.

After his exclusion last year, Cipollini had a war of words with the Tour officials, then trained like a maniac to win the world title in October, on the assumption that they would want the world champion. But on Monday, when the final four slots for the Tour were announced, there was no place for his Domina Vacanze team, whose zebra-striped jerseys are the most distinctive in the peloton. In their place are the worthy but utterly dull Jean Delatour squad, sponsored by a jeweller from Lyon.

The decision of the organisers, headed by the former journalist and Tour rider Jean-Marie Leblanc, looked particularly tactless as it came the day after Cipollini won his forty-first stage in the Giro, and a few hours before he won his forty-second. The figures are significant: 41 stage wins put Cipollini level with the record held since 1933 by Alfredo Binda, the greatest Italian *campionissimo* of the pre-war years; 42 meant the record was his.

It is a colossal achievement. The two greatest Giro riders since the war, Fausto Coppi and Eddy Merckx, are both legends of the sport, and neither got near Binda's record. Cipollini has made hype his trademark, marketing himself as "the fastest man in the world" but his record, a tribute to 15 seasons at the top, justifies the hyperbole. The anger among the *tifosi* has been palpable: "Go Mario, Leblanc is mad" read one banner; "History will be your judge" read another.

The press, too, had bitter words for the Tour de France. In a venomous editorial under the headline "an offence to the world", Angelo Zomegnan, one of *La Gazzetta dello Sport*'s most senior editors, described the decision as "a blasphemy" and concluded "the world title has been emptied of all meaning. Cipollini has lost to some Mr Nobodies.

"Part of cycling's heritage has been stupidly trodden into the dirt," he continued. "Such an act is what we might have expected of one of Leblanc's predecessors, hounded out of the job because they were unable to manage the Tour, or of his successor [Daniel Baal], a man who has never looked capable of taking in sport's culture."

Even Lance Armstrong has expressed surprise: "I don't understand this decision. I've asked for an answer but I haven't gotten a response. There are three good reasons why this decision is absolutely wrong. First, Cipollini is the World Champion and they didn't think only of the race. Second, he is the best sprinter in the world, so even on a technical level it's a mistake not to invite him. Third, he is a really big personality and he's very popular in cycling. He knows how to take his responsibilities, and the Tour should welcome him back."

As is always the case in Italy, it is not as simple as it looks. Cipollini and the Tour have a troubled recent history. He has started the race seven times, won 12 stages, but never made it to Paris. Last time he rode the Tour, in 1999, he won four stages in a row, a feat not seen since the 1930s. The organisers, however, do not approve of the fact that he wins his stages, then goes home when the race hits the mountains, leaving his team as mere passengers.

There remains the chance of a last-minute change of heart. On Friday evening, Leblanc said: "There is a 10 to 15 per cent chance that Cipollini will start the Tour. I am wondering about the decision that we took. The problem is one of logistics and finding hotels."

But Cipollini will not forget an insult lightly. "Now, even if they do invite me I won't go," he said. "And if I had to go because the team asked me then I'd go without enthusiasm or preparation. For me to win a stage at the Tour wearing the world champion's jersey would be the ultimate feat in my career. It will remain an unfulfilled desire."

The Tour organisers accepted that Cipollini probably merited a place ahead of some of the teams who achieved automatic qualification, an admission that their race will be the poorer without him. Not even Armstrong has Cipollini's public profile, as astute marketing campaigns by sponsors have made him far more than a sprinter, and no ordinary world champion. He has, at various points in his career, also been "the Lion King", the "Sun God", "Super Mario" and "Julius Caesar". He has constantly sported colour-coordinated outfits and bikes, usually receiving a fine for having non-standard kit. When the Tour started in Ireland in 1998, out came a green jersey with a "Peace" slogan. When he won his four stages in a row, he was issued a gold racing suit with the words "veni, vidi, vici".

He borrowed an Inter Milan shirt from his friend Ronaldo to wear after one victory, and has moonlighted as a fashion model. His shoe ads created the biggest stir, as he was depicted being fed grapes by topless models, and dressed up as Superman alongside a bodypainted nude. In a sport that has a lengthy tradition of celibacy, he makes much of his liking for *amore*. "Ejaculating costs you all of 100 calories, no more than a bar of chocolate," he once said. Asked if he would like to be in movies, he answered "porn, naturally".

Victory at San Dona was a matter of 15 seconds in the future when it slid away, the perfect metaphor for a week in which the fastest man in the world glimpsed a place in the Tour de France, then lost it. First out, then down and out.

Cipollini didn't make it to the centenary Tour de France, which turned, after a glitch or two, into another Armstrong-fest. The build-up, however, offered an opportunity to give some insights into the history of the race.

From seaweed to EPO – the Tour in four generations
5 July 2003

As the greatest cycle race in the world celebrates its centenary, riders from four golden eras remember what made it so special.

1930s: Roger Lapebie:

Made his Tour debut in 1932, won in 1937. Interviewed before his death in 1996, when the Frenchman was one of two surviving winners from the pre-war era.

"The roads were *épouvantable* [terrifying], filled with huge potholes which we called *nids de poule* – bird's nests – covered in pebbles, dust, gravel. We were given 25 pairs of shorts and 25 jerseys at the start of the race and changed our socks every day because of the dust and the dirt. We had saddle sores all the time because of the dirt and cowdung on the roads. It was easy to get an infection in any wound and the rare red meat we ate would give us boils.

To look after ourselves, we had old wives' remedies. Very hot baths, with three or four kilograms of sea salt, and two or three litres of vinegar after a cold rainy stage. We would have a hard massage, with a lot of seaweed, and we would wear long johns. We'd buy packets of three or four dozen mustard plasters in Paris at the start – American or English were best – and put them on our legs all night if they were painful. In bad weather we'd put them over our livers.

I was the first man to win the Tour using a derailleur gear. Until then they were banned, so we had two freewheel sprockets on each side of the wheel. You would stop and turn the wheel around to change gear, or move it with your fingers. You had to do it at the right moment or you could lose a race. If a good rider stopped to change gear, everyone would attack and he might never see them again."

1950s: Brian Robinson

First Briton to finish the Tour, in 1955; first Briton to win a stage, in 1958. Now retired and living in Yorkshire.

"The Tour was completely open to the public at the starts and finishes, nothing was cordoned off and we would sit in the village squares, waiting for the race to start, talking to the locals. Anyone who could speak English would just come along and practise it on me. The public could rub shoulders with Jacques Anquetil and Louison Bobet, the biggest stars of the day. The British fans would find us, tell us what hill they would be on and ask if we needed anything.

We were always looking for water because we were restricted to two bottles at the start and another two in the bag we collected in the feed stations. We would ride into a town, try to find a cafe where no other riders had stopped, get water and ride on. If there was a fountain, everyone would stop, there would be bikes everywhere, you'd push to get your bottle under the tap, someone else would push it away.

In the mountains, there was no road surface on the passes above the snowline, just gravel. I've seen guys stop, grab a handful of snow and stuff it down their jersey to cool down. The thing that I remember most was the noise. You'd be staying in a town centre and the partying would go on until 2am. Up in the mountains, with the crowds on either side, the noise in your ears would be tremendous.

It was a good wage but you'd have to look after yourself in the winter. There were no contracts until March or April. It was £50 for a stage win and I'd look to put away about a grand in the bank at the end of the year, enough to buy a car."

1970s: Bernard Thevenet

His victory in 1975 ended Eddy Merckx's run of victories and began France's last spell of domination, when the home nation took nine wins in 11 years.

"My Tours were the last Tours of the old generation. Fundamentally there had not been much change since the era of Fausto Coppi, the late 1940s. Cycling was parochial. There was one New Zealander racing and I remember we all went to look at him because we'd never seen anyone from down there. I raced against an American once, at the world championship. At the Tour there might have been 10 nations at the start; this year there will be 26.

There was less pressure on the riders, less of a scrum at the stage finish, although when I took the yellow jersey from Merckx in 1975 people just kept coming on to the podium for interviews, more and more of them. I was standing close to the edge, they all moved and I nearly fell off. There were no buses for the riders, so you got to the start, got out of the car and there were people all round you.

The Tour was smaller, with far fewer media. The press room was about a quarter the size it is now. The riders were not cut off from the media as they are now that the Tour is so huge. We knew all the journalists, relations were good and they would come to interview us in our hotels after the finish of the day's stage. Now they will simply go to a press conference. The riders did not specialise in the Tour; they raced from February to October, so we all raced together and knew each other."

1980s: Steve Bauer

The first Canadian to ride the Tour, finished nine times, wearing the yellow jersey twice, between 1985 and 1995, the period when the event turned into an international extravaganza. Now visits the race with groups of touring cyclists.

"It's incredible to come back and see the Tour from the outside. You see the size, the number of people, the logistics. There was a general trend of internationalisation and innovation during my time, more media attention, more journalists from America, more television crews, a move from an evening round-up of 15 minutes on CBS to continual live coverage. Without Greg LeMond's wins, his comeback, that might never have happened.

A lot of the innovation was driven by Americans, mainly LeMond. It was a mix of business, invention and good sense: try this helmet, try this computer. We started wearing Oakley pilot glasses, really ugly, but now Oakley is cool and everyone has them. There were triathlon bars for aerodynamics, which Greg made popular. We were more open to change, we weren't stuck in traditional ways and the Europeans followed.

The racing in the Tour changed as well. At the start it was more controlled, I remember just touring through Brittany before everyone wound it up for the finish. Bernard Hinault would control things, someone would attack and he'd growl at them, "Cool it, guys. Hard day today." Miguel Indurain never made his presence felt in the same way and I'm not sure anyone does now.

The distances lessened and the stages became eyeballs out. There got to be more roundabouts over my time, so it all got more dangerous. I remember one pile-up on a *rond-point* [roundabout] in the west somewhere in 1994, 65 kilometres per hour, a whole heap of guys on the floor. And I noticed the arrival of EPO in the peloton in the early 1990s, guys kicking my ass who shouldn't have been, whole teams superstrong that shouldn't have been, and it was very discouraging as I came from teams which had a clean philosophy."

Apart from Armstrong's duel with Jan Ullrich, the other story of the Centenary Tour was Tyler Hamilton's battle with his broken collarbone. This interview was a rarity: a one on one with a major rider during the Tour, but it was worth it, because what Hamilton was doing fitted in with the whole Tourman-as-Superman notion. Nine years later, Hamilton revealed that he was blood doping during this Tour. That wasn't surprising, as he had tested positive for blood doping in 2004, but to have it confirmed was depressing. Superman was a cheat. Does it lessen the courage it took to ride through the Tour with a broken collarbone? No. You can be immoral and courageous at the same time.

The pain barrier: Broken collarbone, twisted spine and Tyler Hamilton rides on. His agony and bravery is the story of the race
20 July 2003

One of the great metaphors inspired by the Tour de France is that of the race as a road to Calvary. *Le calvaire* has been routinely used throughout the 100 years since the great race was born to describe the process of a cyclist continuing in the face of great affliction, be it injury, or illness, or the mental agony that follows the death of a close relative.

Tyler Hamilton has put all the past century of two-wheeled battles against pain into a new perspective over the past two weeks. He has ridden on in spite of a broken collarbone, holding a high place overall as the race entered the Pyrenees yesterday. The doctors can barely believe it. Hamilton's is *le calvaire* against which all others will be measured in future.

"I work with the pain, and that's how I go about my daily life," he says. "Accepting the pain has turned into part of my daily routine. In my opinion, it's better to accept it and not resist it. If you resist it, it's even harder." Hamilton, like all Tour cyclists, is smaller than you would expect when seen up close. He has the same deep tan, the same shuffling, strength-saving walk, as the rest. But when he comes into the lobby of his Toulouse hotel, he shakes hands with the left. The right cannot be used.

An unassuming man from Massachusetts, Hamilton is no stranger to pain. A keen and talented skier, he broke several vertebrae in a fall and got into cycling when in rehab. Last year, famously, he came second in the Tour of Italy, bearing a cracked shoulder blade. He ground his teeth in agony so strongly that 11 have needed replacing. He lists his symptoms modestly and emphasises: "I feel I'm complaining a lot." But much of the last two weeks has been spent in silence. Just him and the pain.

The first station on his calvary was Avenue de l'Appel du 18 Juin 1940 in Meaux two weeks ago, where Hamilton's front wheel landed on the prone form of the sprinter Jimmy Casper, catapulting him over the bars at 30mph and on to his right shoulder. X-rays showed a V-shaped double crack in his collarbone, and that, it seemed, was that. But the next morning, Hamilton was on the start line. "When I saw the X-rays, and I saw my Tour de France was over, I'm not ashamed to say it, but I cried. For three or four hours I was devastated. Then I learned it was maybe possible to try."

Critically, there was no displacement of the bones – the two parts remained in a straight line, meaning that in medical terms, it was possible for Hamilton to go on without damaging it further. Riding with three layers of foam on his handlebars and reduced pressure in his tyres to ease the shocks from the road surfaces, Hamilton rode into Sedan that evening as pale as a ghost, but 100th.

His initial target was the team time-trial, to assist his team, CSC, the computer software company, to a respectable placing. That obstacle surmounted, more than respectably, further X-rays last Thursday showed no further movement in the fracture. Even so, he was expected to quit when the race arrived in the Alps a week ago yesterday. But at l'Alpe d'Huez six days ago, he finished with Lance Armstrong to move to sixth overall. Casper, the man he fell over in Sedan, went home the following day. Twenty-two others quit in the Alps through illness or injury.

"A couple of days after the crash I was in so much pain when I woke up that I thought it was over," Hamilton says. "Mentally, it's been a rollercoaster ride. There have been points where I didn't think I would be able to continue. The first night I got four hours' sleep, the second five. I didn't get a decent night's rest for five nights." The pain, says Hamilton, is "constant, numb. On a scale of one to 10 it was 10, now it's seven or eight. On my bike I get sharp pains, and every bump I can feel it. When I put pressure on it, it tells me to stop."

The worst point, thus far, came on Tuesday, when the race left the Alps for Marseille. "I'd had a twisted spine since the crash, and they couldn't put pressure on it to push it back into place. It was putting pressure on a nerve that runs from my back to my stomach. It got inflamed and when I woke up I was in so much pain. Normally, to breathe, I push down with my stomach, but I couldn't push it out an inch."

By sheer good fortune, that day's route was mainly downhill and the peloton relaxed after letting a group of backmarkers escape. "If it had been a mountain stage, I'd have been in trouble, and fortunately the next day was the rest day. They gave me a muscle relaxant and pushed it back. The night before, my body was just too tense for them to do it. I was in so much pain."

Why do it? "One thing is my team, I owe it to them to push on. I didn't want to give up at the first problem." There is also the fact that Hamilton is now 32, and has only lately emerged from a career largely spent working for Armstrong. Time is not on his side.

Last Monday, on the final Alpine stage, he was a few yards behind when the Spaniard Joseba Beloki skidded on a patch of melted Tarmac on a descent, flew over the bars and broke his hip, elbow and wrist. Going downhill through hairpin bends at 50mph is a supreme test of nerves and clear-headedness – with one arm partly out of action and a shoulder in agony from every bump, it hardly bears thinking about.

"You try to relax. If you're tense on a descent, it just makes it worse. The descent where Beloki fell was incredibly dangerous, the Tarmac was melting and it was one of those turns that just kept going." Asked if falling again worries him, he doesn't get the question. It clearly isn't in his mental terms of reference.

"The doctors have said it will heal normally if I crash on it again. Maybe I'd need an operation with a plate in it, but that didn't happen when I broke it the first time. For me it's worth the risk. I worry, but you can only worry so much."

Hamilton's courage may be admired by many – asked how he feels about what his protege is doing, his team manager Bjarne Riis simply spreads his arms as wide as they can go – but his wisdom and that of his team have been questioned. Eddy Merckx, who finished the Tour in 1975 with a fractured cheekbone, feels that that hastened the end of his career, and that Hamilton is making the same error. One rival team manager has alleged that the fracture is not real, and had to be shown the X-rays to prove that it is.

There is one question that Hamilton cannot be asked. That is how he will react if his strength deserts him, or if he falls again, and all the pain of the last two weeks was for nothing. There is no point in asking the question, as it is something that he is just not contemplating.

The Tour has captured the imagination of its followers for 100 years because it drives men beyond their physical limits. Episodes of great courage in the face of pain are the norm rather than the exception. Even so, Dr Gerard Porte, 32 years on the Tour, 22 as chief doctor, says Hamilton's is the most surprising case that he has ever seen.

"A normal person would have to have four weeks off work. It is the finest example of courage that I've come across. It has amazed me. Obviously, medically it is possible, in that there are no counter-indications, no sign that it's getting worse. It's simply down to how much pain he can stand. That he still has the courage to be with the best is incredible."

Porte has seen other men drive themselves through injuries that would normally call for complete rest. He remembers the case of Johnny Weltz of Denmark in the mid-1980s, when the Dane broke a finger on stage six and got to Paris with it in plaster. By happy coincidence, Weltz is now one of Hamilton's *directeurs sportifs*.

In 1983, Porte was forced to look on as the Peugeot squad pushed their leader Pascal Simon from the Pyrenees to the Alps in spite of his broken shoulder blade. Simon became a legend, but he was never the same cyclist again. In 1985, Jean-Claude Bagot of France managed four stages with a broken elbow, simply because his pride would not allow him to quit before the Tour had entered his native Normandy.

"To understand why Hamilton is still here, you have to look back a year, when he fell in the Grand Prix," explains Porte. "There he suffered a real fracture of the collarbone, the bone was scarred and acquired a big lump. He fell in Meaux on the same shoulder, and cracked it in the same place, in the knot of scarred bone. It is an incomplete fracture, two fissures, which are not as bad as a classic fracture which would have sent him home no matter how brave he was."

What chance does Hamilton stand of getting through the Pyrenean stages today, tomorrow and on Wednesday, and of making it to Paris? "I think he has a chance," says Porte. "He's been going for 10 days, it's through the most painful period for a fracture – and it's becoming less painful. The question is whether riding without the full use of his right arm has weakened the rest of his body."

In autumn next year, the first Imax film of the Tour, provisionally entitled Brainpower, will be released. Partly sponsored by America's National Science Foundation, it is being shot on this Tour with a 49-strong team. By freaky coincidence, it deals with the mind's ability to overcome pain, and it is being shot largely with Hamilton and the CSC team. The scriptwriters could not have dreamt of the current scenario.

The film Brainpower was eventually released with the title Wired to Win. Not surprisingly, Hamilton's role was downplayed.

The 2004 Tour de France saw Armstrong ride to his sixth consecutive victory. But by then, his story had gained further complexity, due to the publication of David Walsh and Pierre Ballester's compilation of evidence that pointed to doping, LA Confidential. *If anything, this incident with Filippo Simeoni towards the end of the Tour was actually more revelatory than Walsh's book. It was a public demonstration of two things: Armstrong was a bully, and he was utterly paranoid about Michele Ferrari.*

Simeoni takes a savage beating
24 July 2004

Showing all the diplomatic skills of a playground bully, Lance Armstrong stamped his authority on one of the rebels of the peloton, Filippo Simeoni. Armstrong frequently complains that he is not universally popular with the public but yesterday afternoon's little cameo will have done little to counter the feeling that he regards the Tour as his personal fiefdom.

"Pippo"'s only offence, after all, is that he has taken legal action against Armstrong in his native Italy after the American questioned his testimony against the Texan's trainer Michele Ferrari.

Simeoni rode away from the peloton early in the stage, in pursuit of the day's six-rider breakaway group, and what followed was bizarre. As if to make the point that he has a personal beef with the Italian, Armstrong did not ask his team to chase him, but caught up himself and the pair rode across to the leaders.

The peloton slowed down, as if it could not believe what was going on either. In the little group, Armstrong, Simeoni and the eventual runner-up on the stage, Vicente Garcia Acosta had an intense discussion before Simeoni dropped back, and Armstrong with him.

At the finish, the Italian was a bitterly disappointed man. "I made a super effort to get to the escape, but Armstrong said the peloton would not let the group remain in front unless I let them go," he explained. "I slowed down out of respect for the other riders there. He shouldn't worry about little riders like me."

Armstrong said simply: "I was just protecting the interests of the peloton." If the common interest of the riders is that whistleblowers in drug trials are ostracised, perhaps he was, but it is not a widely expressed sentiment among his fellows.

With Armstrong and Simeoni back in the peloton, normal service was resumed, and the escape duly fought out the finish, where Garcia-Acosta was narrowly beaten by his fellow Spaniard Juan-Miguel Mercado.

The essential contradiction of the Armstrong years is all here in this end-of-Tour piece: a sporting phenomenon that could not be denied, a comeback from the near dead to win six Tours, but undercurrents that could not be ignored, given what had come before and during his reign. The use of the adjective incredible in the headline seems amply justified with hindsight.

Armstrong powers to incredible sixth and glory
26 July 2004

In November 1997 I sat down with Lance Armstrong, his future ex-wife Kristin, and three bottles of red wine on the bare floor of a room devoid of furniture in a borrowed villa on the exclusive peninsula of St Jean-Cap Ferrat, between Nice and Monaco. "We'll go out for dinner," Armstrong had said, and we did – to a supermarket, where we stocked up with wine, salad and pasta, which the couple cooked.

To look back at that evening reflects how far Armstrong has travelled in sporting and personal terms. Back then he and Kristin were so uncertain about his comeback to racing in Europe that they had no idea whether to buy furniture or not. It was just over a year since he had been diagnosed with testicular cancer, and a comeback from tumours as acute as Armstrong's had never been attempted in cycling or any endurance sport before.

The rest is history. Armstrong is now the best Tour de France cyclist to have graced the planet. His marriage has been and gone, leaving three children along the way. When we met seven years ago he had just driven a small rented car across Europe to pick up a borrowed mattress and carried it back tied on to the roof with string. Now he is courting a rock star and courted by the President of the United States, who called Armstrong yesterday soon after he crossed the finishing line to congratulate him on behalf of the American people.

To call him the greatest cyclist ever would be like saying Michael Schumacher is a greater driver than Juan-Manuel Fangio. Like Schumacher he is a creature of his time, "a charismatic leader who has the best means available at his disposal", as Alain Prost said yesterday, but that merely underlines his achievement in getting the best on offer and making the most of it. *[again in hindsight, Prost's statement is masterly in its ambiguity.]*

His team-mate George Hincapie, the only member of the US Postal team to have ridden alongside Armstrong in all six of his Tour wins, said: "He is on the top of his game. He is stronger than ever." Few would disagree: in this year's race he has proved strongest in every domain that matters to a Tour winner, taking mountain-top stages, sprint finishes from a small breakaway group, a mountain time-trial, a flat time-trial and the team time-trial.

Here, too, the transformation is dramatic from even five years ago, when Armstrong led the Tour and was "constantly nervous" because he felt he could lose the yellow jersey at any moment. In this Tour, as in his fourth success in 2002, he is so far ahead of the opposition that he is turning his mind to helping his team-mates to win stages.

Yesterday the lone star of Texas was flying alongside the barriers on the Champs-Élysées. American cycle tourists had chained their bikes to the ornate columns of the Hotel de Crillon on the Place de la Concorde and children in US Postal replica kit were being hoisted on to window sills to watch sporting history being made. Security around the American embassy was intense, as it has been around Armstrong all through the Tour. The wave of cheering rippled up the avenue as eight of the US Postal team led their boss past the grandstands, his face as impassive as ever.

Amid the Armstrong victory parade the green jersey of points winner was the only issue to be settled yesterday. This has been a tight three-way battle between Robbie McEwen, Thor Hushovd and Stuart O'Grady but the Norwegian was balked on the rush to the final corner yesterday behind the stage winner Tom Boonen of Belgium, and McEwen finished ahead of his fellow Australian to secure his second title in three years.

The other unfinished business yesterday was Armstrong's personal battle with the Italian Filippo Simeoni, who is suing the Texan for libel. It will rumble on after the Tour but to make the point that he is not intimidated by Armstrong after the "Boss" prevented him going for the stage win on Friday, the Italian escaped soon after the start and sped away again as the peloton approached Paris.

The convention is that the yellow jersey winner and his team lead the race on to the Champs-Élysées, so Simeoni's attack was akin to breaking wind in communion. He was chased down by the US Postal team and one of Armstrong's domestiques, the Russian Viatcheslav Ekimov, made a "horns" gesture as he overtook the Italian. He escaped again and received similar short shrift from Hincapie.

Simeoni received the day's "combativity" award but the episode was more redolent of the playground than the world's biggest annual sports event. It was, however, a reminder that Armstrong is not a straightforward hero. The drugs suspicions remain largely unanswered and the contents of the biography, *LA Confidentiel*, unexplained and the subject of legal action. The Simeoni episode perhaps helps to explain why Armstrong figured prominently in a poll of the French public's most unpopular sportsmen in a Sunday newspaper yesterday. He was not in the lead but was not far behind Michael Schumacher and Nicolas Anelka. Given that whenever he speaks he seems preoccupied by his popularity, or lack of it, he was probably relieved merely to be third overall.

Mr Popular or not, there seems no chance of Armstrong getting jaded just yet. Seven years ago he said that, when he was diagnosed with cancer, two thoughts went through his mind: "I might lose my career", "I might die" – in that order. After winning the 21st Tour de France stage of his career on Saturday he made it clear he still feels that way.

"This is probably the most fun year I've had racing bikes. I can't explain why a 33-year-old who's been here for 12 years should be having more fun than ever ... It's not about making history or money, just the thrill of getting on a bike and racing 200 other guys."

Speculation about Armstrong and a seventh Tour will remain intense. Perhaps, now, his celebrity is such that he can afford to miss the race, as Eddy Merckx did in his prime, and take a sabbatical at the Giro d'Italia, the Tour of Spain or the World Cup series of single-day races.

That seems unlikely. "No other bike race has a million people by the side of the road, this is the one I love and I can't imagine skipping the Tour de France. I would only come with perfect condition and come ready to win. I can't imagine not being here."

While Armstrong was racing to his sixth Tour, a different story was unfolding in Biarritz and Paris. David Millar, the golden boy of British cycling in the post-Boardman years, had been busted by the drugs police as they investigated doping in his Cofidis team. The day after the Tour finished, Millar gave me an interview, his first since his confession; it was both sobering and salutary to hear the story of a drug-taker from the inside. It was also a journalistic marathon; I drove from Paris to London in the morning, did the interview that afternoon, and filed three long stories for the Guardian *in the early evening. It's a story I was proud to get first.*

The wrong gear
27 July 2004

Had it not been for an oversight in packing his suitcase last September, today David Millar would probably be celebrating finishing his fourth Tour de France, in which he has won three stages and worn the yellow jersey. He would be thinking about the Athens Olympics, about setting out to attempt something no British sportsman has achieved: two gold medals at the same games. He would also still be "living a lie", as he puts it: a highly paid, prestigious lie.

Instead, he is sitting in a bar explaining lucidly and heart-rendingly how he destroyed what could have been a glorious sporting career by using drugs. His eyes are red at the corners and have a distant look. Occasionally, he seems close to tears. One hand drums almost constantly on his knee. He has always seemed somewhat distrait, but now he has the lost air of a man who has fallen from the heavens into an unknown world, and is trying to figure out where he is and what he should do.

On June 22, Millar was detained in Biarritz by drugs police investigating his professional cycling team, Cofidis. He emerged 48 hours later after confessing to having used the banned blood booster erythropoietin (EPO) on three occasions. The key to his downfall was a pair of syringes which had contained the drug, that he had taken before winning the world championship in Canada in October 2003.

"I used them, I forgot about them, left them in my bag, went to Las Vegas, came back, was unpacking and found them. I thought, "What the fuck has my life come to?" and put them on the bookshelf. It's my most private place, a place no one touches. It had scarred me: I had won the World Championship by a huge margin and didn't need to have used drugs. I had got to a point where I had wanted to win so much that to guarantee my victory I did something I didn't need to do. I didn't want to forget about it."

The drug police found them when they searched his Biarritz flat after his detention, and put them in front of him late in his 48-hour detention. "At first I made up a story. I thought I could still get out of it. After 47 hours they started threatening me, they were flipping out because I had not admitted to anything. It was Thursday evening, they were going to keep me, take me to Paris in a van, keep me in for three days then put me before the judge on Monday.

"I could have carried on. I have a good lawyer in Paris and might have got away with it. But I thought, "Fuck this, I can't live with this." It wasn't difficult. I was just thinking, "I can't go through with this, I'm fucked whatever happens, it's not 100 per cent my fault, but I'm not going to live like this." I could have kept fighting, fighting, fighting, but fundamentally, I'm not a good liar."

He accepts that he hung on to the syringes partly because deep down inside he wanted someone to catch him, because he had lost so much respect for himself that he no longer cared if he were caught and it came to an end. "I believe in the power of the subconscious. It was my get-out. I wasn't happy. I wasn't enjoying it. I didn't like the point I'd got to. It was an extreme way of doing it, but it's typical of my style of life."

Born in Malta, brought up in Hong Kong and west London, the 27-year-old Millar is nominally Scottish but actually rootless, a charismatic young man, part grunge kid, part art student, who opted at 18 to be a professional cyclist rather than go to art college. Asked how he made the journey from an idealistic youth who was adamant that he would never use drugs to a cynical professional who needed "guarantees", Millar holds up finger and thumb. The gap between them is half an inch.

"It's that. I was 100 per cemt sure I'd never dope. All of a sudden it escalated out of control." It was, he believes, a form of adolescent rebellion against the demands of his sport. "It was the only thing in life that defined me. I resented that. I didn't think about it, there was no twiddling thumbs and wondering if I should or I shouldn't. I just walked into a room one day and did it."

The turning point came during the 2001 Tour de France. He had won the opening stage in 2000, but a year later he fell in the first stage, and barely clung on for another nine days. Eight days in, he greeted me with hysterical laughter after one tough stage finish in Alsace. "By day nine or 10 I'd started to go mental, the managers said they would fly my then girlfriend in, but when they asked her, she was, 'No, I'm not coming.'" That night, he saw an older professional in the team who introduced him to EPO.

Before the Tour of Spain, that September, he travelled to Italy and was shown how to inject himself with the drug. There was no risk of a positive test, he says, because the drug was used in small quantities and taken well before competition. Nor were there second thoughts. "You don't stop and think, or it's game over. When the line is crossed, it's crossed. It stops being a sport.

"I had taken on a load of responsibility" – his team was invited to the race on condition that he start and perform – "and I was taking that on, being professional." It was "mental insurance", and there was nothing to stop him. "There was very little guidance, few options, no coach, no set-up in the team to encourage you not to do that. No other team would have pushed me through what I went through in that year. I was going bananas."

After winning another stage of the Tour in 2002 "clean", Millar used EPO again in 2003. This time, there were financial pressures as well. In 2002, he "had a crap year apart from winning a stage in the Tour de France. I'd saved the team's arse there, but wasn't in the top 100 in the world rankings. From making a lot of money I went to the basic that I had in 2002. I felt it was wrong. My salary dropped by 300 per cent. It was like, 'I'll make them pay me a shedload of money and run this team.'"

The drugs he took that May and August were in order to keep going during intense training over 10 days: courses of EPO taken to keep up the red-cell count, plus the use of testosterone patches to keep his level of male hormone up. Both red blood cells and testosterone drop as the body becomes fatigued, impairing performance. If they are boosted, more intense training is possible. "It's training hard and taking a certain amount of EPO over 10 days so you can keep doing the training." As before, stopping taking the drugs well before racing removed the risk of a positive test.

In recent years, since the drugs scandal that almost stopped the 1998 Tour de France, many top professional cyclists, particularly those specialising in the great stage races such as the Tours of Spain, Italy and France, have moved away from building condition through racing to high-intensity training camps, but it is impossible to say whether or not they are on similar programmes to the one that Millar used. He knows the solution: out of competition testing, which is currently being beefed up by cycling's governing bodies. People in the sport, he says, genuinely don't know whether their fellow competitors are using the drug. "I only know about me. I didn't ask questions of other guys. Everyone is so paranoid now."

In January 2002, I asked Millar about his attitude to drugs. I didn't ask point blank: are you using them? Sports journalists, and particularly those who work in cycling, don't: it is like asking if someone beats their wife. Millar's answer was, "I don't need to dope. I don't have to live with myself doing that. There will always be guys ahead of me who are one step ahead of the rules. I have to live with it, because it's their choice." There was not an untrue word in the sentence, but it was not a point-blank denial. He looks back and says: "I hadn't refined my answers to be ambiguous." Later, he managed that, but felt uncomfortable.

Ironically, from the start of this year, Millar had turned his back on doping and begun racing "clean" under the influence of a British coach, Peter Keen, and the Lottery funded World Class performance programme. "I wanted to win the Olympics clean, for myself. I wasn't good with myself. I had changed as a person."

He regrets what he has done, and seems relieved that, for the moment, he is through with cycling. "If you go through such a big ethical change in one day it's going to affect you on a deeper level. I was unstable, my self-esteem started evaporating. I was living a lie and that's not good for anyone. It is so hard to explain, because I was capable of winning big races clean. I couldn't explain it to myself. It's very confusing. I haven't slept well for the last two or three years."

More sleepless nights must await. On August 4, a disciplinary commission will decide the length of his ban. He will be stripped of the world title. He will probably sell his "dream home in Biarritz", which he has spent two and a half years having restored, but will never sleep in. Where next? He has no idea. He accepts what he has done, hopes the ban will not end his career, and now wishes to offer his services "to prevent young riders doing what I have done".

For seven years Millar has been known as "Boy Dave" to me and my colleagues. He earned the nickname when he turned professional at the tender age of 19, and brought a fresh face, glamour, and a bit of rock-star chic to the two-wheeled world. Now, the boy faces a painful growing up.

Millar returned to racing in 2006, and has since reinvented himself as a leader in the fight for a cleaner cycling. His personal story of his downfall, rehabilitation and redemption, Racing Through the Dark, *was deservedly a best-seller. Richard Virenque came from completely the other side of the spectrum, however, as this piece on his retirement shows.*

Tainted hero Virenque ends polka-dot era
25 September 2004

Richard Virenque, the French rider described once as "incarnating the issue of doping" finally called time yesterday on a career in which, against the odds, he survived the biggest drugs scandal in sport since Ben Johnson to retain a place in the hearts of the French public, if not in the minds of more dispassionate followers of cycling.

"I was particularly worried about doing one year too many," said Virenque. "Leaving cycling on the right note is something I've dreamed about. I don't see what I can gain by riding the Tour de France next year."

Virenque, who will be 35 in November, had hinted that he might quit the sport after winning a stage of this year's Tour across the Massif Central on France's national holiday, Bastille Day. His final appearance on a bike will be at a touring event on October 3.

The record books will note that July 14 was the seventh stage victory in the great race for the slender, piping-voiced lad from the Var who climbed with all the aplomb of a nodding dog, and that it was a springboard to his seventh King of the Mountains title, an absolute if not absolutely pristine Tour record.

The enduring images of Virenque, however, are not those of a mountain king whizzing up the passes of the Alps and Pyrenees. They are more sombre: his expulsion, face creased with tears, from the 1998 Tour after the police inquiry into his Festina team exposed their reliance on industrial quantities of the blood-booster erythropoietin, liberally laced with human growth hormone and the heroin-amphetamine cocktail known as "Belgian mix".

A few days earlier he had solemnly announced that the allegations that Festina had used drugs were untrue, and Festina's expulsion was followed by police questioning in which he denied using drugs, a claim he continued to make for two further years. His refusal to confess was, he said, a stance he adopted to avoid taking the blame for others who had never got caught.

He was brutally lampooned by *Les Guignols*, the French version of *Spitting Image*, who created a Virenque puppet festooned with syringes mouthing the ludicrous phrase which formed the core of his defence that he had accepted drugs without knowing what they were: "Without my knowledge but of my own free will."

Then came a tearful confession in a Lille courtroom in October 2000, that he had used the drugs "with his knowledge and of his own free will" and a lenient nine-month ban which reduced him to a bloated wreck.

His comeback, initially for a pittance with the Belgian team Quickstep, earned him some redemption, however, with victory in the Paris-Tours Classic in October 2001, and prestigious mountain stage wins in the Tour at Mont Ventoux and Morzine.

Virenque was adamant that he was now racing "clean" and, though his word carried little credibility, the results bore him out. Whereas in his pomp, in the mid-1990s, he could race through the mountains at the front for day after day, in recent Tours an epic mountain performance would be followed by a day or two when he was clearly under the weather.

His Tour mountain titles record this year was not well received by the previous holders, Lucien van Impe of Belgium and Federico Bahamontes of Spain, since four of his victories, between 1994 and 1997, were achieved with the help of banned substances. Asked recently why Virenque had not been stripped of those titles, a senior member of cycling's governing body, the UCI, appeared surprised at the very notion.

The courage Virenque showed in his comeback meant that the public continued to turn out for him. Their red banners in the polka-dots of the mountains jersey lauded Richard "Lionheart" as a god, and recent Tours saw ever more bizarre items along the route: cows in spotty jerseys, polka-dot cars, and a 40ft-high banner on a cliff face in the Alps. Their loyalty meant that his popularity was never in question, but his credibility would never recover.

By 2005 I couldn't wait for Armstrong to retire. It wasn't just the fact that I was certain in my mind that he was doping although I couldn't actually write it, there was the whole "Armstrong show" –

his massive entourage, the sense that he and those around him were bigger than the entire Tour, and thus bigger than the sport of cycling. This piece from the 2005 reflects something of those sentiments.

The cycling world's daily struggle with Mr Muscles of Brussels
4 July 2005

In three weeks' time the Tour de France will not merely bid farewell to Lance Armstrong, but to an entertaining spectacle which has accompanied the American since 2001, played out each morning on whatever vast parking area is hosting the Tour's daily stage start. Yesterday the dance of the bodyguards, the bodies and the bus took place in the industrial hinterland of the town of Challans, between a petrol station and a vast exhibition hall.

The Discovery Channel team's vast blue and grey vehicle, air conditioners humming like a spaceship and windows tinted tantalisingly, is parked up and cordoned off with red ribbon, against which a sweating mass of cameramen, journalists and fans pushes fruitlessly like high tide against a sea wall.

The back door of the bus is guarded by a burly Belgian ex-policeman, Serge, nicknamed the "muscles from Brussels"; at the front stands the bespectacled, slight figure of Erwin, who looks as mild as a kitten in his perfectly pressed shirt. In fact he is a martial arts specialist who has worked protecting George W Bush.

The ribboned area has the forbidden feel of a VIP area at a premiere, and that is heightened when Sheryl Crow – vast black mirror sunglasses, black slinky top, tight jeans – slips under the tape. Those inside wear what seems to be almost a uniform for the Armstrong inner circle: crew cuts, shades, Nikes, and the yellow "Livestrong" wristbands, probably not bootlegs purchased on eBay.

The pecking order – and the way Armstrong's accession to celebrity has turned traditional cycling values on their head – is shown when Crow goes straight into the bus, while her escort, the five-times Tour winner Bernard Hinault (aviators, bald patch, a boxer's walk) waits 10 minutes before entering the sanctum. A rockstar, and a woman at that, taking precedence over a two-wheeled legend at the Tour is something that would have seemed barely credible even 10 years ago.

It is 10 minutes before the start time when the inner members of the inner circle begin to emerge: team manager Johan Bruyneel, bearing a briefcase, Brylcreemed hair and a big grin; Armstrong's team-mates, skinny, impassive to a man under more exotic sunglasses, some chewing energy bars.

They disappear astride their bikes and the "ah-ing" begins. Every time the bus door opens, the crowd emits a collective sigh: perhaps it is Armstrong. *Non, non, non*, comes the response; all of five minutes before the start flag drops he emerges, signs autographs, mouths a few niceties and disappears, with Erwin and the Muscles parting the rows of fans like a speedboat in a choppy sea.

Armstrong has bodyguards, of a slightly different kind, allotted to him during the cycling part of each stage as well. Yesterday, as is usual, two team members, George Hincapie and Benjamin Noval, were instructed to stay close to him to keep him from crashing. There were four *chutes* [falls] during the stage, none serious, but Armstrong came through unscathed, avoiding a prone Frenchman, Samuel Dumoulin, in the hectic finale.

Today, the fourth of July, the yellow jersey will be on the back of another American, a clean-cut lad from Utah with a penchant for Batman. David Zabriskie, who has a habit of putting off-beat interviews with his fellow cyclists on his personal website.

That should not distract, however, from the perfect start that Armstrong has made to his final Tour. The only favourite within a minute after Saturday's time-trial was Alexander Vinokourov, with the rest up to three minutes behind.

The daily performance outside the Discovery bus has a clearly defined purpose, and that will be pursued relentlessly in the final three weeks of Armstrong's career.

Alongside the Armstrong show – on and off the road – the Tour went on, in its uniquely immutable way. There was much more to the race than the Texan, as this diary from his final Tour shows.

The *Observer*
2005 Tour diary: week two
Sunday, Les Essarts

Sudden heat, a rash of holidaymakers in skimpies and Speedos by the roadside, a swelling of support for local team Bouygues Telecom – the stage finishes not far from the elegant chateau that houses their headquarters – and a sprint finish at the end of a stage that is supposed to be by the seaside, but remains at least a field's width from the beach.

Monday, Tours

Literary France today: a quick flip past the birthplace of François Rabelais, a nod to Honoré de Balzac and an exhibition in the tourist office devoted to Antoine Blondin, whose elegies to the race are as integral a part of its 1960s heyday as Anquetil and Poulidor. *Fay ce que voudras* – do as you will – wrote Rabelais. The Tour sprinters would add "as long as you don't fall off", but the race judges do not have such a liberal outlook and relegate Robbie McEwen for a series of headbutts at fellow Australian Stuart O'Grady on the elegant Boulevard de Grammont.

A newspaper ad for a mattress company the next day runs a picture of today's winner, Tom Boonen, arms in the air, with the caption "awake" and McEwen, close behind with his head tucked under O'Grady's arm, captioned "asleep". Two days later, McEwen wins in Montargis, with Boonen in his wake. He jests that Davitamon, the company who sponsor him, should run an ad showing the Belgian finishing second and caption it "he didn't use the same vitamins". Given the speculation about which cyclists use which vitamins and whether they are legal, this does not raise a huge laugh.

Tuesday, Blois

Since Saturday's time-trial, the yellow jersey has been worn by the American David Zabriskie – universally known as Dave Zee – he of the clean-cut college-boy looks, an elaborately rebuilt leg after a close encounter with a lorry in his native Utah and a fine line in delicate sarcasm, as in this answer to a question about his CSC team's winter boot camp: "I stared death in the eye and it helped me grow as a man. It made me what I am because I almost died in the woods and I can't wait to do it again." He will need all his strength after becoming the first rider to lose the yellow jersey because of a crash since Chris Boardman in 1998. His successor is a rather less kooky American, Lance Armstrong.

[Zabriskie would go on to be a witness against Armstrong in the USADA case.]

Wednesday, Montargis

[The day when London was awarded the Olympic Games ahead of Paris.]
The only signs of anti-British feeling after the IOC's 2012 Olympic Games vote are a few catcalls from the crowds near the finish on seeing a car registered in Britain. We are expecting at least a few rotten tomatoes or a demonstration from an angry farmer or two and feel a little let down. The vote, and the Paris 2012 T-shirt we were given in Challans, leaves the *Observer* with a dilemma. Will it be taken the wrong way if we wear it next week, when the weather might finally turn hot again?

Thursday, Nancy

[The day of the London bombings]
The tragic events in London do not seem real in the self-contained, relentlessly festive world of the Tour. I've felt this before, 10 years ago, reading about the massacres at Srebrenica as Miguel Indurain was being given a birthday cake a few yards away. The jarring dislocation between here and home is hard to avoid and is made more acute by the abrupt emotional U-turn: affectionate joshing with French colleagues one evening, condolences the next morning. A planned minute's silence on Friday at the start barely alters the feeling.

Friday, Karlsruhe

If two halves make a whole, there is one British competitor in the race. Reading-born, Scottish-educated Italian Dario Cioni, plus Welsh-domiciled Magnus "Maggie" Backstedt who is married to former Wales cyclist Megan Hughes, surely between them add up to one Briton. Cioni, who is aiming for a place in the top 10, made a fine late bid to win yesterday, while Backstedt fights out today's stage finish in Germany. His aim is to win a flat stage and for a time, as he fights his way up to Robbie McEwen's side, it looks as if Maggie may.

Saturday, Gerardmer

The tide of humanity making its way towards the Col de la Schlucht, the first big climb of the Tour, begins an impressive 25 miles away on the outskirts of Colmar, which is not even on the race route. From there to the summit, every parking space is full of cars disembarking fans on bikes who then ride to the top, dicing with death under the tyres of the cars in the race convoy. At the top is a poster proclaiming "one human being is missing and always in our hearts". It is, predictably, in honour of Richard

Virenque, disgraced in the Festina drug scandal and now working as a consultant for Eurosport. Some things never change.

Armstrong quit at the end of the 2005 Tour, making his famous diatribe from the finish podium against those who did not believe in him. Among several pieces I wrote about his retirement was this one. Describing the legal cases that Armstrong was involved in was a way of keeping the drugs allegations against him out there, meaning the reader could make up his or her own mind about what he was up to. The circumlocutions that were necessary to keep on the right side of the Guardian's *lawyers now look ludicrous, but with Armstrong's legal action under way against the* Sunday Times *they were paranoid, and not unreasonably so.*

Armstrong faces legal marathon
26 July 2005

In keeping with his declaration that he wishes to keep out of the public eye for the near future, Lance Armstrong yesterday denied recent press rumours that he would run for the governorship of Texas in next year's elections.

Armstrong yesterday began his retirement by flying to the south of France for a beach holiday with his girlfriend, the rock star Sheryl Crow – whose next album is inspired by her love affair with the seven-times Tour de France winner – and his children Luke, Grace and Isabelle and close friends. His plan, he said before the Tour ended, was to have a preview of his life "for the next 50 years – no stress".

That may not be quite so easy to achieve in the medium term, if the list of impending legal cases involving him is anything to go by. As in so much that he has brought to his sport, litigation on this scale is a first for professional cycling, where lawyers were hardly involved until the 1980s and where they have tended to limit their activities to the occasional contractual dispute.

All the legal disputes have a common theme: drugs allegations involving either Armstrong or his former trainer Michele Ferrari, with whom the Texan officially cut all ties after Ferrari's conviction in October on drugs charges.

A recent biography of Armstrong estimated that he is employing 11 lawyers on eight cases in three countries: the US, Britain and France. Several of the cases centre on allegations made in the 2004 biography *LA Confidentiel: Les Secrets de Lance Armstrong*, which uses what is apparently circumstantial evidence to support its claim that he may have used performance-enhancing drugs.

Armstrong has brought libel suits against the authors, the *Sunday Times* journalist David Walsh and the former *L'Equipe* sportswriter Pierre Ballester, and against the *Sunday Times*, as well as against two of the witnesses quoted in the book.

Armstrong is also fighting a Dallas company, SCA Promotions, over his $5m (£2.86m) performance bonus for 2004. The company withheld the bonus, saying that it wished to look into the allegations in *LA Confidentiel* further and asking to examine Armstrong's medical records. The case is in arbitration and is expected to stay there until at least the end of the year.

In a further case to be heard in the US, Armstrong faces a case brought by his former personal assistant Mike Anderson, who claims he was sacked by the Texan in February 2004 after spotting a box containing steroids in Armstrong's bathroom. Armstrong denies the claim and has issued a counter-suit.

Finally, Filippo Simeoni's case for "public defamation" against Armstrong will be heard in Paris in March. The Italian cyclist was a key witness in Ferrari's trial and sued Armstrong after the American claimed in an interview with a French newspaper that Simeoni was "an absolute liar".

Whatever the outcome, Armstrong has confirmed that he will return to the Tour next year in a consultant's role with the Discovery Channel team. "I'll be on the Tour a little, probably bothering [the team manager] Johan [Bruyneel], begging for a place in the car." He already part-owns the management company that runs the team.

His immediate task, he accepts, will be to find a new US star to front the team. "The Tour is the only time that cycling crosses over to the newspapers and networks. For the American public to stay interested in cycling and the Tour they have to have an American guy, an American face."

As well as his close friend George Hincapie, Armstrong has named another, younger rider with the team, Tom Danielson, as a possible future leader. *[both Hincapie and Danielson would eventually confess to using banned drugs and would testify against their former boss in the USADA inquiry.]*

Speculation that Armstrong will eventually find his way into politics was heightened when the White House confirmed yesterday that he had taken a telephone call from George W Bush, a fellow Texan, shortly after finishing his final Tour in Paris.

President Bush and last year's Democratic presidential candidate John Kerry are both keen cyclists. Kerry was at the Tour over the weekend and said that Armstrong would be a force to be reckoned with if he went into politics, "but I hope he goes in for the right side".

Armstrong has never openly declared his allegiance; he is on President Bush's cancer commission but apparently opposed the Iraq war, and his girlfriend's left-wing credentials are well established.

Armstrong denied at the start of the Tour that he had any immediate ambitions for a political career, citing his dislike of press conferences. "I don't like this setting," he said. "Why be president and have this setting every day? But politics and the good of my country interest me."

Given the benefit of hindsight, this piece was hard to resist. It ran alongside another, which placed Armstrong in the pantheon of world sporting heroes who had quit while on top of their game: Nicklaus, Ali, Fangio, Herb Elliott, Rocky Marciano, Martin Johnson, Steve

Redgrave. For a few weeks it was possible to put him in that league. But on August 23, l'Equipe broke the story that EPO had been found in urine samples taken from Armstrong in the 1999 Tour. What that meant was that there was finally direct proof to go with the wealth of circumstantial evidence. Unfortunately, for legal reasons, Armstrong could not be described as a drug taker. That was to take another seven years.

5. AU REVOIR FLOYD, BIENVENUE MARK

Eleven months after Armstrong's retirement, the Tour caravan assembled in Stuttgart, well aware that a major doping scandal was looming after Spanish police had broken the blood doping ring centred on Doctor Eufemiano Fuentes, with a host of the biggest names in the Tour implicated.

Tour elite thrown out
1 July 2006

Jan Ullrich's T-Mobile team had laid on a sumptuous buffet in a luxurious golf club a dozen miles out of town where the press were to meet their squad yesterday morning. But as the team bus turned into the drive at Kemperhof, 10 minutes before it forks up, the driver took a call on his mobile phone and was told to do a U-turn.

Their leader was out of the Tour de France, which was at a stroke deprived of the only rider in the field who had actually won the race. Ullrich's team-mate Oscar Sevilla of Spain was also withdrawn, along with Rudy Pevenage, the grizzled, burly Belgian former professional who has been Ullrich's mentor since he turned professional in 1993 and was to manage T-Mobile in this Tour. The public-relations man who had arranged the spread, Luuc Eisenga, was left to face the press on his own, an apposite image of the shambolic embarrassment the race endured yesterday. Never can so many favourites have been lost in the flagship event in any sport in so few hours.

After their implication in a blood-doping inquiry conducted by Spanish police, and reported in the Spanish press on Thursday, was confirmed, the Tour was rapidly relieved of Ullrich and the other big favourite, Ivan Basso, as well as last year's fourth finisher Francesco Mancebo of Spain. The three riders' records put them at the top of the Tour's recent hierarchy behind the now-retired seven-times winner Lance Armstrong.

Ullrich finished in the first three in seven of the last nine Tours, Basso second and third in the last two races and Mancebo has five top-10 placings in the last six Tours. The loss of credibility was the greater with the implication in the investigation of Joseba Beloki, third in 2000 and 2001 and second in 2002.

Last year's fifth finisher Alexander Vinokourov was forced out of the race yesterday evening, even though he was not personally implicated in the police inquiry. His team, Astana, withdrew the five riders in their Tour squad who had been named in connection with the inquiry and as a result, they were only able to field four men, thus falling foul of the rule that Tour teams must start with at least six cyclists. They had owed their place in the race to the clemency of the Court of Arbitration for Sport on Thursday, which reversed the Tour's decision of Monday that they should not ride due to the possibility that they might damage the race's image.

Ullrich, Sevilla and Pevenage went early in the morning, after T-Mobile were sent a fax by the Tour organisers who had received a 50-page memo from the Spanish Cycling Federation, giving details of the police investigation.

Mancebo, who is now considering retirement, and Basso followed at lunch-time, after a lengthy meeting of the international teams association in Strasbourg's Palais des Congres, where it was decided the ethical code agreed on by the teams in 2005 should be rigorously applied. The code specifies that teams should provisionally suspend cyclists who are involved in police drug inquiries, and there have been many since the Festina scandal began the clear-out within the sport.

Critically for this Tour, the teams decided the half-dozen riders who were removed should not be replaced, even though the rules permit this. "We wanted to give a strong message to the outside world by not allowing replacements. That would be too easy," said Patrick Lefevère, head of the teams body, the AIGCP, who added he was "ashamed" by what had happened.

Early in the afternoon Basso's manager Bjarne Riis returned to the conference room in the Palais des Congrès, where he and Basso had sat side by side only the day before, with Basso sidestepping questions about the affair while Riis declared himself powerless to act. "We had a chance to look at the 50-page memo and have established that he is part of the case and under suspicion," said Riis.

There was a certain implacable if unsavoury logic about yesterday's events when they were put in the context of events in cycling since the exclusion of the Festina team from the 1998 Tour. The other great Tours, the Giro d'Italia and Vuelta a España, have been hit by scandals that have made the overall results from certain years virtually meaningless.

The 2001 Giro lost its overall leader and main favourite after a police raid; the 2005 Vuelta winner Roberto Heras was recently banned after a positive test. For the Tour's hierarchy to be shaken in this way on race eve was shocking but not astounding. Whether the credibility of the Tour could be restored, and how long that might take, was what remained to be seen.

Operación Puerto remains the biggest clear-out of major names that cycling has seen. With hindsight it now looks like a turning point. Ullrich's career ended here; Basso returned to the sport after a ban, but has been nothing like the man he was. What is salutary is the difference, compared to the Festina scandal, in the way the riders implicated were treated: they were given no chance of starting the race. This was, in my view, the only option available to the cycling authorities, and for once they actually grasped the nettle. However, as with Festina, Rumsas, and the Armstrong affair, Puerto was not a "conventional" doping case and it served to highlight the weaknesses in the anti-doping system.

Casper triumphs but Hushovd steals blood and thunder
3 July 2006

After 1998's *Tour de Farce*, welcome to the *Tour de Sang*. Most appositely for the city where the Marseillaise was composed, with its references to spilling impure blood, since the Tour caravan arrived here last week corpuscles have topped the agenda. Until yesterday it was a matter of whose blood, in which fridge and being kept for what purpose?

The finish sprints that dominate the opening week, on the other hand, are pure blood and thunder. Yesterday was another reminder of that. Immediately after crossing the line, the yellow jersey wearer Thor Hushovd lay prone, doctors desperately trying to staunch the claret spurting from his right shoulder after a freak accident in the finish straight where the stocky Frenchman Jimmy Casper took victory.

Hushovd looked as if he had been knifed in a barroom brawl but he had actually fallen foul of one of the green 18-inch high cardboard hands that are given out in their hundreds of thousands by the betting company that sponsors the green jersey awarded to the best sprinter. Hushovd, ironically enough, had won the award last year. The hands are prized by the fans, who cannot resist waving them over the crowd barriers in a way that delights the marketing men because the logos and the colour get television exposure. This annoys the sprinters, who have complained that the practice is highly dangerous because they ride so close to the barriers.

The point was made again yesterday after one of the hands sliced open Hushovd's upper arm like a scalpel as he made his move 150 metres out. Then he crossed the line with blood spraying his bike and his fellow sprinters' faces. He was taken to hospital and is expected to start this morning. Tour officials last night said the hands would no longer be permitted in the final kilometre.

"It's very dangerous. It's not the first time it has happened," said Casper, who has been rubbing shoulders with the best of the fast men for several years but had never won a stage in the Tour.

He is a team-mate of Bradley Wiggins in the Cofidis team; yesterday both the Olympic pursuit champion and his fellow Briton David Millar avoided any close encounters with publicity handouts to remain 17th and 18th overall. It is 12 years since two men flew the union flag, or in Millar's case the saltire which is painted on his bike, in the first 20 of the Tour.

The Marseillaise was being sung loudly and liquidly in the streets here on Saturday night, and there were signs encouraging *Les Bleus* on the roadsides yesterday. Casper's win will bring forth another surge of Gallic pride. French stage wins are rare and nationally cherished items nowadays because the French media and teams consider their riders are racing in a "two-speed sport" where French teams are "clean" and those who win rather dubious. If yesterday was *cyclisme a deux vitesses*, Casper had a third.

Hushovd will start this morning without the *maillot jaune* he won in Saturday's prologue time-trial. He finished only ninth in the sprint and was relieved of the race lead by Lance Armstrong's closest friend in the peloton, George Hincapie, who had finished less than a second behind the Norwegian on Saturday.

Hincapie, the only one of Armstrong's team-mates to complete all his seven victorious Tours, saw an opening at the final intermediate sprint, where he sneaked into third place, carrying a time bonus which meant two seconds were deducted from his overall time. That made him yellow jersey "on the road", putting pressure on Hushovd to finish in the first three placings, which also award bonuses.

Armstrong will no doubt be delighted, because he part-owns Hincapie's Discovery Channel team, but he will not have smiled when his old adversary, the president of the World Anti-Doping Association Dick Pound, said he felt last week's drug scandal had left the image of cycling and the centrepiece of its calendar "in the toilet". Speaking on Radio Five Live he repeated the view he expressed in the *Guardian* last October, that cycling had been "close to being in clinical denial".

"If they resolve to do something about it then they have a chance to take some steps they haven't been able to do in the past. Something has to be done about it or the risk is the sport will be ignored by some, marginalised by others, and it won't be a sport any more," he said.

Dick Pound was an old adversary of Armstrong and the UCI; they had crossed swords the previous year after l'Equipe had revealed that the Texan had tested positive for EPO in the 1999 Tour.

The double whammy from the 2006 Tour came in the week after the race ended, when the winner Floyd Landis was confirmed as having tested positive for testosterone.

Landis case erodes all trust in Tour
30 July 2006

Eight days ago Floyd Landis wrapped up what may prove to be a pyrrhic victory in the Tour de France amid the gently rolling hills of Burgundy. Eight years before, over the same roads, between the same towns, another kooky character with a goatee beard, the Italian Marco Pantani, wrapped up his Tour win in 1998.

The circumstances were disconcertingly familiar: France had made it to the final of a World Cup, the Tour had been dominated by a colossal drugs scandal and Landis and Pantani had achieved feats it was believed had put cycling back in touch with its past. In both cases, the vastness of the drug scandals – Festina in 1998 during the race, the blood-boosting ring this year, just before the start – was such that it induced an intense need for something and someone to restore belief, to redeem the event.

It took several years for Pantani's win to unravel amid clear evidence that he was a persistent user of the blood booster erythropoietin (EPO); it took four days for Landis to come unstuck. There is an outside chance that the test on the American's second urine sample will clear him this week. There is every chance it will repeat the initial verdict, ushering in a lengthy legal and endocrinological process (endocrinology being the study of the endocrine glands and their secretions) in which he attempts to clear his name. Whatever the outcome, his reputation has gone.

In happier times in cycling, stars were given the benefit of any doubts going. There was nothing to indicate that Pantani had won the 1998 Tour under the influence of illicit substances other than the fact that he would have been stupid and perverse to do so amid the biggest drug scandal the sport had known. The assumption about Landis this year was the same.

Landis insisted on Friday that he had not taken drugs, although the day before, when asked the same question, he hesitated and said "I'll say no", as if he had a choice in what to reply. But denials mean nothing in cycling because denial in the face of reality is a way of life for some. Pantani went to his deathbed swearing blind he never used EPO. Richard Virenque said the same for two-and-a-half years. The belief among the drug takers is that if you are not positive, you are not taking drugs. And that is stupid and perverse. Tyler Hamilton maintained that his positive for blood-boosting was due to the presence of a twin in his mother's womb, which subsequently disappeared. Roberto Heras, winner of last year's Tour of Spain, is adamant that his positive for EPO is nothing to do with use of the drug.

Landis has hired the same lawyer as Heras, Jose Maria Buxeda, and his defence now rests on the fact that his testosterone count is naturally high and the test is flawed. Of course.

It will, no doubt, all become part of the history of a sport that has taken denial beyond the surreal, that brought us dogs that take steroids, sick mothers-in-law who require growth hormone, wives who use EPO as a fertility treatment. It speaks volumes for cycling that the British racer David Millar stands out as a shining example because, when confronted with the evidence, he came clean, recognised his folly and dishonesty and took his punishment.

On Thursday evening, a few hours after news of Landis's positive test had broken, I received a message from a cycling friend, a bloke in his mid-50s who is absolutely typical of the vast unheard body of fans who race bikes for fun and who ride up mountain passes to see how far they can push their bodies and minds. "I know we are cynical [already] but this is so bloody depressing. Can we ever believe in another great ride?" he asked. Unfortunately, the answer is "no".

No matter how much we want to believe in some feat that harks back to Eddy Merckx and Fausto Coppi, unless we are intimately acquainted with the cyclist in question and know enough of his medical history and his personality to make a rational judgement, we must suspend belief in anything in the Tour that looks unbelievable. Wait for the drug tests, be ready for the police inquiry, expect the spin and denial.

It is, however, utterly imperative that we do not idly believe every Tour cyclist takes drugs. I was asked a few years ago whether it was possible to race the Tour de France "clean"? "Surely not," said my companion. "The event is simply too tough." "Why not?" I said. Cyclists I knew were "clean", such as Chris Boardman, had completed the Tour with a bit to spare. I would say the same about Bradley Wiggins and Millar, and others in this year's Tour. My companion thought for a moment. "But if you can do it clean, then taking drugs to do it is unforgivable, surely?" In recent years that is what too many of the men in the upper echelons of the Tour have forgotten.

The Landis positive was a desperate moment, although its eventual ramifications did not emerge for a further six years. The young American was stripped of his Tour title a year later – the process took that long – and eventually, after four years of denial, brought forward the evidence that led directly to Lance Armstrong's incrimination. He had, however, been strongly advised by Greg LeMond to reveal everything he knew immediately after the positive test, but he ignored him. Had he (and indeed Tyler Hamilton) behaved with the same courage as David Millar, cycling would have looked very different in 2012.

In the surreal parallel world that was cycling in the early 2000s, the Tour was coming to London; whatever the drug issues, the Tour remained the Tour. I was not the only one with very contradictory and confused feelings about cycling at this point.

Childhood dream can help end nightmare
18 February 2007

When the Tour de France visits London in July, it will do so at a time of unprecedented crisis for cycling. The previous year's Tour winner is unlikely to be known, unless Floyd Landis, who finished first then tested positive, is cleared of using testosterone. It is, however, likely that Landis's version of events will be widely known, as he announced last week that his autobiography will be published just before the Tour starts. Its title, *Falsely Positive*, is magnificently hubristic.

Landis is merely the tip of the iceberg. It is impossible to predict whether previous Tour de France winner Jan Ullrich, and the 2005 runner-up Ivan Basso will be at the London start. That will depend on the fallout from Operatión Puerto, the Spanish blood-doping inquiry that led to both men's exclusion from the 2006 race.

Behind the scenes, the men at the top of the sport cannot even seem to agree how it should be run, let alone how to deal with the doping problem. The big-race organisers and the governing body, the Union Cycliste Internationale, are bogged down in a turf war over the UCI's controversial ProTour calendar – UCI want it, the organisers do not – that is set to go to the European Court.

"I can see why people have lost faith in cycling, because there are so many problems," acknowledges Bradley Wiggins, the Olympic pursuit champion and Britain's most successful cyclist. "I'm a fan as well [as a rider], and always have been. The events of the last six months have made me think twice about whether I still love it."

By the end of last August, after Landis's positive test was announced, Wiggins was a demoralised man. "It was one of the best Tours for many years, to be part of it made me proud, but a few days afterwards the whole thing evaporated," he says. If there is one reason why people should go to the Tour when it visits London for the first time this summer, it is because of the presence of men such as Wiggins, who have publicly and proudly turned their backs on the needle and the blood bank. "There are a lot of people like me, not just a few of us," says the Londoner. "A lot of the guys are open about being clean. You have guys in my team [Cofidis] like David Moncoutié who simply loves his sport, but isn't prepared to go to the lengths it might take to win the Tour. He was twelfth on the Tour on bread and water and is something special.

"The Tour was my childhood dream. When you start riding, every kid dreams of riding the Tour when you are training, sprinting for road signs and so on. For that to be reality and to happen to me was amazing. As someone who grew up as a club cyclist it's something to be proud of for the rest of your life."

The birth back in September of his and wife Cath's second child, Isabella, has helped Wiggins to put his sport's struggles into perspective, he says. "That's increased my belief that it's just sport, that there are more things in life than winning in sport. I'm happy with where I am, what I've achieved. If I were to have to do things other riders might do to win a yellow jersey, or a Tour de France, that's not for me. I'd rather bow out and do something else."

In some ways, the Beijing Olympics is nearer at hand for Wiggins than the Tour, even though there are 18 months before he defends his Olympic individual 4,000 metre pursuit title. In competitive terms the 2008 Games are just around the corner. Which is why next weekend's World Cup track meeting in Manchester suddenly has such importance.

"There isn't much time to play with. In terms of competitive pursuits there is this week, the world championship in March, and next year's Worlds," says Wiggins, 26, between training sessions at the Manchester velodrome, where, on Friday, he will take to a track for a world-standard competition for the first time since the Athens Games. "Beijing isn't that far away. It's less than two years and that goes quickly. My priority is a double of golds, in the team pursuit and the individual, at the Worlds and Olympics, and Manchester is a bit of a dress rehearsal." Already, he is eyeing possible rivals for his Olympic title; the good news is that only his old foe Bradley McGee of Australia seems to be in the frame.

The only hiccup in Wiggins's progress this winter was a freak training accident last Thursday when he fell off a treadmill, cutting his forehead and, the physios suspected, straining his groin. He should be fit for the World Cup, however. The good news is that Wiggins is stronger and faster than he was at this time in the last Olympic cycle. In training last week he and his three team-mates in the team pursuit squad were on a time of 3min 58sec for the 4,000m, faster than they managed in taking silver behind the Australians in Athens.

Part of his increased strength can be put down to physical maturing, but the road programme he has followed since leaving the track at the end of 2004 is also responsible. "I feel a different athlete to the one I was in Athens. I feel stronger, more mature, and having done the Giro d'Italia and Tour de France puts [the track] into perspective.

"In terms of effort and difficulty this is easier to do. The Tour is tougher mentally; a four-minute pursuit is awful to ride in the last kilometre, the team pursuit the same, you hurt so much, but in the Tour you are up against the scale of the thing, mental challenges every day. You get to thinking, 'I'm hurting and I've two weeks to go here.'"

Wiggins has spent the winter building up for his return to the track, and he hopes the form he has found will carry him through the spring and up to July, when he will be among the contenders for that Tour de France prologue time-trial in London. "There's a lot of expectation, not so much pressure, but this is a once-in-a-lifetime opportunity. Win or lose, how many guys ride the Tour prologue in their home city? It's an honour and a privilege for someone who set out to be a professional cyclist as a kid. I can treasure that experience for ever."

This interview mirrors one that Bradley Wiggins gave to me for the Observer *at the start of 2005, when he expressed pretty much the same feelings about David Millar as he did about Landis. As I said in the piece, the reason to keep faith in the sport was because of those riders who had openly turned their backs on doping – and because there were others, one assumes, who had done the same but kept quiet about it.*

The third time of crossing
2 July 2007

The roots of the Tour de France's visit to England this summer probably lie in a chance encounter in the spring of 1966. An obscure French professional cyclist, in his first season, is sitting on a seat in the sunshine pinning on his race number. The current world champion, an Englishman, sits beside him as they wait for the race to start. In accented French he fires out questions calculated to put the nervous novice at his ease: Who are you? What are you called? What have you won?

Thirty-five years later the Tour de France organiser, Jean-Marie Leblanc – our youthful obscurity – was still overwhelmed by the charisma of the then world champion, Tommy Simpson. The encounter remained fresh in his mind: he still could not believe that a rider of Simpson's stature could take notice of a nonentity such as he, Leblanc, then was.

Leblanc's partiality for English cycling and English cyclists started then and continues to this day. He will be there in London on July 7–8, burly, genial and perhaps a little less lined in the face than of late because in 2005 he retired as organiser of the world's greatest bike race after 16 years.

The Tour's visit to London may seem like an anachronism for an event which is quintessentially French and has never been won by a cyclist from this country. Cyclists in England, after all, run red lights and get in the way of cars. Whatever the recent success of our track cycling team at the Olympics, Britain cannot be described as a heartland of the sport.

That may be true but it is to ignore the fact that in the 70 years since two British cyclists, Bill Burl and Charles Holland, became the first *Britanniques* to start the great race, a rich heritage has accrued, reflected in Leblanc's experiences since his meeting with Simpson.

He rode his first Tour, 1968, with the last Great Britain team to ride the event; never a star, he remembers sharing the last place in the bunch with John Clarey, who finished in Paris as *lanterne rouge*, last man in the pack. As a journalist with the newspaper *L'Equipe*, Leblanc was a rare English speaker and he moonlighted for an English cycling magazine. He was a big fan of the talented Mancunian Graham Jones, who reminded him of Simpson with his chequered Peugeot jersey and his roman nose.

"*Mon favori*" he still calls Jones, who works on the Tour for Radio Five Live. He looked on as Robert Millar challenged for the King of the Mountains prize in the 1984 race and admired the Scot's colossal talent, even if he found him the devil to interview.

With a confirmed Anglophile at the helm, it was no surprise that as soon as the Channel Tunnel made it practicable for the

Tour to visit England, Leblanc brought the race over, making the decision three years after being appointed organiser in 1989. An earlier visit, to Plymouth in 1974, had been blighted by delays at Exeter airport as the riders transferred back to France. The experiment was not popular and made the organisers aware that the travel had to be impeccably organised.

The Channel Tunnel was not actually open to the public when the riders and cars piled into the shuttle wagons – in many cases after a lengthy wait, because the tunnel still had teething problems – for the two stages of *Le Tour en Angleterre* in 1994. And here it was legitimate to ask the question: would the public turn out?

By then, 57 years after Burl and Holland had boarded the Golden Arrow to head for Paris, the Tour had its place in the national consciousness. The process had been slow, however. Simpson made headlines in the 1960s but for the wrong reasons, dying in tragic and controversial circumstances having overdosed on amphetamines. The sprinter Barry Hoban won eight Tour stages in the 1960s and 1970s but complained bitterly that no one in his native land knew who he was, even though he was a popular figure in Ghent.

The broadsheets began to look across the Channel in the late 1970s but the breakthrough was the inception of a new television channel with a brief to think outside the broadcasting box. With Robert Millar and the Irish stars Sean Kelly and Stephen Roche as the *points d'appui*, Channel Four began showing nightly highlights in 1986 and remains synonymous with the Tour in many minds, even though it has long given up the race, initially in favour of cricket.

To set the seal on *Le Tour en Angleterre*, a British hero appeared in the form of Chris Boardman, who had come from nowhere to wear the yellow jersey a few days earlier, although unfortunately he was relieved of it a few hours before crossing the Channel. The scenes were unforgettable: a swath of southern

England transformed for the day into a passable replica of *la France profonde,* with an entire population taking the day off work to set up camping chairs and roadside barbecues as the show travelled past.

And having seen two million people on the roadsides of Hampshire, Kent and Sussex, Leblanc declared he would bring his Tour back as soon as was practicable. He has been as good as his word. All it needs now is for Bradley Wiggins or David Millar to emulate Boardman but this time to carry *le maillot jaune* into Kent.

The London départ *saw two key debuts by British cyclists in the Tour: Mark Cavendish and the future double Olympic gold medallist Geraint Thomas. The following piece was the first large profile of Cavendish the* Guardian *ran, although we had pinpointed him as a man to watch back in 2005.*

Rookie Cavendish dreams of leaving England in yellow
6 July 2007

If all British eyes will be on Bradley Wiggins and David Millar tomorrow when the Tour de France's prologue time-trial comes to a climax in Whitehall, on Sunday as the sprinters jockey for position on Canterbury's Rheims Way the figure to look for will be the diminutive, pink-clad Mark Cavendish, the first British fastman to start the Tour in 19 years.

With six wins under his belt in his first professional year "Cav", inevitably, will be tipped as a possible stage winner for T-Mobile, and if he gets an opening the dream finish may indeed happen, but these are uncharted waters for the 22-year-old, as he acknowledges. "The Tour is a lot faster than any other race," he says. "I've heard everything – uphill, downhill, the finish sprints – is three to five kilometres per hour [2–3mph] faster than other races. I've no apprehension at all about the finishes, only getting to the finish."

The bunch sprints that decide most of the early flat stages are the Tour's most spectacular and dangerous side, a maelstrom of bodies and bikes heading for the line at 40mph. Crashes are inevitable, so too physical contact, be it merely brushing shoulders – scary enough at that speed – or butting, pushing and, on one memorable occasion in 1997, bottle-throwing.

No sprinter admits to nerves, and Cavendish says simply: "It doesn't bother me a bit. I love it. Since I was young I've loved watching sprints on television. If anything I think the smaller races can be more dangerous than the big races – you can have 150 guys going for the win in a small race, but maybe 30 sprinters in the Tour. It looks worse on television than it actually is. I hate people shouting and as long as people ride cleanly that's fine, but if they flick you deliberately, that's different."

Only a handful of British sprinters have figured in the Tour's results: most recently Malcolm Elliott, but that was in 1987 and 1988 and the Sheffield flyer never won a stage. Before Elliott, the best known is Barry Hoban, winner of eight stages, the British record, in the 1960s and 1970s.

"I wrote a career plan when I was young, and I thought then the Tour was coming to London in 2009," says Cavendish. "It came two years earlier than I expected so I thought it would never happen again in my lifetime and I'd miss out. It makes it extra special. I just hope people who aren't into cycling come and appreciate how beautiful the sport is."

Cavendish is the first Isle of Man cyclist to start the Tour and is the best in a long and distinguished line of riders from the island, the product of a rich, close-knit two-wheel culture born of the now defunct Cycling Week of races, notably on the TT circuit. The island produced a Commonwealth champion in the 60s in the late Peter Buckley, and another notable sprinter in the 80s, "Pocket Rocket" Steve Joughin. Another former Manx cycling star, Mike Doyle, trains Cavendish when he returns to visit family.

Thanks also to the fact that it competes as a separate entity in the Commonwealth Games – where Cavendish won a gold medal last year – the island is currently punching above its weight on two wheels, with Jonny Bellis earning selection for the world track championships this year at only 19, and Pete Kennaugh, "another possible Cavendish" in the view of Rod Ellingworth, head of British cycling's under-23 academy programme. Cavendish pays tribute to Ellingworth, whose academy has produced another Tour debutant this year, Geraint Thomas. "He turned me from a fat wanker to a world champion in 15 months. The best thing he did was teach me the ethics of hard work."

[In his autobiography Boy Racer, *Cavendish states specifically that I misheard him when I scribbled down "fat wanker" rather than "fat banker" – a reference to the fact that he had worked in a bank before turning professional. I apologize for the misquote; such things can happen – if only very rarely – during telephone interviews. But the point he was making remains – his progress under Ellingworth was outstanding.]*

"He's got a boxer's attitude, massive self-belief," says Ellingworth, who remembers that when he first met Cavendish he saw "an 85-kilo lad – 15 kilos more than he is now – saying how quick he was, how he would never let me down. You go "Yeah yeah yeah" and accept it, a bit of lip service. But, looking back, he believed in himself and was already a winner."

Ellingworth adds that Cavendish has incredible clarity of mind in the hectic final kilometre, as the sprinters fight for position, and he already has a team leader's ability to "put an arm around someone, give them a bit of sympathy, get behind them, which is why he will be a success.

"And he's not scared to say when he's not good; he takes responsibility as the team's sprinter. He's not going to the Tour thinking "Great, I'm riding the Tour" – he's thinking he's absolutely cacking himself, he seriously doesn't know what he's getting into, he doesn't take it lightly at all, and in the next breath he says he's fast enough to win a stage."

Kennaugh has since gone on to become a gold medallist at London 2012 and a hot prospect on the road; Bellis would win a bronze medal at the under-23 world championship that autumn, but his career was wrecked by a near-fatal scooter crash in 2009.

The 2007 Tour was a complicated, emotional race, probably the low point of all the post-1998 Tours as far as I was concerned, because it went from a magnificent beginning to an ignominious ending, offering a vision of what the sport could be with a gruesome reminder of what it was. It's best read as a whole, via the Observer *diary for the complete four weeks.*

The *Observer*
Tour 2007
Wednesday 4 July

Driving into central London, the heart lifts as the first Tour posters are sighted – and the first notices warning that Westminster will be shut down on Saturday afternoon and Sunday morning. It finally hits home: the *Grand Départ* is actually happening and it's happening here.

Something else hits home as, a little later, I drive into the race headquarters in the ExCel Centre: no matter what the attractions of the host city, the initial venue on any Tour is usually an anonymous barn – the ExCel Centre is actually more redolent of a giant logistics warehouse or airport freight terminal. On the plus side, it is neither a cattle market in Holland nor a ruined castle in the middle of nowhere, as has been the case at *Grand Départs* in the past.

Thursday 5 July

L'Equipe has stopped being pessimistic about doping for a day and looks at the weather. It has been raining. As their reporter apparently feels it often does in these parts. On the hunt for further cliche in central London, I take a taxi through the area where the *Grand Départ* is to be held. The driver, it seems, has not bought into Mayor Ken Livingstone's culture of cycling in the capital just yet.

He will not be watching Wiggins, Millar et al. He hates cyclists. He hates them more than anything he can think of. Ninety per cent of them should not be on the road, because 90 per cent of them cannot ride their bikes. In the interests of equity, however, he approves of the 10 per cent who can, and he is not a fan of "90 per cent" of car drivers, either. Given the dodgy manoeuvres that are performed hourly by the four-wheeled Tour caravan, perhaps it is as well he is not going to view the race.

Friday 6 July

Most teams content themselves with a bland press conference at ExCel to present their squad for the Tour but T-Mobile, befitting the sponsor with the most interest in the British market, set their sights higher, inviting the press to breakfast at Jamie Oliver's restaurant Fifteen near Old Street. The relaxed ambience, accessible riders and positive talk about fighting doping is in contrast with the tense questioning of the previous evening when the Tour favourite Alexander Vinokourov met hacks at ExCel. If T-Mobile's do is indeed what cycling might be like if the sport's drug problem is tackled head on, it is a promising prospect. So promising that the head of the International Cycling Union, Pat McQuaid, makes a point of turning up to endorse the team in pink.

Saturday 7 July

Radio Monte Carlo call to get the views of an *Anglais* on the *Grand Départ*. After exploring traffic chaos (bad but normal for the Tour), *les Britanniques* in the race (five of them), the views (Buck House is a great backdrop) and cycle use in London (growing in spite of rabid taxi drivers) we turn to Wimbledon. The presenter points out, smugly, that the French are way better than the British. The reply is obvious: in the Tour this weekend, thanks to Mark Cavendish and Bradley Wiggins there is more chance of a British stage win than a French one. Long live the old rivalry, says RMC, and signs off quickly.

Week two
Sunday 8 July, Canterbury

An unforgettable day in Kent, with a variety of surreal juxta-positions. To start, there is the sight of the Victoria memorial outside Buckingham Palace without a car nearby, with the road closed for the Tour. To celebrate, we do a few extra laps of the statue *[in the Tour car]*. Then we spend as much of the stage as possible driving on the right, simply because we can. Strangest of all is an invitation to provide an English voice from the *Départ* on French television, which offers an insight into how *les rosbifs* are seen on the other side of the Channel. With me on the chat show are a red phone box and two bulldogs.

To cap the weirdness, France 2 have dug up an ageing Beatles tribute band, but what is striking is how their singer manages a near-perfect John Lennon impersonation. The Tour offers its share of surreal moments, but none can match standing in Trafalgar Square playing the role of fifth Beatle next to four middle-aged moptops with guitars.

Monday 9 July, Ghent

Overnight, the decor changes: for warm bitter, brown Trappist beer; for roadside pubs, cafes with net curtains; for rolling hills and green hedges, first world war battlefields. And windswept fens where the occasional large wind farm is a big improvement on the natural scenery. To underline the lack of home-grown cycling stars in Kent, every community along the way has bred a Flandrian cycling star: Freddy Maertens in Nieuwpoort, double Tour winner Sylvere Maes in Gistel, a double world champion in the evocatively named Briek "Brick" Schotte in Tielt. The British connection comes at the finish, birthplace of Bradley Wiggins and former home of Tom Simpson.

Tuesday 10 July, Compiègne

Team managers, particularly from the French squads, have been advising their riders not to burn up all their energy in fruitless escapes in the opening week. Nicolas Vogondy and Matthieu Ladagnous, the day's *echappées*, take the instructions to the letter and can be seen at various times during their 145-mile spell at the front during the race's longest stage going at speeds that a decent amateur could manage out training. But, bizarrely, the bunch go slightly slower because they have no wish to catch the pair and prompt a resumption of hostilities. The result is a slow race that lasts six-and-a-half hours and mystifies many of the cyclists. The sight of everyone pedalling at tourist speed to preserve the status quo is unprecedented.

Wednesday 11 July, Joigny

A rapid spin south from Champagne vineyards to the land of Chablis, where bottles of the flinty white wine are handed out liberally at the finish at a groaning *buffet de terroir régional*. It is a literary excursion, too, starting in Villers-Cotterets, the

147

birthplace of Alexandre Dumas, passing through La Ferté Milon, that of Jean Racine, and ending up in the town of Marcel Aymé, who wrote of one hero: "He believed that God was interested in bike races and of course he was right." Deity of the day is none other than Thor, second name Hushovd, who flies over the line for his fifth Tour stage win.

Thursday 12 July, Autun

The hopes of Kazakhstan go tumbling with Alexandre Vinokourov when the leader of Team Borat, as Astana are affectionately known, comes a cropper in the Morvan massif, during an unusually hectic stage for the Tour's first week. It is the fruit of a policy by Christian Prudhomme, the new Tour director, who wants to make greater use of France's hills to liven up the opening phase. As a former head of sport at France Televisions, he is presumably happy with a 41 per cent share of the viewing audience, rising to 50 per cent as Vino's desperate, unsuccessful attempt to regain the bunch reaches a climax.

Friday 13 July, Bourg-En-Bresse

British Cycling performance director Dave Brailsford visits the race en route to riding the *Étape du Tour* cyclosportive in the Pyrenees. He is photographed before the start with the four riders in the race involved with the Lottery-funded squad: Geraint Thomas, Bradley Wiggins, Mark Cavendish and David Millar. "Cav", "Wiggo" and "Gee" are in the Tour largely through Brailsford's policy of placing riders with professional teams who put them in races such as this, thereby increasing their strength for when the Olympics come round.

It is probably not a coincidence that in a single afternoon Wiggins comes within seven kilometres of winning the stage after a 190-kilometre solo escape, Thomas shows his increasing confidence – at only 21 – by finishing fifteenth and Cavendish is in the mix at the finish for the third time this week, until another sprinter puts a pedal in his front wheel, taking out half the spokes.

Add to that Millar's strong late attempt to win the previous day's stage and Charly Wegelius's unsung contribution to Liquigas leader Filippo Pozzato's stage win and the British influence has lasted well beyond Kent. The Britain Olympic squad are fast movers: while Wiggo is speeding south from Sémur-en-Auxois to Bourg, Brailsford is done for speeding by the *gendarmes*, an occupational hazard in the Tour convoy.

Saturday 14 July, Le Grand Bornand

As well as Lance Armstrong's controversial former trainer Michele Ferrari, Vinokourov has hired one of his bodyguards, Serge Borlee, a bullet-headed man-mountain nicknamed "The Muscles from Brussels", and his old chef, the Swiss Willy Balmat. It is tempting to chant: "Are you Armstrong in disguise?" The answer so far is no; the cancer survivor never went into the mountains with a two-minute handicap. You can buy all the help in the world, but good fortune has no price.

[There was a double entendre *here, which I hoped the reader would pick up. Vino was done for blood doping 10 days later.]*

Week 3
Tignes, Sunday

A victory for "Chicken", as Michael Rasmussen is known, which turns the Tour on its head on a day of crashes. Worst off is Stuart O'Grady, who piles off a bend on the Cormet de Roselend and breaks bones in his back and a few ribs. He is carrying eight water bottles in his jersey to refuel his team-mates and the consensus is that they acted like airbags and saved him from more serious injury. Britain's Charly Wegelius slips a gear coming

149

out of a roundabout at 40mph and falls on his head. The impact can be measured in the fact that his helmet is broken into four pieces. He gets away with whiplash and abrasions. T-Mobile lose three riders: Michael Rogers with a dislocated shoulder, Patrick Sinkewitz, who breaks his nose after colliding with a spectator while riding to his hotel, and Mark Cavendish, whose cuts from his crash six days earlier have become infected.

Val d'Isere, Monday

Like hundreds of other amateur cyclists, the *Observer* sets off to share the roads around the stylish ski resort with the Tour pros as they spin their legs on the rest day. There is, however, only one road, and it goes up the Iseran pass, to 2,770 metres above sea level. All the Tourmen are riding it, even though they will race up it the next morning. I start the climb with the Agritubel team. Their little string is led by former French darling Laurent Jalabert – out for a spin with his brother Nicolas.

Near the top, I am overtaken by two pros from Quick-Step who whizz past at twice my speed, wearing full training kit – tights, arm warmers, warm tops – in the 30C heat. They are not sweating, although the impression they give of being untouchable gods lessens when I catch a glimpse of them taking photos of each other on their mobile phones. Back at the foot of the climb, I encounter Bradley Wiggins and we float gently up the ascent to Tignes. Gently is relative. Wiggo is not apparently breathing, but after 2km I am a sweating, shivering wreck.

Briancon, Tuesday

The politicians weigh in. The new French president Nicolas Sarkozy makes a flying visit and mouths a few platitudes about how the Tour makes the French people happy and how he is there to support the organisers in their fight against doping. In which cause he hops up on the podium after the finish and kisses

Richard Virenque on both cheeks. Perhaps he asked Virenque whether he remembers the last visit by a French President to the race. That was Jacques Chirac, in Correze in 1998, the day Virenque made a tearful exit from the Tour after being thrown off during the Festina drug scandal. (They didn't meet.)

A more meaningful intervention comes from the Kazakh defence minister Danyal Akhmetov, who sends a text message just before the stage finish to Marc Biver, manager of Astana. Alexander Vinokourov has crumbled during the stage and Biver is ordered to put the team to work for Andreas Kloden instead of the oil-rich country's national hero.

Marseille, Wednesday

German cycling's *annus horribilis* deteriorates further. *[There had been continual revelations about Jan Ullrich and T-Mobile since the Operatión Puerto scandal.]* Sinkewitz is positive for excessive testosterone (subject to a second test) and German cycling crumbles within days: TV stations ARD and ZDF suspend coverage – the first time any national broadcaster has pulled out of the Tour mid-race. Adidas abandon sponsorship of T-Mobile and the French national squad. Audi contemplate following suit. The world championships in Stuttgart in September are in question. All three major team sponsors, T-Mobile, Gerolsteiner mineral water and the Nordmilch dairy co-op, are to reconsider their future in the sport. As an illustration of how rapidly and destructively doping can impact on a sport, it is deeply sobering. On past experience, however, it probably won't make the cheats think again. *[T-Mobile were to pull out later in the year; Gerolsteiner and Nordmilch – backers of Milram – followed suit in 2008.]*

Montpellier, Thursday

Three records are broken. Attacking in a crosswind to catch a rival unawares is something all textbooks mention and a move team managers love to try. For the first time in recent memory on the Tour, it works and Christophe Moreau is the victim. Sporting France goes into mourning, although "Titou" will no doubt merely become even more popular now that he has been unlucky, because that is how France loves its cycling stars.

The stage win is the first for a South African, Robert Hunter, which means the low-rent Barloworld team (budget €2.5million) has outplayed all the other teams in the race bar Quick-Step and CSC. Finally, the vast amount of road furniture in the Midi means the Tour breaks the record for the number of roundabouts in a single stage. There are 49. God help us if the Tour ever visits Stevenage or Milton Keynes.

Castres, Friday

There has been much grumbling among the *suiveurs* this year about the dearth of gifts, but nostalgia for the freebies of yesteryear is nothing new. Time was, when you returned from the Tour laden with largesse from the stage towns, like Crusaders weighed down with booty, wrote Geoffrey Nicholson, the *Observer's* late cycling correspondent, in 1992.

This year we thank London for a bag, Ghent for a computer memory stick, Autun for a bottle of Chablis and Briançon for a business-card carrier and a bit of cloth, the purpose of which confused us all. (Sunglasses cleaner? Napkin? Hankie?) But Castres comes up trumps with a bag containing a Tour survival kit: energy bars, sun cream and shower gel. There are a few nasty odours emanating from Germany and Denmark right now, but at least the press corps will smell sweeter.

[The Denmark reference was to Michael Rasmussen; questions were being asked about his failure to register his "whereabouts" for random testing during pre-season training.]

Martin Johnson, captain of the England team that won the Rugby World Cup in 2003, turns up at the race for the second day running. While Jonno's love of American football is well documented, his passion for cycling is less well known. "I am amazed at what they do in the mountains," he tells French television. The feeling is mutual: most cyclists can't quite believe the things that go on in the scrum.

Week Four
Plateau-De-Beille, Sunday

An opinion poll in the *Journal du Dimanche* reveals that four out of five of those questioned doubt the probity of Tour de France stage winners, or any professional cyclist winning any race anywhere. That is hardly surprising, given the nine years of almost unbroken scandals in the sport since the Festina drugs bust of 1998. There is a paradox here, though: television audiences are up, with a 52 per cent share of the viewing French public, and the roadside spectators are as numerous as ever.

Loudenville, Monday

Further fall-out from the collapse of German cycling following the wave of confessions about doping, the departure of the national TV stations ARD and ZDF from the Tour and the withdrawal of Adidas. Other key backers such as Audi, VW and Skoda are thinking again. So too, still more traumatically, are the bike companies who sponsor Didi Senft, the bearded crazy who dresses up as a devil and runs down the road after the riders waving a trident and yelling "Allez, allez, allez". Senft is famous for his BO – the red suit rarely seems to get washed – so without him at least the Tour would smell a little sweeter in one sense.

Pau, Tuesday

We have been here before. Grilled "Chicken" is on the menu as the press question Michael Rasmussen. By the neatest of ironies, the setting, Pau's Palais Beaumont Congress Centre, was the venue for the legendary confrontation between Lance Armstrong and the media in 2001 over Dr Michele Ferrari. During Rasmussen's 40-minute press conference the race is not mentioned once.

An hour or so after "Chicken" runs for his hotel, the racing seems even less relevant as the news of Alexander Vinokourov's positive test *[for blood doping]* interrupts a press conference given by David Millar. The Scot leaves the room in tears. Vino's departure leads to one funny, if slightly sick moment. A rumour does the rounds that Vinokourov's blood may have originated from his father. The rider's riposte is: "If that's the case, it would test positive for vodka." That the Tour has come down to jokes about whose blood is where reflects its dire state.

Col D'aubisque, Wednesday

Jeers for Rasmussen from French fans on the roadside and cheers for the backmarkers after a protest at the stage start by the teams in the race who consider they are racing "clean". One rider, Lilian Jegou, of Française des Jeux, states: "You have more sporting credibility if you are at the back of the race." To celebrate this new phenomenon, the paper *Libération* announces that it is now supporting only the *lanterne rouge*, as the last rider in the race is nicknamed, after the red lantern that hangs on the back of a train. In the old days, cyclists in contention for this position would "race" to lose time, without actually losing so much that they had to leave the race, because there was a certain notoriety – and lucrative appearance contracts – for the last man to finish the Tour. Acting no doubt on the biblical principle that the last shall be first and the first shall be last (in terms of credibility), *Libé* exhorts the current incumbent, the Belgian domestique Wim Vansevenant, to "go slower!"

Castelsarrasin, Thursday, Angouleme, Friday

Two days wending our way from the Pyrenees to the Cognac region, in hourly expectation of a fresh positive test or two. In Angouleme, we receive the final free gift of the Tour, a bottle of brandy. Most are duly grateful.

With no more scandals, for the moment, the caravan indulges in its favourite pastime: gossip. Rumours and late-night text messages proliferate: that this rider or that from this or that team is positive, that new revelations from retired cyclists are imminent.

Cognac, Yesterday

As in 1998, the year of the Festina drugs busts, the Tour's final time-trial has no real meaning. No doubt when Lance Armstrong turns up in Paris to glad-hand potential sponsors for [*Alberto*] Contador's team, Discovery Channel – which the Texan part-owns – he won't be putting it that way, whether or not Contador is in yellow. I remember exchanging words with Armstrong in a Paris hotel at the end of the "Festina" Tour. He believed the vast scandal was all for the good and the sport would change its ways. I was with him on that one, most Tour followers were. After this year's events, our naive optimism now seems like a bad joke.

The diary makes it clear how my mood developed during that Tour; the Vinokourov positive was what disgusted me most, simply because of the level of denial. He had been under fire from the start of the race, as this piece shows.

How Vinokourov was blooded into the Tour of infamy
25 July 2007

One of the hallmarks of cycling's most notorious drug cheats is hubristic denial, on the most colossal scale. If his control test is confirmed, Alexander Vinokourov will end up right on the top row of the pantheon of infamy along with Tyler Hamilton, Richard Virenque and Raimondas Rumsas.

Asked repeatedly about his regime before the start of the Tour in London, Vinokourov cast his eyes to the floor and replied: "Why do you think that training means doping? I have done my work and I have nothing to reproach myself for."

Vinokourov went down the same road after his second stage win of the Tour on Sunday, accusing the president of the International Cycling Union, Pat McQuaid, of "trying to make me look like a cheat. We are always made to look like animals without brains," he continued. "I am not a criminal. I am only trying to do my work in the best conditions I can." By then, the blood had apparently been put in, the stages won.

So much for the "campaign of harassment" that Vinokourov and his intense, shaven-headed manager Mark Biver complained about before the Tour started. Biver, so quick to get behind his leader when the questions were answered, wasted no time in declaring him "guilty until proven innocent" yesterday.

It is worth looking back a few weeks to what Biver referred to as "harassment." There were the nods and winks when Vinokourov rode the Dauphiné Libéré stage race in a state of grace, seemingly winning or setting his team-mates up to win as and when he chose. There were the rumours that he and some of his team mates were the "men in black", said by the International Cycling Union's head of anti-doping Anne Gripper to be training in anonymous clothing in far-off places to avoid random drug tests. There were the rumoured sightings of Vinokourov at Col de Madone near Nice, in the Canaries. With hindsight, it all has a new complexion.

The *Guardian* was among those who questioned Vinokourov's ethics before this Tour de France began, only to be slapped down by Biver, who said that we "had not quite understood". Perhaps we understood all too well. It all makes a horrible, grim kind of sense, as did the case of Hamilton, as did those of Virenque and Rumsas.

Vinokourov had raised eyebrows on Saturday, simply because his margin of victory was so vast, particularly for a rider who had been on his knees – literally – for the previous nine days, who had been unable to get over the biggest Alpine cols with the best the previous Tuesday. As Britain's 1992 Olympic pursuit gold medallist Chris Boardman said, "If it looks too good to be true, it probably is."

By the time the time-trial came around on Saturday, Vinokourov had his back to the wall. His tour had fallen apart when he crashed on the stage to Autun nine days earlier, gashing both knees so deeply that 30 stitches were required to keep him in the race. On occasions he had barely been able to climb the podium to register in the mornings. He had clung on initially in the Alps only to lose, as it then seemed, all chance of overall victory on the stage to Briançon, when he was unable to hold the pace set by the Spaniard Alberto Contador and the young Colombian Juan Mauricio Soler. He ended the stage in tears, convinced his race was over.

This was to be Vinokourov's last chance to win the Tour, just as the 1998 version looked set to be Virenque's best opportunity ever. He is now 33, well past the age at which a cyclist is at his best. He had the pride of an entire nation, Kazakhstan, and the weight of its oil millions riding behind him. He had an entire group of his countrymen riding alongside him in the country's national colours, bearing the name of their capital city. He had pulled strings with the politicians to put the financial package behind the team together.

David Millar could easily be understood when he said that Vino was his favourite rider in the bunch. Vinokourov was the best road racer in the peloton, with an ability to produce the winning attack at the right time, and a never-say-die mentality which delighted the fans. His final kilometre move to win the last stage of the 2005 Tour on the Champs-Élysées was the high point of a routine seventh Tour win for Lance Armstrong.

He is a legendary hardman, who originally turned professional in France for the Casino team. The turning point in his career came when his best friend and fellow Kazakh, Andrei Kivilev, died of head injuries sustained in a crash in the Paris-Nice "race to the sun" in 2003. "I know he is always at my side. His strength is always there to support me," he repeated.

But Vino's connections, in hindsight, appear suspicious. From 2000 he was part of the T-Mobile team alongside Jan Ullrich, with whom he escaped to take silver to the German's gold in the Sydney Olympic road race. Doping, if not necessarily systematic, was clearly endemic in the German team, if the spate of recent confessions of drug use and administration – by the team's doctors – is anything to go by. Ullrich is now disgraced, although still in denial.

In 2006 Vinokourov moved to the Liberty Seguros team, run by Manolo Saiz, the team manager who was subsequently implicated in the Operation Puerto blood-doping investigation. Last year, to fuel his competitive anger further, he was denied entry to the Tour in spite of the fact that he had not been obviously involved in any wrongdoing.

His ejection from the Tour came after a lengthy saga in which Liberty pulled out following Saiz's implication in Operation Puerto, upon which Vino went to Kazakhstan and put the finance together to relaunch the team as Astana. But when the Tour purged itself of cyclists involved in Operation Puerto, Astana – formerly Liberty – lost five men, which put them below the minimum required to ride the Tour.

Vino was out, the Kazakh baby with the Puerto bath water. Astana was rebuilt, with entirely new management and in what now seems like an exquisite irony, Biver went to great lengths to underline that this year's Astana had nothing to do with the squad run by Saiz. Perhaps, but they do have this in common: Saiz also lost his leader, Roberto Heras, to a positive drug test, in Heras's case for erythropoietin.

Vino went on to win the Tour of Spain last September, in a dominating performance in which he won a total of three stages. That performance will now be tainted with suspicion, as will Vino's other major wins – the Liège-Bastogne-Liège Classic in 2005 and the Amstel Gold Classic in 2005.

Vinokourov's positive was not the only major event of the 2007 Tour; Rasmussen was removed by his team, Rabobank, late on the rest day after contraditions in his whereabouts in pre-season training made his position untenable, and the day after, a positive test for Christian Moreni (testosterone) led to the exit en masse *of Cofidis, including Bradley Wiggins. I found the fact that Wiggins had to leave the Tour utterly disheartening; it summed up the way that "clean" riders were victims of the drug cheats. The Vino and Rasmussen scandals were different – eight years on from Festina, much of the press was alert to lies, contradictions and evasions – so although we knew something was up in both cases, there was little we could do other than write what we knew and hope they got rumbled eventually.*

The 2008 Tour was the last – one hopes – to experience a flurry of doping scandals, but before those erupted, it enjoyed a significant moment: Mark Cavendish's first stage win.

Cavendish sprints away from the field and into the history books of the Tour
10 July 2008

British sportsmen who walk the walk as well as talk the talk are rare creatures, but Mark Cavendish proved yesterday that his self-confidence is merited. Having said he would do his utmost to win a stage in this Tour, and that this was possible because he has been faster than the other sprinters on seven occasions this year, he duly delivered on Avenue de la Chatre *[in Chateauroux]*, with the triple world road champion Oscar Freire struggling to keep pace.

It is five years since the last British stage win in the Tour, David Millar's victory in a time-trial at Nantes, but a huge 33 years had elapsed since Barry Hoban's win on the Bordeaux velodrome in 1975, the last time a Briton took a bunch sprint in the Tour. Hoban managed eight stages in his career – that was the last – and if Cavendish is looking for other omens, the last Tour winner in this town was Mario Cipollini, king of the sprint for a decade in the Tour and Giro.

This was a magisterial sprint to close the Tour's longest stage, 145 miles. The last of his pilot fish, Gerald Ciolek of Austria, pulled off at 250m to go, just after the field swept up the last breakaway of the day, the French champion Nicolas Vogondy.

Initially Cavendish sprinted side by side with Thor Hushovd, the huge Norwegian who took Sunday's stage into Saint-Brieuc, but as the Crédit Agricole leader faded, Freire and another wily old fox, the near-veteran German Erik Zabel, edged into the picture. Cavendish, however, never looked like he was going to be caught, and finished over a bike length clear.

"I've won a lot in the last year and a bit and there was only a Tour win that I had still to achieve," he said afterwards. "People always say, 'He's got some scalps, beaten some good people', but I've been one of the best in the last year. I thought of myself as a big name in sprinting, but unless you've won a Tour stage you can't count yourself a great sprinter."

Yesterday was his 18th victory since turning professional last season although Cavendish has some way to go before he matches Hoban – twice a Classic winner as well as those eight Tour stages – but if he continues as he has begun in the last 15 months, it is perfectly attainable. After that, who knows?

Cavendish has spoken frequently about the spirit in his Columbia team and yesterday they performed in exemplary style, putting all nine men on the front in the final kilometres to counter a stubborn display from the day's three-man escape, Vogondy, the Breton Lilian Jegou and the lanky Florent Brard.

This was a first truly major win for the American squad, born out of the ashes of T-Mobile when the German team went under last December. They launched a new-name sponsor at the Tour and are also trying to set the pace in riding "clean" under their US owner, Bob Stapleton.

This victory has implications that go beyond the Tour, too. In five weeks Cavendish will take part in the Madison relay at the Olympic Games with Bradley Wiggins. He feels an Olympic title to go with the duo's world title will be more straightforward than winning a Tour stage, and his confidence should remain high for Beijing.

Yesterday's win will also have inspired the British team, already electrifying in trials last week, and it will have given the team's head, Dave Brailsford, a major selling point as he seeks to pull together a sponsorship deal for a Tour de France team in 2010. Cavendish is the first product of the British Under-23 academy, run by the former pro Rod Ellingworth, to win at cycling's flagship event. *[That squad would eventually see the light of day in the form of Team Sky – based solidly on the foundations laid by Ellingworth's academy.]*

For the future, Cavendish says he will not go for the green jersey in this Tour – "This year it's a bit out of my reach" – although it may fall to his team-mate, Kim Kirchen. However, he will now "give it 100 per cent" to win another stage. "I have the team to do it, for sure. I'm getting a bit tired now, but the team have been remarkable the way they have looked after me and kept me fresh."

His next likely target will be Toulouse on Saturday. Yesterday was about the Isle of Man, with a first stage victory in the Tour for an island community that has always punched well above its weight since the days of the 1966 Commonwealth Games road race champion Peter Buckley. But today, possibly, could be one for Millar, a Scot who is in third overall as the Tour tackles its first mountain-top finish at the Super-Besse ski resort.

Whether the Garmin team leader can dislodge Stefan Schumacher or Kirchen will depend more on the tactics of the day than brute strength. The pair seem to have plenty of that at present, as Kirchen showed in setting the pace for Cavendish yesterday. It is a long call, but Millar remains optimistic. Cavendish, on the other hand, was simply ecstatic.

The following day's time-trial was won by Stefan Schumacher, who then tested positive; Millar did not take the yellow jersey. By the next year, 2009, Cavendish was established as the best sprinter in the pack, and Bradley Wiggins was waiting in the wings.

French have only memories as British eye success
28 June 2009

It has often been said that the Tour de France is to the French what Wimbledon is to the British: a global sports event in which the founding nation can no longer triumph. Andy Murray may be about to make the comparison redundant *[he didn't win Wimbledon that year, sadly, but the proviso had to be put in just the same]*, but this year it is business as usual for the French in the Tour.

No Frenchman will start with a hope of making the podium. None has a remote chance of winning the green jersey for points, or the King of the Mountains. Any French stage wins will be a major national achievement rather than a matter of routine. For the first time in the race's 103-year history, British fans will await the start of this Tour with infinitely more optimism than their counterparts on the other side of the Channel.

The fastest sprinter in the sport, Mark Cavendish, is from these shores – the Manx shores – and will be the nailed-on favourite to repeat his four wins of last year and win the green jersey, assuming his skill and good fortune do not desert him. David Millar and Bradley Wiggins, meanwhile, have shown enough this season to be candidates for a stage win or a respectable overall placing. The length of the current French famine was thrown into stark relief recently with the news that the last Frenchman to have a real shout of winning the Tour, Laurent Fignon, is suffering from advanced intestinal cancer, which has spread to his pancreas. He is only 48.

Fignon is an intelligent, likeable man nicknamed "*Le Professeur*" because he has a degree and wears spectacles. He won the race in 1983 and 1984, but is remembered as the man on the receiving end of the Tour's narrowest defeat. Fignon led going into the final time-trial of the 1989 race, only for Greg LeMond to snatch the win by eight seconds.

Since Fignon's day, the only Frenchman to have been on the podium was the discredited climber Richard Virenque, who came second to Jan Ullrich in 1997, then fell foul of the Festina doping scandal a year later. Fignon doped too, according to his recently released autobiography *We were Young and Carefree*, but quit in 1993 just as cycling entered the era when EPO became widespread. Unlike Virenque, however, on his day Fignon was one of the last of the traditional cycling champions, capable of winning major one-day Classics or a Grand Tour.

Since retirement, he has gone through various business ventures and, most recently, was commentating for French television. His illness will cast a shadow over the race, but will also lead to a feeling of nostalgia for the days when the French won stages left right and centre and when there always seemed to be a Frenchman in contention for the yellow jersey.

There are various reasons for France's lack of success, something which was already beginning to be a theme when I first covered the Tour in 1990. Some put it down to lack of effort, most notably the five-times winner Bernard Hinault, the last home rider to win the race, in 1985. "The French earn too much money and don't make enough effort," Hinault said. "There are champions who simply go through the motions when they turn pro. You have to put a knife to their throats to get results. The French don't go training. No one slaps them in the face to move them forwards. They need part of their salaries blocked off, to be given back if they win."

The respected journalist Jean-Francois Quenet says the reasons are complex. "Firstly, since the 1980s, we've never seen a super-class French cyclist. The raw material isn't exceptional. Our riders have also been handicapped by doping: after Festina [in 1998], all the French teams except one, Cofidis, virtually stopped using drugs. If you have no super riders and you don't dope, you can't be competitive against super riders and riders who dope. We've had big-budget teams, but that means that anyone with any small results becomes a star, so they have a lack of motivation."

There is another explanation, summed up by the emergence of Cavendish. His achievements underline that the sport is now far more open than in the days, which ended in the 1980s, when the French had the race largely to themselves. The Australians began emerging as a force in 1981; the Irish followed with Sean Kelly and Stephen Roche; the Colombians improved at the same time, and from 1989 onwards the collapse of the Berlin Wall meant that every impoverished cyclist from here to the Urals could look longingly at the cash on offer at the Tour.

Fignon's plight has highlighted something else: the presence in the Tour of world sport's most celebrated survivor of cancer, Lance Armstrong, who was quick to offer his support to the Frenchman. The seven-times winner will come into the race as a wildcard, in several senses. After three years out, no one knows what he is physically capable of. His 12th place in the Giro d'Italia was in spite of poor preparation following a broken collarbone.

It is also unclear how or if he will collaborate with his co-leader at the Astana team, the Spaniard Alberto Contador, the clear Tour favourite from his results over the past two years. But, most of all, Armstrong's comeback has been eventful and controversial. It has to date survived his abortive attempt to construct a personal anti-doping programme, a spat with French drug testers, a dispute with the Giro d'Italia organiser and the near-collapse of Astana for financial reasons. In the next few weeks, anything is possible with Armstrong in the Tour.

The 2009 Tour was the first one I had missed in its entirety for 20 years; partly I felt I needed a break, but I also wanted to avoid the Armstrong show. His comeback was not something I anticipated with any joy. But I did bump into Bradley Wiggins the week before, at the national road race championships in Abergavenny.

Wiggins wants top-20 place in Tour de France
2 July 2009

On form, Bradley Wiggins will be the favourite for Saturday's opening time-trial stage in the Tour de France in Monaco, but has longer-term ambitions for the overall standings. Wiggins is aware that the make-up of the Tour's opening week means he will have a chance of taking the yellow jersey, and he has also set himself a target of a place in the first 20 overall.

"I think I'm going well enough to be up there," said Wiggins. "The top 20 is achievable as my own personal goal. In one sense it's not that big an achievement but it would be something to build on for the future. I don't think I can climb with the likes of Alberto Contador or Cadel Evans, but you have to look at the second echelon of riders, the guys who are going to finish between 12th and 20th."

The triple Olympic gold medallist showed up well in the early mountain stages at the Giro d'Italia, but saved his strength from half-distance so as to keep something in reserve for the Tour. "I was up there for 10 days there. It's hard to concentrate every day in the Giro, because there is always a finishing circuit or a little hill in the last miles, but the Tour is more straightforward. The first week should take care of itself. If I can get close in [Saturday's] prologue time-trial, not too far behind someone like Fabian Cancellara, and then we can do a rattler of a ride in [next Tuesday's] team-time-trial I might have a chance of taking the yellow jersey."

Wiggins is apparently at his lightest-ever race weight, 5kg lighter than a year ago when he was focused solely on winning Olympic gold medals in Beijing.

"I'm in the ballpark as regards power and weight, but the big thing is going to be how I recover. The big thing for me will be the third week, but I've never gone into the final week of a big Tour in [a high] position. The Ventoux on the final Saturday will be a killer, but I'm in the best shape I've ever been for a stage race."

Wiggins went on to finish third in that Tour (fourth at the time, but he was subsequently bumped up the order after Armstrong's disqualification); privately, he felt before the start that he could finish in the top 10, but he was not keen to make it public.

6. RISE OF THE BRITS, FALL OF LANCE: 2009–2012

Since 2009, the Tour has been transformed for the British media and fans. Suddenly, this event, once so marginal, has gone centre stage. That centres on three factors: Mark Cavendish, Bradley Wiggins, and Team Sky.

"He was a plumpish bank clerk"
19 July 2009

It was always tempting fate to put down in black and white that no Briton looked likely to match Barry Hoban's UK record of eight Tour de France stage wins, but I have a cast-iron excuse. Five years ago when I wrote that, in a history of British cyclists in the Tour, *Roule Britannia*, Mark Cavendish was a plumpish bank clerk struggling to find his feet in the Great Britain Olympic team's under-23 academy.

The scale of what Cavendish achieved on Wednesday, when he equalled Hoban's achievement, has to be put into perspective. It took Hoban 14 seasons to win his eight stages. It has taken Cavendish only two. Hoban was glad to see his record equalled. "It's about time, and it's about time we had someone who can win stages in the Tour. He's an amazingly superfast sprinter. He's got an amazing jump, an amazing turn of speed. I think he's matured; as a first year pro he was falling off all over the place but now he realises where he has to ride."

The bare statistics are invidious in one sense, because comparing Hoban and Cavendish is like putting, say, the careers of Graham Hill and Lewis Hamilton side by side. When I last saw Hoban, he was living quietly in mid Wales with his wife, working as a rep for a cycle-component importer. And while his Tour stage wins and one-day Classic successes might have given him a bit more cachet when it came to flogging frames, there was no celebrity stardust about him.

The sport has changed hugely in the past 45 years. When Hoban set off to France to make his fortune on two wheels in the early 60s, European cycling was a closed, conservative world. His first team manager, Antonin Magne, had won the Tour twice in the early 30s, wore a black beret to emphasise his peasant roots, and was not particularly interested in his *anglais*, other than as a team man to support his leader, Raymond Poulidor.

It barely registered with him that Hoban won two stages back to back at the Tour of Spain in his first year as a pro, 1964, and was a few yards from winning a Tour de France stage. Cavendish was also initially designated as a team rider rather than a leader but quickly broke through at T-Mobile. Similarly, Hoban never enjoyed the support that Cavendish does now, because teams were far less sophisticated.

Lower fitness levels and relatively poor communications meant a sprint train like Columbia's was hard to establish. "Sport evolves and, if you go back to the 1970s, I never, ever had a lead-out man, not once," Hoban said this week. "Everyone was there, man to man. The way they do it now, with a team like that, if they are leading out at 65kph very few people are going to come over that. Anyone to challenge Mark going at 65kph has got to do 70kph."

There are obvious similarities between the pair, however. Both used track cycling to hone their speed and bike handling – Hoban has compared Cavendish to Patrick Sercu, a track specialist who took the Tour's green jersey in 1974. And Hoban was the last rider to win a Tour finish on a velodrome, in 1975, at the age of 35, when he zipped down the banking at Bordeaux to outsprint a bevy of youngsters. Cavendish would have been at home there as well.

Both men complain that they are better known in Europe [than in Britain], but only Hoban is correct. Cavendish's frank autobiography, *Boy Racer*, rightly made headlines and he has many more years ahead of him in which his profile will rise. In his autobiography, published soon after he retired in 1980, Hoban was bitter that his achievements went largely unnoticed: "It would be nice not [to be] pushed into oblivion as if it didn't count. No one knows who the hell Barry Hoban was." Right now, it's hard to see Cavendish suffering the same fate.

There has been another key player in recent Tours: Alberto Contador. Whatever one feels about his ethics few can deny his influence. This piece was written before he took his third win in the Tour, and many months before that third win was taken away from him.

The gunslinger firing at a place in the pantheon
27 June 2010

For the past two decades the Tour de France has belonged to the USA and Spain. The Americans have followed their national stereotype to the letter: global stars such as Greg LeMond and Lance Armstrong, both of whom managed the greatest comebacks in the sport's history and took salary levels to stratospheric heights, accompanied by, in Armstrong's case at least, whirlwinds of controversy – bigger arguments, juicier doping allegations, and meatier lawsuits.

The Spanish, on the other hand, have gone to the other extreme. If Armstrong is the equivalent of a jet fighter – very fast, cracking the sound barrier as he goes, shaking those around him out of their slumbers, and leaving an unmissable slipstream – the Spanish resemble those black triangular things made largely of carbon fibre that zip about under the radar. They are stealth cyclists, remaining largely unnoticed before and after the racing is done.

Miguel Indurain was the first Spanish stealth champion, dominating the Tour from 1991 to 1995, five Julys in which the most dramatic event was the annual ritual of watching him receive his birthday cake. As Indurain was about to win his first Tour, a Spanish journalist came up with the phrase that was to sum up Big Mig: so impenetrable was the great man, said the writer, that the woman in his life would never know the man she had married. Oscar Pereiro and Carlos "the silent assassin" Sastre, respectively 2006 and 2008 winners, were so obscure that no one even went to the trouble of dreaming up such a line about them.

This year, Spain's fourth stealth cycling champion, Alberto Contador, is expected to win his third Tour in four starts, if the form he has shown this year holds. Three Tour victories would be key, as that marks the point at which a Tour winner joins a small, elite club: only eight riders in the race's history have managed three victories or more. Equally strong in the time-trials and the mountains, Contador is the perfect all-rounder, and has won every major Tour he has entered since 2007, taking the Giro d'Italia and Vuelta a España in 2008, when he did not start in France. Only four other cyclists have won all three Grand Tours during their careers. It is a remarkable record for a rider still only 27.

Yet he has remained in the shadows, emerging to take the plaudits before returning to live the life of a normal man in Pinto, an anonymous dormitory town in the Madrid hinterland. No tax exile in Monte Carlo for him. As far as indulgences go, Contador's are decidedly modest: a Porsche he bought after his Giro win, a BMW that was his personal reward after last year's defeat of Armstrong, a Weimar dog called "Tour" bought after his first win in the French race. Birds are one of his hobbies, but he has given up his aviary of 20 canaries.

"Off the bike he is a simple, humble guy, but on the bike ... There are two different faces to Alberto: one in the saddle, the other in front of the press," said his *directeur sportif*, the Italian Giuseppe Martinelli, who ironically enough was Marco Pantani's manager in the 1990s. The same was said of Indurain, time after time. Contador's one concession to the charisma-seekers is the victory salute: he mimes a shooting gesture like a child playing cowboys and Indians, which has led to him being nicknamed *pistolero* or gunslinger.

Spanish stealth cyclists are a recent trend, some would say a historical aberration. On two wheels, Spain was once known for producing charismatic, quixotic figures such as Federico Bahamontes, a child of the civil war famed for two episodes, one in which he was (wrongly) claimed to have left the field behind on a climb, then stopped at the top for an ice cream, another in which he set about an opponent with a pump. Luis Ocaña was a tormented champion of the 1970s, who regularly attempted to defeat Eddy Merckx only to implode dramatically en route. Perico Delgado was an equally unpredictable character who lost the 1989 Tour by turning up late for the start of the prologue.

Perhaps this sea change helps explain why Spain is no longer a major cycling nation, if its representation in the Tour is any measure. There is one fully Spanish team in the Tour, but it would be insulted at that description: Euskaltel is Basque, not Spanish. The Caisse d'Epargne squad is French-sponsored, but largely Spanish-managed. And that is it. Ironically, Spain has the strongest stage racer in the world, but no team for him to ride in. As a result, Contador will line up in the colours of Astana, financed by the Kazakh national development fund Samruk Kazyna, with largely Italian management and inevitably known as Team Borat.

Contador began riding a handed-down bike from his elder brother Francisco at the age of 15. On their first ride together, on a little hill outside Pinto, he was faster than his brother, and that seems to have sparked his interest in cycling. From his earliest races he was given the nickname Pantani, because like Pantani he would always sprint for the King of the Mountains award in every event he rode. By the age of 20, he was a professional, under the tutelage of Manolo Saiz, who had a knack for discovering emerging stars until busted during the Operación Puerto blood doping scandal of 2006.

One reason why Contador has remained relatively unsung is because each of his Grand Tour wins has been overshadowed by other events. His 2007 Tour victory, riding for the Discovery team, was a relative anti-climax as the race tried to get its collective head around a series of drug scandals. His 2008 Giro and Vuelta wins were emphatic – the more so as he rode the Giro at a week's notice – but what mattered more was the fact that his team, Astana, were refused entry to the Tour due to involvement in the 2007 drug scandals (in which Contador had not been implicated). No Tour winner had ever had to suffer such humiliation.

2009, of course, was the year of the reprise of cycling's greatest comeback, with Armstrong in the starring role. Contador may have won, but the main strand in the plot was his relations with the Texan, who was then also riding for Astana and employed every psychological trick up his sleeve in an attempt to destabilise the younger man. Armstrong attacked Contador on a cross-wind stage early on, and then criticised him publicly for not following the team's gameplan in the Pyrenees. Afterwards, Contador said there had been "a tendency to prioritise other people's interests". In other words, Astana were racing for Armstrong even though Contador was the strongest.

It might have seemed astonishing that Contador was not destabilised, but in fact it is no surprise once his past was taken into account. In 2004, Contador crashed at the Tour of Asturias. It seemed an ordinary fall, but Contador noticed something: he had abrasions on the back of his hands, not the palms as would be expected. In other words, he had been unconscious when he fell. It was discovered that the fainting fit was linked to a cavernoma, an aneurism: he was offered the option of a risky operation to solve the problem, or remaining handicapped in the sense that he would not be allowed to ride his bike or drive.

The operation left him with 100 stitches running from ear to ear, but it left him with something else, according to those close to him: maturity. "He has said this escape has helped him recognise what is important in life: every time he looks in a mirror he can see the scar, which is as if a doctor had opened his head to look at his brain," says Jacinto Vidarte, the former journalist who handles press for Contador. "He looks older than his true age, because he matured quickly. It always surprises people: he seems far older and more experienced than they expect."

There are question marks over Contador's ability to notch up a third Tour win. One involves the strength of his team: Astana was left virtually riderless when Armstrong moved on with all his mates, and has been rebuilt with a core of strong Italians and Spaniards, including Pereiro. It has never looked poor this year, but whether it will come apart in the crucible of the Tour is another question. There are also doubts about Contador's capacity to get through one specific stage, the third, which includes several sections of the cobbles used in the Paris-Roubaix Classic. But if he is in with a shout when the Tour enters the Pyrenees in the final week, the Spanish stealth fighter will take some shooting down.

Contador won the 2010 Tour after a tense duel with Andy Schleck, but was eventually disqualified after a lengthy dispute over a positive test for clenbuterol, which the Court for Arbitration in Sport ruled was probably due to a contaminated food supplement. He rode the 2011 race with the shadow of an impending suspension hanging over him, and was not present in 2012. He will return to the Tour in 2013.

The other story of the 2010 Tour was the arrival of Team Sky, formed by Dave Brailsford on the back of British Cycling's Olympic success –

of which more later. With Bradley Wiggins in the leader's role, their Tour debut was not a happy one.

Lifting the lid on Sky's icy precision
18 July 2010

Just inside the wide-open door of the Team Sky doctor's hotel room sits the ice bath. It is not much to look at: a paddling pool with a pipe to bring in water at 10 degrees and another to pump it out. Something small and yellow is sitting in the water. It is not a climber who has caught jaundice. It is final confirmation that here is a team that covers every detail: it is a rubber duck. "You've seen all our secrets now," jokes Dave Brailsford, the team principal.

On which note, let us backtrack for a moment and make a more serious point. Team doctor. Hotel room door. Wide open. Doctor absent. "He's very trusting," says one staff member, but that's only part of the point. There is nothing to stop me – or a WADA (World Anti-Doping Agency) patrol, or one of the French television crews who like to do this kind of thing – popping in and rootling around in search of incriminating performance-enhancing stuff.

Open doors are not the norm in professional cycling. Trust has been a rare commodity since well before the Festina scandal of 1998, and if you believe only half the stories of the stuff that has gone on behind locked hotel room doors you can see why. But back in February 2009 when Sky's sponsorship of a British-centred professional team was announced, Brailsford said he would have an open-doors policy: come and see what we do. The team doctor has clearly taken Brailsford at his word. So here we are.

The doctor's room is not empty for long. The sports scientist Matt Parker – the trainer who guided Britain's pursuiters to a world record and a gold medal in Beijing – brings along the team's Norwegian starlet, Edvald Boasson Hagen. Haagen-Dazs,

174

as he is inevitably known, sits on the bed and Parker wraps his legs in two contraptions that resemble outsize moon boots.

NormaTec space boots are used for treating circulatory conditions, putting pressure on the legs to pulse upwards; the team are using them to speed up recovery. The ice bath performs the same function – as used by rugby players – but has a more important role: with the temperatures on the Tour, 35 to 40 degrees by day, 20-plus at night, the riders take a quick dip before bed, to drop their core body temperature, so that they sleep without sweating.

These are all part of a panoply of ways in which Sky are trying to improve their riders' performance: recovery is key in the Tour and sleep is a vital part of that. To that end, Sky have brought their own mattresses, duvets and pillows on the race. They are all hypoallergenic, so that the riders do not wake up with the sniffles hotel beds often produce. They are new, so they contain less dust. And some of the pillows contain built-in iPod speakers so that as the riders go to sleep, they can listen to what they want without disturbing their room-mate, who may well be in a bed just inches away, dying for peace and quiet.

"Eighty to 90 per cent of what we do is the same as other teams, but the aim here is to try harder to help the riders in areas such as nutrition, recovery, what goes in their bottles," says the most senior *directeur sportif,* Sean Yates, a British icon as a cyclist and as a manager a veteran of major teams such as CSC and Lance Armstrong's Astana. "They are going into everything."

Enhancing every area that can be controlled means two things: the riders' performance should improve, over time, and they should have no reason to use doping as a psychological crutch. But it all takes more time and application. That morning, the team helper designated to move the bedding explained it takes him an hour on his own to get duvets, sheets and mattresses into vast bags, and load them into the big black van.

Not far away, Parker and another helper were filling the day's 40 ice bags. These are women's stockings filled with handfuls of ice (the hotels have to supply Tour teams with a designated amount; Sky, naturally, have their own back-up ice-maker); Yates hands them up from the team car to cool the riders down during the stage. Cooling being critical, the team have ice bowls on the bus for after the stage, when the riders wear silicone neck scarves, as used by the military.

The morning briefing has been transformed, with the use of military terms (wingman, tailguard). "In a lot of team meetings there isn't much clarity about what the roles are," Bradley Wiggins says. "It needs to be very clear, so that I won't be complaining to someone that he isn't getting bottles when it isn't his job. A lot of guys are shocked by how advanced it is, others have said their teams were just appalling for communication."

At the briefings, the riders seem to do as much of the talking as the management, with Wiggins and the Canadian Michael Barry in a lead role. "Most teams do what they do because they are run by ex-cyclists and that's what they've always done," Barry says. "Here, no one individual thinks he has an answer to anything. If issues arise, we get them off our chests. From day one, they opened up lines of communication, we were made aware our opinions mattered and that if we expressed them things might change."

Sitting alongside Yates on a very hot day on the Tour, you become aware of the "80 to 90 per cent" that Sky have not changed: the *directeur sportif* constantly handing up bottle after bottle, warning his riders of road conditions through the helmet radios, juggling supplies of ice and bottles. You note also that some of the riders – Steve Cummings, Boasson Hagen – have their own bottles, with different electrolyte mixes, because they sweat in a different way.

Watching the group of 180 cyclists deal with 40-degree temperatures, a vicious dry headwind and climb after climb, a bigger point rams itself home: the Tour is light years away from the track racing that Brailsford and his team dominated in Beijing less than two years ago.

The variables of terrain, weather, inter-team tactics and the agendas of the rest of the bunch have almost infinite variety. Comparing track and Tour is like setting martial arts against pure war. That military terminology is not misplaced.

Among the bustle of the 13 Sky-badged vehicles and the 32 staff and riders, it is easy to forget that this is a project in its infancy. So much has been written and said about Brailsford's new brainchild that two points have been overlooked: this is year one of a five-year project to win the Tour, and Wiggins and company in the Tour is just part of a larger picture for Sky and its partner, British Cycling.

Team Sky at the Tour de France is just the tip of the Sky iceberg: down below are mass-participation rides, taking cycling into schools, and putting 125 Sky employees into today's *Étape du Tour*, the chance for amateurs to face the kind of challenge the pros must deal with. Sky have a director of cycling, Corin Dimopoulos, who has between seven and 70 employees working for him. In the nation's bike shops, opinions have been divided about the project, but the Tour's roadsides tell another story: on the evidence of a week driving, the route, the black, white and blue strip is more popular than any other pro-team jersey.

What of the future? In terms of signings, speculation is naturally centred on the fact that Mark Cavendish has an opt-out in his contract at the end of the season. But on the bigger picture, race coach Rod Ellingworth, for one, notes that Sky are only at the base of a long learning curve: senior Tour teams can have up to 20 years behind them.

"If you look at the majority of us on the Tour, apart from the riders, we haven't done it before," he says. "It is a big enough challenge for many teams, for us there's the moulding-together process, Sean [Yates] has never been a lead *directeur sportif* at the Tour and that needs developing, we are trying out different techniques, trying to find out what works best, whether it's equipment, bikes, clothing, trying to build a coaching model. In a business, the building period is 18 months from when you start, so that means two Tours. By the third, we should be bang on."

It's rare that you have a pay-off as prescient as this quote: in year three Team Sky went on to win the Tour with Bradley Wiggins. That's more credit to Ellingworth's vision than my ability to foresee the future. There would be changes, however: Yates left Sky at the end of 2012; Cavendish came in for 2012 and left at the end of the season as well.

Mortal Armstrong hits the wall on the rock of hell
12 July 2010

Most of the Tour's greats are forced to endure a moment of brutal clarity, when they are reduced to the ranks of mere mortals. For some a particular time and place always denotes the point where they have visibly taken on *un Tour de trop*.

After Lance Armstrong's disastrous showing yesterday the next 13 days will show whether or not signing up for one last Tour at the age of nearly 39 was the two-wheeled equivalent of the boxer who cannot resist one final bout and ends up sprawling on the canvas after two rounds.

Halfway up the Col de la Ramaz, a sign offered leisure cyclists the chance to take part in a circuit of the rock of hell. The heat beating off the asphalt definitely had an infernal quality about it, and the steepest part of the climb leading to a series of tunnels and avalanche shelters through a rocky gorge marked the start of Armstrong's personal purgatory as he slipped inexorably off the back of the group that included all those with pretensions to a high placing overall.

The group still numbered some 35 and that made the point: the seven-times winner was about to have the worst day he has endured in 12 Tour starts. As if by magic – but more probably on the orders of an Astana team manager who had seen the television pictures of the team's former leader in trouble – two of Alberto Contador's team-mates appeared at the front of the group and upped the pace.

The chance to put such a major rival out of the reckoning could not be missed but it was hard to resist the obvious conclusion: Contador was taking revenge for the mind games Armstrong played with him as they jostled for team leadership last year.

Even before the race hit the Ramaz Armstrong's day had a nightmare quality. As the field accelerated before the foot of the climb, the Texan touched a pedal on a roundabout, his front tyre came unstuck from the rim and he fell on the right side of the road.

His jersey was ripped, his knee cut but critically his saddle broke, meaning he needed a new bike, and there were no kind souls in the field to stage a go-slow. Instead he had to fight to close a 45sec gap, with the help of four team-mates, and when the climb started, he had still to fight his way to the front of the peloton.

All those efforts must have taken their toll. The luck that had assisted Armstrong to seven Tour wins – marred by one *chute* that had any true gravity, in 2003 – had finally deserted him. It was not his first crash of this Tour. He fell, along with many others, on stage two to Spa and he had suffered an ill-timed puncture on the cobbles of the Arenberg stage.

"I've never been so unlucky," he said later. The counter argument runs that in the Tour good luck tends to follow the men in form, because the slightest weakness means a fractional slowing in reaction time and a minute increase in stress levels that can make a cyclist simply try too hard.

The rest of the stage was what the French love to call *un calvaire*, a road of the cross. Atop the third category climb to Les Gets, Armstrong was nearly involved in another crash. His head shake spoke volumes. He climbed to Avoriaz in 61st place, nearly 12 minutes behind, pedalling at normal speed rather than his usual frenetic cadence, alongside also-rans such as the French national champion Thomas Voeckler, in happier times the recipient of largesse from the Texan, who "permitted" him to take the yellow jersey in the 2004 Tour.

"I was behind, so starting the Ramaz was hard and then it went from bad to worse," Armstrong told French television. The company unwittingly underlined the extent of Armstrong's misfortune by switching from live coverage a few minutes after Andy Schleck's stage win, including a lengthy ad break and a fulsome preamble to their World Cup coverage, before eventually going back to live pictures of Armstrong crossing the line. He was that far behind.

The Texan's mentor, Eddy Merckx, lost his mystique in 1977, when he rode up the Col du Glandon in a daze due to stomach trouble. Miguel Indurain was never the same again after blowing up at Les Arcs in 1996. For those places and dates, read Armstrong, Col de la Ramaz, 2010.

He spoke bravely yesterday of continuing for his team but those with long memories remember the fate of the first man to win the Tour five times, Jacques Anquetil, who set out on his "one Tour too many" in 1966, and ended it anonymously on a roadside near Saint-Etienne. Armstrong is now in 39th place overall with a kicking to digest: this is uncharted territory for the Texan.

Seventeen years after his first stage win at Verdun in 1993, this will remain the final image in my mind of Armstrong on the Tour de France: grovelling up the climb to Avoriaz with the no-hopers. Given the way he had made plenty of also-rans suffer thanks to his blood-fuelled racing, it seemed only just. The man's trajectory through the race cannot be disconnected from his doping. He was at one and the same time, Armstrong the hero, Armstrong the cheat. From now on, his battles would be fought elsewhere.

Vendée takes detour on road to redemption

26 June 2011

The Tour de France is back in the Vendée and back at Madman's Hill. Yet again. This week, the region south-west of Nantes will host its fourth *Grand Départ* of the Tour in 18 years, after 1993, 1999 and 2005. That is astonishing given the demand from cities and regions all across Europe to host the five-day junket that brings in millions in revenues from the Tour and its vast caravan. There is, however, a good reason for this.

It boils down to a partnership going back 20 years between a politician, Philippe de Villiers, and a former professional cyclist, Jean-Rene Bernaudeau, who was chief lieutenant to the five-times Tour winner Bernard Hinault in the late 1970s and early 1980s. De Villiers, president of the Vendée general council from 1988 until his resignation in 2010, wanted to promote his region. Bernaudeau, who is now 55, wanted to set up a cycling club that would nurture young riders, as he himself had been nurtured in his youth.

Symbolically, next Sunday's stage two will start and finish in front of the Manoir de Saint Michel, an attractive 19th-century manor house in the village of Les Essarts which is the headquarters of Bernaudeau's project. On Thursday, the riders of the Tour will be presented to the public at the Puy du Fou – Madman's Hill – theme park, dreamed up by De Villiers as a way of simultaneously bringing the public to his region and promoting his "traditional" view of French history.

In a sport that has been buffeted by drugs scandals for a dozen years, it is a success story and possible role model for the future. The amateur club founded by Bernaudeau, who twice finished sixth in the Tour, ran for 10 years before he founded a professional team to sit at the top of the structure; now, sponsored by Europcar, they are France's most successful Tour team, having taken two stage wins last year with Thomas Voeckler and Pierrick Fédrigo, and the King of the Mountains title with Anthony Charteau. Bernaudeau and his riders are the *régionaux* of this weekend's racing, and will be warmly supported.

Below the pro team sits the 20-rider strong Vendee-U amateur team, a feeder squad sponsored jointly by the Vendee departement and a supermarket. The bottom of the pyramid is the *sport-etudes* project, also known as Pole Espoir which has two full-time staff overseeing 50 young cyclists combining cycle training and studies.

"The goal was to create a philosophy of cycling which combined education and work and cycling," Bernaudeau says. Among the centre's intake are cyclists from outside the sport's mainstream: France's Pacific and Atlantic islands. Three-quarters of the Europcar team have come through the structure, notably the team leader Voeckler, pictured left, probably the most popular cyclist in France. "The advantage of the Pole Espoir is that you can combine study and sport and come away with a qualification," Voeckler says. "It's important because in sport you don't always make it."

Bernaudeau's project was founded in 1991, seven years before cycling woke up to its endemic doping problem but it clearly offers a solution. His pro team has never had a positive test, which speaks for itself. "The key to preventing doping is education," he says. "It's a matter of the way people are raised and nurtured. Someone who dopes is just as capable of stealing from a shop. After all, they are riders who steal results and glory from others. They are hooligans."

Bernaudeau believes cycling has taken the wrong approach. "I tell my riders that I could have won a Tour de France stage at l'Alpe d'Huez; I made a mistake with my gears but today, that hasn't changed my life. Cycling doesn't need to be about winning at all costs. It's not boxing. It's a sport where you can race 100 times a year but that doesn't mean you have 100 chances to win."

He is known for having trenchant opinions on some of his fellow team chiefs but says: "I don't believe some of the other managers can get the pleasure I can take in what I do. Where is the satisfaction in having a rider like Riccardo Ricco [who tested positive for EPO in 2008] in your team? I pity those guys. For me, the satisfaction is in seeing a rider come through from the beginning, seeing a rider go to another team, then come back to me and begin winning."

The problem, as he sees it, is that it is hard to know how to measure success because of wave after wave of scandals. "We need to wipe out 10 years because we have lost our reference points. Some of the results in the last 10 years are simply meaningless. There are riders who make sense to me: [Thor] Hushovd, for example, hasn't come from nowhere. Bradley Wiggins has been fast since he was 18 or 19. You can't wipe out 10 years of the sport, but in my mind I don't use those years as a measure of reference.

"We are on the right road. We are seeing things that make sense again. You can see the riders grimacing as they ride up the mountains. I don't like seeing riders climbing mountains with their mouths closed, or the same guys riding super-strong on the flat and in the mountains."

With that return to normality, he believes, the French will again begin to shine in their home race. And the chances are that Bernaudeau's riders will play a lead role in any French renaissance.

Bernaudeau's riders had a great Tour in 2011, with Voeckler wearing yellow and finishing fourth and Pierre Rolland winning at l'Alpe d'Huez. But this piece was satisfying for other reasons. For one thing, amidst all the hype around Wiggins, Cavendish and Sky, it was good to write about European cycling, and for another, Bernaudeau's upbeat approach and ethical philosophy was something I had wanted to write about for several years.

Havoc reigns as rogue car takes out two of the leading riders
11 July 2011

The Tour de France is "a massive televisual spectacle" to quote the organiser Christian Prudhomme, but the small screen's contribution was less than glorious 36km from the finish [*in Saint-Flour*]. A car driving personnel from the French channels that cover the Tour collided with the cyclists in the winning escape, sending Juan-Antonio Flecha of Team Sky crashing to the floor while the Dutchman Johnny Hoogerland went flying over him and landed in a barbed wire fence.

The incident happened as the five leaders who had survived the toughest stage of the race so far were speeding towards the finish. Car No800, bearing stickers from French television, attempted to overtake the escape – a daily procedure for the many vehicles in the race that have "all areas" passes – but they did so driving along the left-hand verge, and disobeying an order from the race's internal radio system to move aside to permit team managers to drive up to the riders to provide feeding bottles.

The driver saw a tree in his way, and swerved into the road, colliding with Flecha, who was leading the string. The second-placed rider, Thomas Voeckler of France, narrowly avoided the Spaniard, but Hoogerland, who was lying third, rode into him then catapulted down the left hand verge into the fence and was lucky to suffer only deep cuts.

"It was unbelievable, they were going at 60kmh, I just saw him flying into the air," said his *directeur sportif*, Michel Cornelisse. "He's bleeding a lot, he has deep cuts in his legs. He was lying in the barbed wire, completely in it, his shorts were completely off, he was completely naked." Flecha suffered a bruised elbow and multiple abrasions. "It is a scandal," said Prudhomme, a former television journalist himself. A communiqué from the race organisers described the incident as "intolerable".

"I did what felt like a few somersaults. I don't know where the car came from," said Hoogerland. "Before I knew it, Flecha was on the ground and there was nothing I could do. I landed on the fence and I looked at my legs and thought, 'Is this what cycling is about?'"

The Dutchman, who figured prominently in the Tour of Britain last year, was in the lead in the mountains jersey standings when he fell. He crossed the line nearly 16 minutes behind the stage winner, Luis León Sánchez, went on to the podium to receive the polka-dot jersey and then was taken to hospital. "I have three cuts that are about seven centimeters long and quite deep too. I think I'll need about 30 stitches at least."

Sanchez, who outsprinted Voeckler for the stage win, said that in his view there were too many cars getting too close to the riders. "It's terrible. There were guest cars following us all day and they were often overtaking us to try and follow the race more closely. Several times when the roads got narrow they were coming close. If there is an accident it's our bodies against a car. Things like that should not happen in the world's best bike race. The organisers need to get the message." Sky will assess Flecha's injuries during the rest day but are not sure he will continue.

Last night the car and its driver were thrown off the race, which was the minimum possible sanction. The same sanction was issued to a Getty Images motorbike which caught the handlebars of the Saxo Bank rider Nicki Sorensen and sent him flying out of the bunch on stage five in Brittany. "Two accidents due to media on the Tour de France is two accidents too many," said Prudhomme. Team Sky and Vacansoleil were last night reserving comment until the rest day.

The incident had a major bearing on the result of the stage by eliminating Flecha and Hoogerland, two of the strongest cyclists in the five-man escape that dominated the day. However, the mass pile-up on the descent from the Col du Puy Mary that did for Alexander Vinokourov and Jurgen van den Broeck also decided the fate of the yellow jersey. The crash was so severe that the peloton slowed up for several kilometres to permit the pedaling wounded to regain contact – as they did after last year's mass pile-up on the stage to Spa – but in doing so the escape's lead rose from three minutes to a far less manageable seven.

After the crash, the yellow jersey Thor Hushovd's Garmin team were left short-handed in the chase, and in any case the Norwegian was not in the best of shape. Voeckler will start stage 10 on Tuesday in yellow, the second stint in the *maillot jaune* of his career and the culmination of a season in which he has won eight races. Since his defence of the *maillot jaune* in 2004 he has become France's most popular cyclist, and this will do him no harm.

This was one of the craziest Tour de France stages I can remember, along with the Les Arcs day in 1996 (see chapter two). So much incident, so much drama. And it had a massive bearing on the final outcome, as Voeckler was to wear the yellow jersey for the next 11 stages. The other outcome, after the Hoogerland-Flecha crash, was that there are now much more draconian restrictions on cars driving within the Tour's protected "bubble".

Bradley Wiggins had left the Tour with a broken collarbone the day before the Hoogerland crash. While he was building for his return in 2012, I spent a couple of days at his high-altitude training camp in Tenerife in late May. As an insight into the sacrifices, hard work and radical thinking called for as Team Sky attempted to win the Tour, this felt pretty telling.

Volcano gives Wiggins the fire for Tour assault
23 May 2012

The Parador hotel in the Teide national park in the centre of Tenerife is eerily quiet and surreally isolated, 15 miles from the nearest village. It sits in a desert of solidified igneous rock where clearly no farmer has dared set a hoe or graze a sheep. High above rise the vast cone and threatening black lava flows of a volcano that looks dormant rather than extinct. The one road that passes through goes from nowhere in particular to nowhere else, through a hostile wilderness where sudden winds whip up dust storms that sting the eyes and burn the sinuses. There is no tumbleweed blowing past the chapel outside the hotel but there should be.

Four hours flight due south of Britain, on the same latitude as the Sahara, the hotel hosts three kinds of visitors: astronomers who want to take advantage of a lack of light pollution and observe the stars, weekenders who want to escape the stag parties of Playa de las Americas in total solitude, and professional cyclists such as Bradley Wiggins and his Team Sky cohorts. The cyclists come in little groups but in sufficient numbers for the hotel to boast a fully kitted bike room, where the carbon fibre machines hang neatly on hooks, and teams such as Liquigas and Astana have left bike bags and cool boxes ready for their next visit.

One can feel what draws the cyclists as one tries to sleep in the hotel. Breathing does not come easy in the thin, dry air at 2,100m above sea level. The lungs struggle from time to time. The nose and throat burn a little, as if breathing in acid. The hotel is at high altitude and it has drawn a select group of Tour de France contenders over the years. Lance Armstrong has slept here. Maxim Iglinsky, winner of one of the biggest Classics of the spring, Liège-Bastogne-Liège, is breakfasting two tables away from Wiggins and his probable team mates in the Tour: Michael Rogers, Chris Froome, Kanstantin Siutsou, Christian Knees and Richie Porte.

The presence of Wiggins and Co can be traced back to the Tour de France of 2010, which the triple Olympic gold medallist describes as "a disaster". He had come into that race under a massive weight of expectation, having just signed with the big-budget new boys of Sky and having finished fourth the previous year, although that happened, he says, without his knowing quite how or why.

In terms of the hopes invested in him he bombed, finishing 23rd, prompting a complete rethink of his approach. "We had no data or information about how I did it, not even a VO2 max test." He invested his trust in two men: one was the former professional Shane Sutton, who had been key to the British Olympic cycling's team's effort in Beijing, "the only person who could tell me exactly how it all was". The second confidant was also Australian, the sports scientist Tim Kerrison, who had trained Olympic swimmers and rowers but knew nothing about cycling when he joined Sky with a brief to look outside the box for ways of improving performance.

Wiggins had struggled in the 2010 Tour whenever the race hit high altitude. With the 2011 race including some of Europe's highest passes, with more kilometres than usual at over 2,500m above sea level, Kerrison decided to begin by focusing on that area of weakness. In January 2011 he visited Tenerife to assess the roads for training. An experimental two-week training camp was followed by the biggest victory of Wiggins's road racing career, the Dauphiné Libéré stage race.

Tenerife, Kerrison explains, provides everything lacking for a Tour contender in Wiggins's home in Lancashire: heat, altitude, 20-mile mountain climbs, and peace and quiet. There is a benefit for athletes merely from being at altitude, which enhances the body's ability to utilise oxygen, but there are other pluses here. "Unlike some high-altitude venues, it's possible to train at sea level, which is less damaging at high intensity; unlike Alpine locations the weather is relatively stable in April and May."

"I said I wanted to train for the Tour without any compromise," Wiggins says. "I'm getting to a point in my career where I want to look back with no regrets." That meant beginning training earlier than usual, training harder from the off and interspersing long training camps with races which have to be tackled flat out, to win. The traditional cycling concept of training through competing has been jettisoned. The new philosophy has given Wiggins two major stage race victories this year – Paris-Nice and the Tour of Romandie – out of the four he has started.

The training schedule Kerrison and Sutton devised began on 1 November 2011. It used data gathered by Kerrison in the 2010 and 2011 Tours, which he believes demonstrates the power outputs an athlete needs to win the race. A graph shows the power output levels against the time they need to be sustained, with a second line showing what Wiggins, or other Sky Tour riders, can achieve relative to what they need to do. The goal is to get the two lines as closely matched as possible. The training programme builds into the latest three-week spell of training through mid-late May, the point where Wiggins takes his form to a level which he hopes will win him the Tour. We visit on a rest day, when he spins his stick-thin legs for 30 minutes to the nearest coffee bar while gossiping on the bike with Rogers, and returns, at a modest pace.

But the previous three days have been six-hour stints, with some 4,000m of vertical climbing per day: he is aiming for a total of 100,000m climbing leading into the Tour. The menu is repeated in subsequent days. Whereas on his previous visit in April the workloads were "mid-range", the levels of intensity, pain and lactate have been increased this time. "Yesterday was 25-minute efforts in 35C heat, three of them. It's hard to tell a layman what it feels like: it's hard in a very sweet way, all mixed up with the endorphins."

The work is at the near maximal intensity he might adopt in a prologue time-trial, followed immediately by what amounts to weight training on the bike, a big-gear effort at low-pedal revolutions, at close to breaking point, all at an oxygen-deprived altitude between 1500m and 2,200m. After a rest he repeats it. All this, Kerrison believes, will prepare Wiggins's legs for the steepest climbs on this year's Tour. "When I came in, people believed Brad was only good up to about a 7 per cent gradient; now he can cope with up to 13 per cent."

"Three of the lads were wasted by the end but you realise that, if you can do that effort now, it's the Tour winner," says Wiggins. "You can hardly breathe but it's the kind of effort that wins the Tour." Such a workload, he emphasises, is possible only after six months' continuous building, to ensure that, when he does the work, his body can cope.

Back at the hotel another attraction is clear: isolation. "When you are training as hard as we are it's nice to have no distractions. You don't end up sitting at a computer while you rest, you do basic things like reading a book or watching a DVD. It's very peaceful." The phrase "living like a monk" is often used to describe an athlete's total focus; here there is truly something monastic about Wiggins's reclusiveness where, as Rogers puts it, "anything could happen in Europe and you'd never know".

Wiggins feels it will be worth it. "After 2009 I didn't really believe I could win the Tour. I thought, "That's for someone else, kids from Kilburn don't win the Tour." But I really believe I can win it now." If he does, or merely comes closer than any Briton has done hitherto, the groundwork has been done here, next to an extinct volcano with only the blue sky and Saharan breeze to distract him.

FIVE STEPS TO A STELLAR SEASON ON THE ROAD

1: A large amount of low-intensity, high-volume work in December and January to act as a foundation for the major training efforts to come

2: Two-to-three week training camps in Mallorca and Tenerife to enable training on long climbs in intense heat, with no distractions

Wiggins was the favourite for the Tour, in the middle of a golden spell of form which lasted from September 2011 to August 2012. Hopefully, this piece helped to explain how he got there. On the other hand, the drama that had lasted since 2001, the Armstrong story, was entering its final act.

Armstrong attacks saga's final stage
17 June 2012

Few of those who were present in Paris in July 2005, when Lance Armstrong retired from professional cycling for the first time, will forget the speech he made as he stood victorious on the podium, resplendent in the yellow jersey, with seven successive Tour de France victories behind him. He attacked "the people who don't believe in cycling, the cynics, the sceptics; [I feel] sorry for you. You need to believe in these riders. I'm sorry you can't dream big and I'm sorry you don't believe in miracles".

The episode summed up Armstrong's Tour de France career: glory and dominance going hand in hand with controversy and virulent rebuttal. At the time he quit in 2005, it was estimated he had 11 lawyers working on eight legal cases in three countries, ranging from libel suits to a disputed bonus and alleged unfair dismissal.

On Thursday afternoon, the controversy that may conclude the saga – and could end with Armstrong losing some or all of his record seven Tour titles – began, inevitably, with a bevy of vitriolic clauses, this time a pre-emptive strike against the United States Anti-Doping Agency (USADA). Before the news emerged that USADA was to place formal charges against Armstrong and five long-time associates, he got his denial in first: the allegations were "discredited", "baseless" and "motivated by spite."

Armstrong went on the offensive again yesterday morning, challenging USADA through his Twitter account. The Texan tweeted: "Dear usantidoping – we have now sent you THREE letters requesting all the relevant info in order for me to respond to your 'review board'. Until now there has been no response, not even an acknowledgement of receipt. The knife cuts both ways – it's time to play by the rules."

The charges brought by USADA are extremely serious. Its 15-page letter to Armstrong, his team manager Johan Bruyneel, his trainer Michele Ferrari and three doctors who worked with the US Postal Service (USPS) team and its subsequent incarnations, is potentially as devastating as the brief release that caused the Festina team to be thrown off the 1998 Tour de France. The Festina statement cited a systematic doping programme that had been financed by the riders and devised by the team managers at the French team.

The USADA case against Armstrong and company is described within the letter as a "consolidated action" against the six named individuals because it alleges they are part of "the USPS conspiracy", which was, the letter claims, "to engage in the use of doping substances and techniques which were either undetectable or difficult to detect in routine drug testing in order to advance the athletic and sporting achievements, financial wellbeing and status of the teams and their riders … as well as to prevent the truth regarding doping on the teams … from being revealed".

The letter, leaked to the Wall Street Journal, includes the claims that drugs used by the US Postal team included the blood-booster erythropoietin – nicknamed Edgar Allan Poe – testosterone, allegedly taken in a cocktail with olive oil, growth hormone and cortisone. It is also alleged that the use of drugs was covered up over the years.

Armstrong is the only rider named, says the letter, because – of the riders summoned to give evidence to the agency – he was the only one who did not respond. Bruyneel issued a statement on Friday asserting his innocence. "I have never participated in any doping activity and I am innocent of all charges," read a statement on his personal website, adding that he would co-operate fully with any inquiry. Ferrari, for his part, has always denied administering drugs and was acquitted of the charge in an Italian court in 2004.

Armstrong's career since his comeback from cancer in early 1998 to win the 1999 Tour de France has had two parallel paths. He has become a major US celebrity, dating rock star Sheryl Crow after his divorce, before starting a second family with girlfriend Anna Hansen. He is a man with whom presidents Clinton and Bush wanted to be photographed, whose cancer charity made yellow Livestrong wristbands into a national symbol, and who has become a hero for the cancer community.

Simultaneously, his career has been wracked with controversy, allegations and investigations. He has persistently, vigorously denied doping, beginning with a press conference at the 1999 Tour de France after a positive test for traces of a corticosteroid. At the time, the governing body accepted his explanation that it emanated from a skin cream.

The event that appears to have tipped the balance came two years ago. Armstrong was preparing for his final Tour, having returned to the sport from retirement. His goal was to ride and win to prove he was clean ("I can come with really a completely comprehensive programme and there will be no way to cheat," he said in a Vanity Fair interview at the time). That spring, Armstrong's former team-mate Floyd Landis went public on his years of doping while riding for US Postal and presented a lengthy document to USA Cycling, the American governing body, which was forwarded to USADA. Landis had tested positive – he was the first rider to be disqualified from victory in the Tour de France, in 2006, after a legal battle that lasted almost a year. With nothing to lose, he produced detailed, if rambling, allegations against Armstrong and US Postal.

He was followed, a year later, by a second former team member, Tyler Hamilton, who had tested positive and been banned for blood doping in 2004. Hamilton, it was claimed, had told the grand jury hearing in the federal criminal inquiry that was launched after Landis's allegations, that he and Armstrong had doped together. Armstrong's denials were vigorous.

The FDA inquiry was dropped, abruptly, in February, but that was not as surprising as it seemed. The only case that could have been brought against Armstrong involved allegations of fraud, but no government agency has managed to make such a charge stick against athletes accused of doping, which is not a criminal offence in America. But after the criminal investigation closed down, USADA resolved to continue the process. Whether they have used evidence gathered by the FDA is unclear, but the document states 10 cyclists – who remain anonymous for the present, but can be assumed to include Landis and Hamilton – have given information.

Armstrong appears to be weighing his options. Robert Luskin, one of his attorneys, said: "He certainly would like to fight it; that's Lance's nature. The question is whether or not the process is going to be sufficiently fair and credible, and give him an opportunity to prove his innocence." It seems likely that, if he fights, a key line of defence will be that witnesses were coerced into saying Armstrong doped. "We're focused on what we understand to be a corrupt bargain USADA made with other riders and said, essentially: 'Here's the script and, if you co-operate, you get a complete pass. And if you refuse, we'll use Landis and Hamilton against you and you'll never ride again.'"

Recent history of major doping cases suggests the "USPS conspiracy" will not be resolved soon, and may well conclude with an appeal to the Court of Arbitration in Sport. In one sense, the outcome should be the same whether Armstrong emerges with his reputation as intact as it is now or whether he and his associates are found guilty. It is hard to imagine the years of controversy continuing beyond the final verdict in the USADA case. Cycling, finally, should achieve the closure it has long wanted and needed.

TEXAN DOGGED BY CONTROVERSY

July 1999: After coming back from cancer, wins Tour de France, but tests positive for traces of a banned corticosteroid. His explanation that it was in a cream being used to treat a saddle sore is accepted.

Aug 2000: A French judge opens inquiry into his US Postal Service team after the discovery of a bin bag with bloodstained compresses and containers for the calf's-blood extract Actovegin, not then on banned list. Case goes nowhere.

Jun 2001: It is revealed that Armstrong works with Michele Ferrari, who is being investigated by Italian authorities. Armstrong says he will work with Ferrari until the case is resolved.

Jun 2004: Promotions company SCA refuses to pay Armstrong's win bonus on the grounds he may have won the Tour using banned drugs. Case is settled out of court two years later.

Apr 2005: Armstrong questioned by Italian police over alleged intimidation of rider Filippo Simeoni, a witness in the drugs trial of Ferrari. The case peters out.

Jul 2005: Retires from the sport after seventh Tour de France win.

Aug 2005: *L'Equipe* claims EPO was found in six urine samples taken from Armstrong during the 1999 Tour, an allegation the Texan rejects. A report by anti-doping expert Emile Vrijman says he has no case to answer. WADA dismiss the report as "so lacking in professionalism and objectivity it borders on the farcical".

Sept 2008: On Armstrong's return to the sport, the ICU waive their rule that athletes must be in the random-testing system for six months before competing so he can race in January 2009.

May 2010: Former team-mate Floyd Landis accuses him of blood doping. Armstrong strongly denies the claim. The Food and Drug Administration (FDA) opens an inquiry into his US Postal team.

Feb 2011: Armstrong retires again.

May 2011: Former team-mate Tyler Hamilton alleges he and Armstrong took EPO in 1999, 2000 and 2001. The CBS programme 60 Minutes claims two other team-mates, Frankie Andreu and George Hincapie, told federal investigators Armstrong took drugs. Hincapie states he has never spoken to 60 Minutes. Armstrong denies the claim.

Feb 2012: FDA inquiry is closed. USADA say they will continue their inquiry into Armstrong and his team, hoping to use evidence given to Federal investigators.

June 2012: USADA bring doping charges against Armstrong and five associates.

While the conclusion didn't come for Armstrong, Ferrari and company until October 2012, this was the beginning of the endgame. It was hard to doubt that USADA would find him guilty, given what Landis and Hamilton had already made public, given the positives from 1999 and the circumstantial evidence put out there by David Walsh. What surprised when the verdict came was not the bare facts of doping, but the depth and complexity of what had been going on at US Postal Service between 1999 and 2005.

The next story, on the other hand, was a mood-lightener; it was also hard to grasp, given that here was a rider I had known since the Observer's *then sports editor Brian Oliver had got me to begin ghostwriting his columns for the paper back in 2004. It was also a chance to call on contacts who in some cases went back 20 years.*

The rise and rise of the golden boy in the yellow jersey
28 July 2012

Few of those who had dealings with Bradley Wiggins in his formative years thought he was a potential Tour de France winner, but as his first coach Sean Bannister says, that is precisely the point. "I didn't think for a second he would be a Grand Tour contender, but no one knows at that stage in a rider's development. He was strong, and cool-headed in a race situation, but it's a mistake for any youngster to be told he could be a Tour winner."

Bannister may not have envisaged it, but 16 years later it is about to happen. With the usual condition – barring an act of God – Bradley Wiggins will race up the Champs-Elysées in the yellow jersey tomorrow as Britain's first Tour de France winner. Asked about that possibility this week, Sir Chris Hoy said it would be "the greatest sporting achievement by any British athlete ever".

Wiggins set his sights on winning the Tour late in his career, but the signs that he was out of the ordinary as an athlete have long been there. Bannister began coaching Wiggins when he was 16. It was Wiggins who asked for his services, not the other way around. Bannister would ask all his potential charges to give an answer to one question: what do you want from cycling? Here, the young Wiggins surprised. "He gave very, very mature, genuine answers, not just what he thought I wanted to hear. He wanted to be national champion by this age, ride the Tour by 25, win a one-day classic."

Sam Collins, now a doctor in Dorset, was Wiggins's main opponent on the West London racing circuit. "The first race I won was the first one he ever did, we were both about 12. We raced together pretty much every weekend from 1992. He was a sprinter, he'd zip off my wheel, he'd come first, I'd be second. He had natural zip."

Wiggins himself has spoken about his love of the sport's history, and that was something that struck his manager at the Great Britain road race team, John Herety. "He had a wealth of knowledge of road racing. He knew all about the riders with a fan's passion. He knew all about my career – as a kid it seemed like he had watched videos of races over and over where others would watch Thomas the Tank Engine. He even knew what shoes I'd been wearing."

Bannister and Herety recall two episodes, a few years apart, which had hints of what Wiggins would show on the Tour this year. Bannister remembers a club ride for coffee and cake in Marlow, after which the route went up Winter Hill, a major challenge. "You can imagine it, everyone went tearing off up the hill and fell to bits before the top, but Brad was cool enough to go up at his own pace, keeping comfortable. I thought: 'That's a bit special, he knows just what he's doing.'"

Herety harks back to a stage race in Mallorca, when Wiggins was 20. "There was a mountaintop stage finish and we thought he'd never get up it. He said he would be OK, so the team rode for him in the same way Team Sky have ridden at the Tour; he limited his losses and won." Clearly, what Wiggins has done this July is not new. *[See chapter 7.]*

All who came across Wiggins say he was quiet and shy except in relaxed circumstances in company where he felt confident. "When you get one drink down him he's hilarious," says Rob Hayles, a former Olympic track cyclist.

"Brad is close to his family, and that's why he comes across as elusive," says Shane Sutton, coach of the Great Britain Olympic team who has been close to Wiggins for the last 10 years. "The hardest thing in making a programme for him is putting in family time." Wiggins and his wife, Catherine, have two children, Ben and Isabella. Cycling runs in the family; Catherine organises races near their Lancashire home and her father works for British Cycling.

Born in Belgium, Wiggins grew up in Kilburn, north London, and has always projected a sense of urban cool off the bike, complemented by his fluent French. He is a self-confessed mod, owns a collection of classic scooters and his principal commercial endorsement is the Fred Perry range of clothing he has helped design.

His trademark sideburns were this week reshaped by a cartoonist at the French sports paper *L'Equipe* into a map of France and children practising at London's Herne Hill velodrome, where Wiggins cut his teeth as junior, have been spotted wearing replica facial hair. He is fast becoming the breakout star of Britain's summer of sport.

A sense of style has always been important to him. Simon Jones, who coached Wiggins to his first Olympic gold, recalls a meeting at the end of 2002, called to discuss Wiggins's flop at the Commonwealth Games. The 22-year-old was called in front of Jones and the other senior British coaches – Dave Brailsford, Chris Boardman and Peter Keen – to discuss his options. "He came dressed up for a wedding," says Jones. "I asked why, he said: "This is important." In the meeting, we were all in our tracksuits, he was calling the shots. It was a pivotal moment as he then took on Chris as his mentor, but as for the meeting, he power-dressed us out of it."

Jones left the British programme in 2007 and Wiggins was then trained by Matt Parker, who oversaw his transition from Olympic gold medallist in Beijing in 2008 to Tour de France contender less than a year later. "It felt like it was a conscious decision," says Parker. "He had done everything he could do to be successful on the track and he made the switch [to road] in his head."

To be so switched on in 2009 was quite remarkable, says Parker. "He had just come off a two- or three-year Olympic campaign, but he didn't miss a beat that next year. Before, he had continually switched from road to track and back again, but now he didn't have to keep making the transition. He had never been far off it on the road. He had incredible power, and in 2009 he stripped down in terms of weight."

Parker underlines that to achieve this over nine months took epic commitment. "Not many would sign up for that, to lose 8kg, mainly muscle mass." Wiggins was lucky to find a professional team with openings for him, and joined his fellow British rider David Millar at Garmin. "Dedicated, driven, self-obsessed and ultimately sensible," was Millar's description of him, although the Scot wrote in his autobiography: "We had absolutely no idea he would become a Grand Tour contender."

Looking back, Jones now wonders if he and Wiggins could have achieved more. "Perhaps I was too limited but I never saw him winning the Tour de France. As kids we put that event way up there, with godlike characters." His current coach, Shane Sutton, believes Wiggins didn't fulfil his true potential early in his career. "One of the things he said to me is that he never really trained and he regretted it. We've never seen the real Brad in all those six Olympic medals. Think of the records that could have fallen … but he didn't apply himself as well as he could."

"He could be one of the best athletes there's ever been," says Parker. "To be a multiple Olympic champion, world champion at Madison, Tour de France winner, it's a hard record to beat." For Hayles, it is simple: "When he puts his mind to something he is unstoppable."

In January 2013, while Wiggins was building towards the defence of his Tour title and a tilt at the Giro d'Italia, the Lance Armstrong saga reached another turning point when the disgraced former seven-times Tour winner – by now banned for life after the USADA inquiry – was interviewed by Oprah Winfrey. Armstrong admitted doping, but showed the bare minimum of contrition and looked to be working towards agendas of his own rather than trying to help rebuild the sport he had damaged so spectacularly. The Oprah interview at least ended the years of denial, but the story wasn't going to end there. This piece was written in response to the second and final episode of the interview.

The Lance Armstrong Confection: a peerless display of shaping narratives
19 January 2013

There was an elephant in the Four Seasons hotel room throughout the two hours in which Lance Armstrong's eyes swivelled downwards, upwards and sideways in the second episode of his ordeal under the Oprah spotlight. The elephant was this: what narrative would cycling's greatest liar and cheat produce? How would the process of concession – look at the lack of revelation on night one and substitute this for "confession" – fit into the story he would want us to believe? For those who may wonder why Armstrong took the risk of appearing on Winfrey's show, the tale he wished to tell may hold the key.

The elephant broke cover a few minutes before the end of the second episode. If part one of the Lance and Oprah show could loosely be termed What and When (certainly not How), part two was How It Felt. The ground was prepared with the subtlety of an emoting rotovator: how Armstrong felt when telling his son Luke he was a liar and a cheat (not good – Armstrong looked close to tears); how Luke had had to defend his father's name at school (at which point the stomach did leap, because how could it not?); how Lance's mom, Linda, took it (she was a wreck, but it took a call from her partner to alert her son).

How about the trauma of losing $75m in sponsorship in a day, and perhaps struggling to make more in future? That lost a little impact if you wondered how much of his ill-gotten gains from the doping years remain in his bank account, and cursed that Oprah was charitable enough not to ask him. He is in therapy, he confirmed, going through "a dark time". Having established How It Felt, Oprah teed up the big moment by asking: "Will you rise again?" Unintentional it may have been, but the vision it conjured up, momentarily, was that of Voldemort emerging out of the cauldron in Harry Potter and the Goblet of Fire.

The elephant sprinted out into the foyer of the Four Seasons when Oprah changed her questioning tone. From soccer mom reproving a child who had mislaid his lunchbox she, very briefly, became Torquemada dealing with a mentally deficient suspect. "Did-this-help-you-become-a-better-human-being?" she intoned, the enunciation of every syllable at half-speed making it clear that this was THE CLIMAX. "Without a doubt," Armstrong said, twice, and then the narrative emerged.

"This has happened twice in my life. When I was diagnosed [with cancer] I was a better human being. I lost my way. This is the second time. I can't lose my way again. I'm in no position to make promises ... the biggest challenge for the rest of my life is not to slip up again." He added a few seconds later: "It's an epic challenge."

In other words, the story Armstrong wants the world to read when he tells the tale of his doping is the second coming of Big Tex the comeback hero. In this narrative, the dope scandal is the equivalent of a second cancer. His way back into hearts and minds after the fall, from the hell of losing his seven Tour de France titles, the terrible whirlwind that has engulfed him and his family, will be a second great comeback. Utterly nauseating it may be, profoundly offensive to anyone who has had cancer or knows anyone who has, but that is it.

"It's an epic story," breathed Winfrey. In the sense that it features the hero's descent into the underworld, perhaps the Armstrong story could be termed an epic. But any purgatory the disgraced cyclist is living in is of his own making. The distancing mechanisms he used with Winfrey are intended to create the opposite impression: that Armstrong resembles Icarus, who aimed too high thanks to his soaring ambition, and was felled by superior forces outside his control.

Defrauding sponsors of millions, perpetrating the biggest robbery in sporting history, crushing minnows such as Christophe Bassons and Filippo Simeoni, bullying and intimidating witnesses, more than a decade of lies, some under oath, became a "slip-up", a euphemism comparable to the "flaws" in his character he had revealed the previous evening. He rammed home the point: "I had it, it got too big, things got too crazy." If he had cheated his way to seven Tours, the blame could be placed on "it" or perhaps the "things".

Armstrong's wider agenda became clear as well. There was an obvious bid for a lower sanction – or at least an attempt to lodge in the public mind that he is being unfairly treated – when he referred to his life ban as a "death sentence" and said he was not saying it was unfair, an outstanding piece of doublespeak. There were few moments in the entire pantomime when he appeared to be genuine, and one was when he said he would "love the opportunity to compete" and would like to be running the Chicago Marathon at the age of 50.

The first volume of Armstrong's memoirs, *It's Not About the Bike*, tugged heartstrings worldwide and became a must-read for cancer sufferers and their families. The follow-up, *Every Second Counts*, was more self-serving. The plotline for the third volume laid out in those few minutes under Winfrey's prompting can be summed up as: *How I Returned From The Doping Hell That Wasn't My Fault.* The title would need to express the utter selfishness of the man and his utter detachment from the reality of what he did in his doping years. One quote he gave Winfrey when asked about the prospect of competing again might work: "I think I deserve it." As a summary of why cheats dope, lie and bully, that would suffice.

7. GREAT BRITAIN – ATLANTA TO ATHENS

The other main strand running through my cycling work at the Guardian *is the progress of the Great Britain team from also-rans to world domination. This is where it all began...*

Official opening of Manchester velodrome
8 October 1994

Britain's Chris Boardman tops the bill at today's inaugural meeting at the £9 million velodrome in Manchester. Although the Wirral rider has a virus he will take on his GAN team-mate Francis Moreau in a re-run of the world pursuit final in Palermo where Boardman won gold.

Boardman, who wore the yellow jersey in this year's Tour de France, has contracted the three other major crowd-pullers in the meeting through his company Beyond Level Four Ltd. It set up his match against Moreau and the other likely focus of interest, a pursuit match between the women's world No 1 Marion Clignet of France and Britain's Commonwealth Games gold medallist Yvonne McGregor.

Peter Woodworth, of Beyond Level Four, said: "We have paid for race fees, transfers and accommodation. The organisers of the meeting had no money, so someone had to step in." In addition, Boardman's company has had to get the French riders to fit the meeting around their other engagements.

The other major attraction today is the unveiling of a bust of Reg Harris, Britain's five-times world sprint champion, who died last year.

What is telling here is that Boardman's company had to finance the meeting as there was no money in British Cycling to do it, and no backers willing to put in the few thousand pounds it took to get those four big names in. But the opening of the velodrome was the key to Britain's eventual success, as we shall see. The bust of Reg Harris was commissioned by a memorial fund set up when Harris died by then Cycling Weekly editor Andy Sutcliffe. As we shall see, without the velodrome there would be no Chris Hoy, no Victoria Pendleton and no Bradley Wiggins.

Data bank funds Boardman
11 February 1995

While all eyes will be on the 4,000 metres head-to-head between Chris Boardman and Switzerland's Tony Rominger at the Manchester velodrome tonight, the sports scientist who has played a key role in the Briton's rise will as always be present in the background.

Peter Keen, a senior lecturer at the University of Brighton, has been Boardman's coach since January 1987, when the Wirral racer, now the leader of the French team GAN, was a 17-year-old stripling with a taste for riding fast in local time-trials. At that time Keen's own career in cycle racing effectively came to an end.

Since then Boardman has regularly made the trek to Sussex to be put on a test rig where his power output, pulse rate and oxygen uptake are monitored, giving Keen data on his rider's reaction to every nuance of racing, training and diet.

Their joint haul has included a string of British championships on road and track, the Olympic pursuit gold in Barcelona in 1992, the world one-hour distance record in 1993 and last year's successful attack on the Tour de France, which netted Boardman Britain's first yellow jersey since 1962.

For all their success, Keen describes his work with Boardman and the other riders in his computer files – Britain's top woman road cyclist Marie Purvis, top mountain biker Caroline Alexander and national cyclo-cross champion Barrie Clarke – as essentially a sideline to his academic career.

"It's a symbiotic relationship. I gain intellectually, they gain in terms of their career. My path is an academic one and coaching is part of it. You can't stand in front of a class and teach if you haven't seen an athlete for 30 years." He agreed that Boardman was to some extent a test bed for his academic work: the research they put in together during Boardman's build-up to the hour record in 1993 enabled him to form mathematical models of track events such as today's pursuit match.

"You get a better picture of how fast various people can go and what training, what equipment, what position on the bike gives an increase in performance. You can discover what is restricting performance." Paradoxically Keen maintains that his most interesting discovery with Boardman has been "not to predict the limits of an athlete.

"I learned that some people can develop beyond what you think is possible. You can't attempt to predict what people can achieve and what they can't achieve." Boardman's rise from regular winner of local time-trials to a man expected to take on Miguel Indurain is living proof of that.

For a British time-triallist to take the hour record was inconceivable to continentals convinced that a deep foundation in road riding was necessary. Keen simply worked on the figures. The next target is the Tour de France, the ultimate test for rider and scientist.

Together they have won over the management at GAN, who come from the most traditional of professional cycling backgrounds. Last year Boardman professed shock at their casual attitude to sports science norms such as monitoring mineral levels by taking blood tests.

His results in 1994 mean that is no longer the case. "Sport in general is traditional, dogmatic," said Keen. "I aim to question things, examine them, test them and, if they don't work, I reject them."

He offers as an example the long-established idea that athletes should base their diet around high carbohydrate and extremely low fat intake. "It's stock advice and I was doing it up to a year ago but, if you do that, within a few hours you're hungry again because the body burns up the carbohydrate so fast. By carefully increasing Chris's fat intake, he became less hungry and more fresh."

Before Keen the thought of a cyclist training on a treadmill to simulate the mountains of the Tour de France would have been dismissed as fantasy. But this winter Boardman has been pedalling for up to 45 minutes on a device which replicates, in pedalling speed and effort, the notorious Alpe d'Huez.

Not surprisingly, Keen has never made it into the British cycling establishment. "I resigned twice as a national sports coach by the age of 28," he chuckled. "There was no funding and I wasn't prepared to put in the effort for £2,000. It will never change unless people like me make a stand."

Nowadays it seems that behind every great cyclist, a sports scientist stands in the shadows. Rominger is umbilically linked to Doctor Ferrari of Ferrara University in Italy, as are a whole host of other top riders.

Keen is unwilling to be compared to the *eminence grise* of cycling: "I have a view of knowledge as an academic would see it. I suspect the problem with professionals like Ferrari is that they see information as having financial value, a way of earning a living." That Corinthian approach will be tested to the full this summer when Boardman takes on Rominger and Indurain in the Tour de France.

This piece makes amusing reading now. Keen would go on to head the lottery-funded World Class Performance Plan when it was founded in 1997, putting in place the system which has produced

Sir Bradley Wiggins, Sir Chris Hoy, Victoria Pendleton et al. He then went on to head UK Sport's performance side. The approach he was taking with Boardman – investigating marginal gains across all areas, questioning traditional approaches – is mirrored in that of Team Sky. And Dr Michele Ferrari – whatever happened to him?

No joy for Boardman as Indurain is invincible again
5 August 1996

Four years on, it is all so different. When Chris Boardman took gold in the track pursuit in Barcelona in 1992, it was a precisely won victory over a small group of specialists who operated in a field somewhat removed from the mainstream events such as the classics and Tour de France.

On Saturday, when he took bronze in the road time-trial, run for the first time in the Olympics, he finished just behind the Spaniards Miguel Indurain, the man who has dominated the Tour for five of the past six years, and Abraham Olano, the current world road race champion.

Although the Briton said "1992 was better, because I won", he was quick to underline the extent to which he has progressed. "These are the best cyclists in the world. When I rode the pursuit I rode against the best guys in that discipline, but it is a very narrow field. Today you can see the very best riders in what I think is the toughest sport in the world."

Just to emphasise the point, Boardman caught and passed Bjarne Riis who, two weeks before, had dominated the Tour. Though admitting that the Dane could not have been at his best after two weeks celebrating his and his country's first Tour victory, Boardman said gleefully: "It's still great to give him a kicking."

[Riis would confess, much later on, to the use of EPO during his Tour win – presumably he had come "off the programme" at this point.]

A professional career has its price, however, and the fact is that if Boardman had been able to devote the same amount of time to preparing for the time-trial as he did to the pursuit four years ago, gold might well have been the result. Instead, Saturday's was just one of 90 or so races he will ride this year, and there was no special training, no real acclimatisation to the heat and humidity. "It was simply a question of recovering from the Tour de France and getting to the start as fresh as I could."

As a result there was no joy in this medal. Max Sciandri was a happy man after taking bronze in the men's road race on Wednesday after he had shaped the race for half the distance; Boardman was merely "content" after being forced to compromise, something he finds utterly frustrating.

"The difference between now and Barcelona is that there I started knowing that the next 4½ minutes could completely change the course of my life," he said. "There was none of that unpleasant pressure on Saturday."

Underlining the change in Boardman's status, the man who yelled encouragement at the Wirral rider from the team car bearing the words "Great Britain" in large letters was not an official of the British cycling squad but a Frenchman, Roger Legeay, manager of Boardman's GAN professional team.

Four years ago Legeay was still trying to make sense of the declining career of America's triple Tour winner Greg LeMond and probably knew nothing of Boardman until he read the results from Barcelona.

Typically, Boardman is already looking four years ahead, beyond the tests for the hour record which he will undergo in the next two weeks, beyond his try for a world pursuit title at Manchester at the end of this month, and beyond the world road championships in October. "Sydney will probably be my last Olympics, and there will be no compromise. If I get bronze there it will simply be because that is how good I am."

Boardman produced this ride just a few days after finishing his first Tour de France and it heralded his best ever spell of form in which he set a new record for the 4,000m and put the Hour Record on the shelf. Atlanta marked Great Britain's lowest medal haul since 1952 and its lowest ever place in the table, so in that context, Boardman and Sciandri's bronze medals were perfectly respectable. Critically, Boardman's performance against Indurain provided Keen with a key plank of his argument for Lottery funding for a cycling programme: British cyclists, properly trained, could compete with the best in the world. The funding was awarded in 1997.

Race stopped after cyclists pedal into a dead end
27 May 1998

THE PruTour, Britain's most prestigious cycle race, turned into the Tour de Brierfield yesterday. Direction arrows went missing, and the main field and cavalcade in the round Britain event – 90 cyclists, 40 following cars, and some 20 motorcycle marshalls – disappeared into the middle of a small town somewhere between Burnley and Nelson, Lancashire.

About half the 116 miles of the stage from Manchester to Blackpool had been covered when the men from the Pru got lost. "We turned right at some traffic lights where we should have gone straight ahead," said leading British cyclist Matt Stephens. "The roads just got narrower and narrower, and we went round the back of some shops into a car park. It was a dead end so we thought we'd better stop."

The result was less a miniature version of the Tour de France than a two-wheeled rerun of the charge of the light brigade. There was chaos as the mile-long cavalcade attempted to find their way back to the course. "There were lost riders and their cars doing a circuit race of the town centre, with pedestrians leaping out the way," said the manager of the Scottish team, Robert Millar. "We were going down streets to T-junctions and we'd see riders and cars going across in front of us – in both directions."

The South African, New Zealand and Australian team cars disappeared the wrong way down a one-way system and were last seen heading westwards, direction Clitheroe. "I saw a motorbike marshal coming towards me and thought 'beauty, he'll tell me where to go'," said Australian manager Brian Stephens. "His first words were 'where am I?'"

Once the cavalcade had turned itself around, with all the finesse of an oil tanker performing a U-turn, and the judges had worked out precisely where they all were a different problem arose. Out on the fells of the Trough of Bowland, the five leaders of the race and their smaller cavalcade had ploughed on in blissful ignorance while the 90 men who had been chasing them disappeared into the East Lancashire Triangle.

They had to be stopped, because the race rules in multi-day events specify that if riders finish more than a certain time behind the day's winner they are eliminated. The organisers had no choice, unless they wanted the field for today's 95-mile stage to be reduced to five. The race referee spent several miles leaning out of his car pleading with the quintet to slow down before they stopped.

After a half-hour halt they sprinted down off the fells and into Blackpool where the finish line had been positioned with curious prescience. The chequered flag fell in front of the Casino, where "master magician Richard De Vere" was offering "a magical mystery". He could so easily have added the word PruTour.

The PruTour has a permanent place in my heart – a well organised Tour of Britain at a time when the sport did not enjoy its current prominence. This was a hilarious episode on the first edition – note that Robert Millar, no less, was managing the Scotland team. This piece was also that rare thing at the time – cycling on the front page of the Guardian *– so there was no mention of the stage winner. The scene where the* commissaire, *Gerry McDaid, had to cajole the break into waiting could have graced any Ealing comedy. The PruTour had* *a second edition in 1999, but Prudential then pulled out. Five years later the British Tour was relaunched. In 2013 Prudential returned to cycling sponsorship.*

A woman in hot pursuit going for a Burton record
24 August 1998

The essence of the Italian cyclist can be summed up in a single image – that of a rider ascending a mountain alone, way ahead of the chasing pack. *Un uomo solo* was the sentence which immortalised Fausto Coppi in the 1950s and it was used again this summer as the little climber Marco Pantani won the Tour de France.

The image that best sums up the British cyclist is that of a solo cyclist on a velodrome, not riding a road race such as the Tour de France but engaged in the track pursuit. British cyclists have earned more medals in this slightly esoteric cycling discipline in the post-war years than in all the others put together. They include the only post-war Olympic gold, won by Chris Boardman in the pursuit at Barcelona in 1992.

Boardman travels to Bordeaux this week in quest of a third pursuit gold medal in the World Track Championships. But, even should he win in spite of his disastrous crash in this year's Tour de France, he will be well short of being the best Briton ever in the discipline. This honour is still held by the late Beryl Burton, who won the women's title five times between 1959 and 1966.

Just as Boardman has picked up the torch from Hugh Porter, four times champion between 1968 and 1973, Burton has her heiress in a fellow Yorkshirewoman Yvonne McGregor. After taking fourth in Atlanta she went to Perth, in Australia, to take the bronze medal in last year's World Championship.

Compared to the Tour de France, the pursuit is a brief, if repetitive, assault on the pain barrier. The principle is simple: two riders start on opposite sides of an oval velodrome – usually in a stadium these days, as at Bordeaux, and its British counterpart, Manchester – and pursue each other over the set distance. For Boardman and company this is four kilometres, for McGregor three.

In theory the object of the exercise is for the stronger cyclist to make up the half-lap. In practice this happens only when the difference in ability or strength is particularly marked, and usually the two cyclists are simply timed for the set distance, and the faster wins. Aerodynamic bikes mean that McGregor will be in action for barely three and a half minutes in each round.

A qualifying round decides the fastest eight and then it is sudden death to the final. Compared to the infinite nuances of road racing, pursuiting is barely tactical. It is principally a question of the cyclists calculating how much energy they can expend to keep their opponent within or just out of reach before the crescendo into exhaustion. The physical effort is intense but not as obvious as, say, Pantani climbing l'Alpe d'Huez. So what intrigues is the psychological battle, the more so now the cyclists' faces are hidden by aerodynamic helmets.

Coping with pain is not a problem for McGregor, who regularly broke bones in her early years – she managed to smash collarbone, shoulder and cheekbone in 1995 alone. A wry sense of humour helped her cope with four major accidents in three years. Like Boardman, she has held the world distance record for one hour, the toughest feat, in terms of distilled agony, that cycling has to offer outside the Tour.

The Boardman connection runs deep: since 1993 she has been part of the team which Boardman set up to bring on Olympic prospects; famously Boardman has helped repair her bike on occasions in the past, and she has shared the expertise of the sports scientist Peter Keen, who guided the Wirral racer to his Barcelona gold. Their training plan for Atlanta's humidity included riding a stationary bike in the bathroom with the central heating on and the shower running.

McGregor has moved across the Pennines to be close to the Manchester velodrome but she is all Yorkshirewoman in her accent and her penchant for plain speaking. The Leeds-born Burton is her model; McGregor, from Bradford, was inspired to take up cycling when she took Burton's autobiography *Personal Best* out of the library after an Achilles tendon injury put paid to her running career.

She has taken several of Burton's British time-trial records but, whereas her fellow Yorkshirewoman remained a British-based cyclist throughout her career, making an annual sortie abroad to pick up her medals in the World Championships, McGregor has recognised the need to race on the women's circuit in Europe to improve her strength and moved into the top five on the world road rankings earlier this year.

The next few weeks are vital ones for her and Keen, who for the last nine months has been performance director of British cycling, responsible for turning Lottery money into medals. McGregor views this week in Bordeaux as a dry run for the Commonwealth Games, where she took gold in the track points race in 1994; Keen is well aware that the Games will be the first high-profile display of what he has achieved, and that McGregor is one of his few reliable hopes for a medal.

McGregor's annus mirabilis *came in 2000, when she won bronze at the Olympic Games and gold in the world pursuit championship. She retired a couple of years later, and was made an MBE. Like Boardman, she was a vital part of Keen's medal strategy in the early years of Lottery funding.*

To Sydney via Stourbridge
9 September 2000

Chris Boardman's road to his final Olympic Games will take him through a time warp today, when he goes back seven years to his roots in British amateur time-trialling to compete in the Stourbridge Cycling Club's hilly 26-mile event on the sedate back lanes around Astley, Shrawley and Great Witley in deepest Worcestershire.

His entry is born of a dire need to race: because he is retiring at the end of the year his French team, Crédit Agricole, have declined to enter him in any events in favour of team-mates who may be able to earn world ranking points to help the team qualify for next year's Tour de France.

Until he turned professional in 1993 Boardman rode time-trials weekly. But for a former Olympic champion and three-times wearer of the yellow jersey in the Tour de France to return to this world is the equivalent of Mike Atherton turning out in a village cricket match to prepare for a Test.

British time-trialling was born 100 years ago, when cycle racing was banned by law, and it maintains many "private and confidential" traditions. The course on which Boardman will compete at 1pm today is known as K22/14, under the coding system devised at the turn of the century to ensure the police had no idea what was going on.

He will get changed in Astley village hall and his finish time will be taken "at the field gate approximately 100 metres before the junction of Pearl Lane and the A451", according to Stourbridge CC's decidedly unconfidential website. Having paid his £9 entry fee, he will be favourite for the first prize of £100 and a "silver trophy donated by the Albury and District Cycling Club".

So removed from the main stream is the British time-trial world that he was almost refused entry because the Road Time-trials Council does not recognise Crédit Agricole and would not permit him to race in their jersey. "Funnily, they aren't affiliated," chuckles his manager Peter Woodworth. Instead he will race in the colours of the North Wirral Velo Club.

To underline the contrast, Boardman's final preparation event in eight days' time is the Grand Prix des Nations in Rouen, the most important *contre la montre* on the European calendar, where he is expected to come up against Lance Armstrong, the double Tour winner's neck injury permitting.

Today the unlucky man starting two minutes before Boardman is British time-trialling's man of the year Michael Hutchinson, a Cambridge graduate in European human rights law. He is a full-timer "making a living even if it's not a very good one".

Having won RTTC national championships this year at 10, 50 and 100 miles, plus the 12-hour distance event, Hutchinson would have been the favourite. But he feels no resentment at having his party gatecrashed. "It will be interesting to see how soon he comes past me. It's great for us to measure ourselves against him; we can all work out how we would have done in the Olympics."

The sports desk at the Guardian *loved the idea of the British Olympic gold medallist riding an obscure time-trial in the middle of the countryside; this was a great – and rare – opportunity to bring the wider story of British time-trialling and its culture to the paper. The course is also well known to West Midlands cyclists as a popular road racing circuit.*

Michael Hutchinson, cycling aficionados will note, is still racing today, having written a fine book on the history of the hour record, and he is also working as a writer at Cycling Weekly.

So where has this band of British cyclists sprung from?
18 September 2000

Two days, four cycling finals, two medals, one near-miss. Thus far in Sydney Britain's strike rate on the velodrome has been unmatched in any other sport. But Jason Queally's gold medal in the kilometre time-trial and his team's silver in the Olympic sprint are the fruit of a quiet, unseen and relatively unsung revolution in British cycling which has, according to its driving force, only just begun. Britain's man with the two-wheeled plan is the sports scientist Peter Keen.

Eight years ago he took Chris Boardman to his dramatic gold medal on the Barcelona velodrome and just under three years ago this cerebral former schoolboy cycling champion gave up his post as a senior lecturer at the University of Brighton to take over at the head of the lottery-funded performance side of British cycling.

Keen, never part of the British cycling establishment, had twice resigned in the past as a national coach due to the dismal lack of funds. Suddenly he had £2.5m to play with – about 50 times the previous year's budget. However, Keen had a dilemma. An entire system had to be put in place, while at the same time medals had to be won, or at the least tangible progress made towards those medals, in order to gain fresh lottery funding each year.

His answer was to target specific areas such as the power-based disciplines on the track like the 1km time-trial and the Olympic sprint where, due to the absence of tactics as on the road, training input directly equates to performance output.

Track racing – traditionally the Cinderella alongside the more glamorous road racing – was highlighted in Keen's Performance Plan, simply because 14 of 18 Olympic medals are on the track. Women's cycling, with only a small band of elite performers worldwide, was another target: another medal contender, the 20-year-old Ceris Gilfillan, has appeared from nowhere.

The change was simply put by Keen back then: "We will be going from a situation where riders have been getting the occasional tyre and jersey – where there was no direct funding of the athlete and limited national team funding – to a budget of £30,000 to £40,000 a year for every rider on the programme." There have been warm-weather training camps during the British winter, full international racing programmes for the first time. Unprecedentedly in British cycling teams, everyone rides the same bike.

Overnight, across British cycling, the catch phrase among top performers went from "getting international selection" to "getting on the plan": those who met Keen's performance targets – such as Queally, and his fellow medallists Chris Hoy and Craig MacLean – were turned overnight into full-time athletes and, by happy coincidence, a world-class training venue was available: the velodrome built for Manchester's abortive Olympic bid.

The velodrome was where Queally first caught the cycling bug. It is, says Keen, the envy of major cycling nations such as Australia and France, which do not have an indoor facility and train outdoors, subject to the weather.

An entire infrastructure has been put in place. At the end of 1997 there were three full-time staff dealing with the competition side of British cycling. Now there are 34. Famously, earlier this year Keen was attacked for "having more coaches than Wallace Arnold" by one of Britain's best ex-professionals, Sid Barras. For all that Keen has, for example, a fan in the sports minister Kate Hoey, there have been frequent grass-roots rumblings about how the money is targeted.

Since he abandoned the union flag on the British team strip at the start of his reign, to break decisively with the past, Keen's single-mindedness has mystified most of Britain's amateur cyclists and British cycling's "blazers".

This weekend Keen must finally have made them lose their doubts but he has only just begun. "We are just at the starting line," he said yesterday. "In years to come there may be a whole raft of young riders coming in to contest all 18 gold medals across the board."

This was one of the first pieces in any British paper to explain what Keen and his backup team were trying to achieve and how they were going about it; it was written as Britain's cyclists surprised everyone – particularly the British media – by taking gold in the kilometre (Jason Queally), silver in the team sprint (Queally, MacLean, Hoy), bronze in the women's pursuit (McGregor) and bronze in the team pursuit (Wiggins, Manning.) The final quote sums up where Keen felt he could take cycling: his vision has been realised, and more.

Queally buckles up to take the pain with the fame
25 October 2000

As Jason Queally clicks his back wheel into the start gate on the Manchester velodrome this evening and attempts to add the one-kilometre time-trial world championship to his Olympic title before his home crowd, he will be hoping that history does not repeat itself.

At the same venue four years ago, when Queally was competing in his first world championship as a complete unknown – it was his first year of track racing – his foot parted company with his pedal as he started the Olympic sprint. He and his team-mates Chris Hoy and Craig MacLean were unable to continue.

It was a farcical episode purely due to Queally's inexperience – he used shoe fixings which were inadequate for the sheer power he can transmit to the pedals – but with hindsight it underlines the dramatic extent of his progress: from novice to shock Olympic gold medallist in four years.

Not surprisingly the 30-year-old from Chorley is a little overwhelmed by it all. "I went to Sydney as Mr Anonymous and came back as someone the general public has been exposed to." He is noticed in the street and gets to disagree with Sue Barker over which German pursuiter is pictured on the BBC's *Question of Sport*.

The transition has, inevitably, affected his readiness for tonight, when he will come up against the reigning world champion Arnaud Tournant, a colossus from the plains of northern France. Tournant was shocked by his defeat in Sydney, which he described as "on the limit of the supernatural", and believes Queally will be his principal adversary for the title in the future.

"I've known about him since the world championship in Bordeaux in 1998. He was eighth and no one paid him the slightest attention, but he finished fifth last year [in Berlin], so we should have known about him," says Tournant. "I know very well who he is now, though."

Fame has its price; Queally has missed valuable training since Sydney due to the welter of television appearances. "I just hope the crowd lift me. I remember how it was in 1996; the atmosphere was incredible."

As Queally circles the empty velodrome at Manchester there is a curious rumbling – hollow carbon fibre wheel on hollow wooden banking. The speed cranks up lap by lap as he trains until he is whizzing past at 40mph, head twisted slightly to one side, the faintest hint of the pressure showing through his shoulders. It takes a long time to recover from this single effort, leaning against the rails.

The kilometre is cycling's most concentrated test of pure, unadulterated power and speed. For the minute he is racing, at more than 35mph from his standing start, Queally puts out an average of about 1,000 watts of power, peaking at 2,000 watts. That is five times what it takes the "average" Tour de France star to climb l'Alpe d'Huez, although that lasts 40 minutes.

The pain may not last as long but Queally has been left writhing on the floor by the trackside for half an hour after a bad "kilo". "You have to train your body to cope with it but bizarrely, the fitter you get, the more you can hurt yourself."

But the potential for gain amid the pain is somewhat limited. Whereas Britain's only other recent Olympic champion, Chris Boardman, turned his individual pursuit skill into a lucrative career in the Tour de France – a career which will be brought to an end on Friday on the velodrome – that option is not open to a kilometrist, especially one who is the wrong side of 30.

Apart from product endorsements – and this front has been quiet, Queally says – there are two opportunities open to him on two wheels: exhibition sprint events during the circuit of winter track meetings across Europe and the eight-week season of keirin races on the Japanese velodromes. A vast betting industry is based around these events, where six or eight riders are paced by a motorbike before sprinting for the finish, and a place is worth about £100,000.

Beforehand, though, Queally will have to conquer his fear of riding in a bunch of other cyclists on the track. His qualms are understandable in the light of his last outing in company on the boards: a Frankensteinian scar stretches from his left armpit to the small of his back where a lengthy splinter of the Meadowbank velodrome in Edinburgh was removed in 1996. "It's a mental thing and I'll have to get over it."

There has been much to cope with in the post-Olympic weeks. Strangest of all, he says, was receiving fan mail – from Germany, Finland, Sweden. In what may be a first for a British cyclist, he was sent a pair of black ladies' knickers through the post. "The lads swear it wasn't them, although they weren't an expensive pair, a g-string. They came with a note saying, 'I've been watching your progress in Sydney and look forward to meeting you in Manchester.'"

The note, rather than the lingerie, pretty much sums up the reaction of British cycling fans. They will fill the velodrome tonight to watch their new hero and cheer him to the echo. He does not seem fazed, however, and is keeping his feet on the ground – and, he hopes, securely clipped into his pedals.

This piece, like the one before it, comes at the point where the track cyclists began to enter the British sports mainstream: as with the McGregor piece earlier on, the intricacies of track cycling had to be explained in some depth because the sport was so obscure. That world championships in Manchester was a resounding success. Queally's role in the run of British medals since Sydney is one that has rarely been recognised.

Boardman suffers blood, sweat and tears for his finest hour
28 October 2000

It is, Chris Boardman said yesterday, "amazing how long an hour can last". The final, and perhaps the most emotional, 60 minutes of Boardman's professional career must have taken time, and pain, into a new dimension as he set a new one-hour record distance by a mere 10 metres at the Manchester velodrome.

Aiming to overtake the 49.431km set in 1972 in Mexico by the great Eddy Merckx, Boardman was comfortably ahead of schedule at half-distance but weakened to slip behind the Belgian's pace with 11 minutes left. An all-out sprint in the final few minutes, with every spectator on his feet yelling himself hoarse, brought him the record on the last lap.

One man riding round a track on his own it might have been, but it was high drama. Like Merckx 28 years before, Boardman had to be lifted off his bike and an hour afterwards he was still unable to sit down. "I have never been in this much pain in my life," he said.

"For half an hour it looked pretty good, then I started dropping back, but I was still on the limit. I was hoping that I would lose just enough to get it back if it came down to a sprint.

"I started sprinting with three minutes left. I had no idea if I would pass the distance. I just wanted it to end. It was most unpleasant for a couple of minutes, which felt like a couple of years."

Boardman's place in cycling will be indelibly linked with the hour, so this was an appropriate way to close, in front of his home crowd. The first record, 52.713km at Bordeaux in 1993 on the day the Tour de France passed through, was deliberately timed to gain maximum attention, and earned him a professional contract. His second, 56.375km on this track four years ago, will remain a high point to rank with his first yellow jersey in the Tour.

Both his previous distances have, however, been sidelined in a bizarre, Canute-like attempt on the part of the governing body, the Union Cycliste Internationale, to rewrite history and halt technological progress in cycling. Boardman's distance will in future be known as the Athlete's Hour Record. The key part of the name is the first word: it is vital, in the eyes of the men who run cycling, to distinguish future records from those of the past, where they feel an unhealthy amount of attention was paid to the bike rather than to the athlete sitting on it.

So Boardman had to ride on a machine based on that used by Merckx, which the UCI regards as the benchmark, with no modern aerodynamic equipment. Whatever the bike, the athletic effort necessary to ride "on the limit" for 60 minutes has applied to every cyclist who has ever attempted what has always been viewed as the sport's Blue Riband: the fastest a man can go unpaced using the technological aids of the day. And, ironically, there was much talk about the bike yesterday.

The BBC spent many minutes with Boardman's management attempting to understand the details, while cycling's Murray Walker, the veteran broadcaster David Duffield, who has consistently opposed the UCI's attempts to turn back the clock, walked out of the velodrome as Boardman appeared, refusing to commentate on the event for Eurosport.

Whatever the niceties of equipment rules, it was a glorious, if nailbiting, end for the Wirral racer. "What kept me going was the fact that it was the last thing I was doing," he said. "I'm glad I was able to make people walk away happy. It was a privilege."

There were hugs and tears afterwards, and among those who threw their arms round Boardman's neck was Yvonne McGregor, who has had advice and support from him through her career, and who today will improve on the bronze she achieved in Sydney in the women's individual pursuit. She qualified fastest yesterday, ahead of the defending champion Marion Clignet of France, then came smoothly through her quarter-final against the Russian Lada Kozlikova to guarantee herself at least silver.

Boardman went on to work for the World Class Performance Plan under Dave Brailsford; prior to the Athens Games his job included mentoring Bradley Wiggins and in the run-up to Beijing he was one of four senior managers supervising the team, while up to 2012 he was the team's head of research and development, heading up their squad of boffins. He quit the team after the London Games to devote his attention to his cycle company and work as a commentator for the BBC and ITV. This was a historic moment in another way: the last high-profile attempt on the hour record, which has lost all credibility and meaning due to the UCI's changes.

Sport in brief – Cycling
2 April 2001

Britain's Bradley Wiggins, an Olympic and world championship bronze medallist on the track last year, scored the biggest road victory of his career yesterday in the five-day Tour of Majorca. The 20-year-old defended the overall lead throughout the race after winning the first two stages.

No need to underline the significance of this one: a first major stage race win by Bradley Wiggins. We gave it 45 words. But at least we got it in the paper.

Enduring challenge of "the Hill"
14 April 2001

There are places and times when past, present and future seem to merge seamlessly. Yesterday, at this venerable venue *[Herne Hill]*, was one. On July 22–23, 1892, proclaims a plaque in the grandstand, "the first 24-hours cycle path race for the Coca-Cola Challenge Cup" was "promoted here by the London Cycling & Athletic Club".

Anyone trying to race on a cycle path these days is liable to be arrested but yesterday at the Good Friday meeting – first promoted by the Southern Counties Cycling Union in 1903 – the current generation of British track Olympians and, perhaps, some of the next, were riding in the wheelmarks not only of the Victorian pioneers and of the competitors in the 1948 London games but of later legends.

When Reg Harris, Tom Simpson, Jacques Anquetil and Fausto Coppi were brought here in the heyday of "the Hill", they drew so many fans that bikes had to be neatly stacked dozens deep outside. Chances to see Britain's Olympic cycling medallists are rare but yesterday the shallow bankings of the 500m concrete bowl were lined rather than packed to watch the men of Sydney. Riders such as Bradley Wiggins, Bryan Steel and Chris Hoy took on locals from outfits such as the exotically named Team Blazing Saddles, plus a smattering of specially flown-in foreigners.

The wafer-thin Wiggins, fresh from his victory in the Tour of Majorca, was clearly the strongest in the pursuit, in a sadistic variant unique to "the Hill", where six riders – rather than the usual two – start at set intervals and "pursue" each other for 10 minutes rather than the usual four.

Trailing in his wake was a minor legend: Sean Yates, perhaps the most popular British cyclist since Simpson, the veteran of a dozen Tours de France, until January manager of the ill-fated Linda McCartney racing team and now racing as an amateur in between work as a builder.

Yates was not the only throwback. This is the only British venue where racing takes place using "the big motors" – customised, full-sized motorbikes behind which a cyclist can draft at up to 50mph.

Steel was the only Olympian to brave these behemoths, driven by Hell's Angel lookalikes sporting battered black leathers, mirror sunglasses and a variety of bizarre facial hair. The drivers sit bolt upright, as if on the lavatory, to give maximum shelter to their charges, themselves on bikes with tiny front wheels and reversed forks in order to get as near as possible to the pacer.

Steel led for much of the 40 laps, covered at well over 40mph, overtaking a local hero, the motor-mouthed Eurosport commentator Russell Williams, but he was outpaced by the German Marko Ulbricht, spinning as dizzily as a hamster on a wheel as he swooped off the banking to overtake.

The motors are firmly of the past, no longer included in major championships, but a glimpse of the future came in the White Hope sprint, held since 1948 for riders under 18. This year it went to the junior David Heald, tipped for a place in next year's Commonwealth Games.

The future of "the Hill" is less certain, for all that it is the only venue in London for those out to emulate Wiggins. Its lease, currently held by Southwark Council, is up at the end of the year, and, ironically given cycling's glut of Olympic and world championships medals last year, there is doubt over its funding.

Getting the Good Friday Meeting into the Guardian *was satisfying, given its tradition. It's amusing to speculate how big a crowd Hoy and Wiggins would draw today – if the Meeting was lucky enough to hit a dry day. Bryan Steel was a mainstay of the team pursuit squad in the early years, and retired after Athens. I have no idea what became of the "White Hope" winner David Heald.*

Wiggins finds solace in new pro deal
27 September 2001

Bradley Wiggins, Britain's finest up and coming cyclist, was unable to overcome a broken wrist yesterday and qualify for today's individual pursuit final *[in Antwerp]*, but at least he could console himself with achieving a longer-term aim: a place on a top European professional team.

The music for the opening ceremony had included the theme from *Mission Impossible*, and that summed up the task facing the west Londoner last night. After qualifying seventh out of eight in the morning for the semi-finals, Wiggins was eliminated yesterday evening by the German veteran Jens Lehmann, last year's champion.

[Lehmann was, coincidentally, the rider lapped by Chris Boardman in the final of the individual pursuit in Barcelona in 1992 – the German was that old.]

It was a bitter end for the 1998 junior world champion, who raced with a plaster cast on his wrist and specially modified handlebars. Lehmann, who won the silver medal in the 1992 Barcelona Olympics behind Chris Boardman, started faster and caught Wiggins after less than three of the four kilometres.

"It was quite painful because the pins in my wrist are coming up through the skin and the plaster cast presses on them," Wiggins said. "I missed a vital part of my final preparation, and I never got my best ride out in qualifying, but I'm still close to the best guys. It's definitely there for the future."

Shortly afterwards, however, he signed a professional contract for the next two years with La Française des Jeux, the team sponsored by the French national lottery and managed by the former top French rider Marc Madiot. He is likely to be based in western France, near Nantes, or will move to Biarritz to join David Millar and Rob Hayles. *[At this point, Hayles was a team mate of Millar's at Cofidis.]*

"To ride with a top professional team is what I always wanted," the 21-year-old said. "The Madiot brothers who manage the team believe in my ability and I am very happy. Having a professional contract has certainly helped my morale. They are talking about putting me in the one-day classics and perhaps the Tour de France."

Wiggins had signed a contract with the Linda McCartney Racing team for this season, only to see the team fold in January before he had turned a pedal in anger. But after that setback he won two important second-ranking stage races this spring while riding with the Great Britain track squad.

228

In yesterday morning's qualifying round on the bumpy wooden track in the vast Sportpaleis, which dates from 1933, Wiggins was clearly hampered by the injury, which occurred two weeks ago when he was brought off his bike by a tarpaulin which blew off a skip.

Britain's Olympic one-kilometre time-trial champion Jason Queally is taking a sabbatical from the distance this year to concentrate on his world speed record attempt next week. Not surprisingly the Scot Chris Hoy found him a hard act to follow and finished only eighth behind the Frenchman Arnaud Tournant, who won his fourth consecutive world title.

Wiggins's injury was one of a series of freak accidents which hit the British team pursuit quartet that year; the last paragraph makes amusing reading given that Hoy would go on to win Olympic gold in the kilometre in 2004.

Cooke ready to take on the world
12 October 2001

No Briton has ever started a world road race championship as the overwhelming favourite but that is the status Nicole Cooke will enjoy in Monsanto Park this morning when she defends the women's junior title she won last year in Brittany.

"Enjoy" is perhaps not the most appropriate word: Cooke will be a heavily marked woman. The rest of the 64-rider field know full well that her back wheel is the best one to follow, and that if they can stay in her slipstream to the finish they may stand a chance of winning the gold medal.

Surprise is a key weapon in a road race but it is no longer part of Cooke's armoury. Since she sprinted across the line in Plouay in October with a yell of delight to become Britain's first ever junior road race champion, male or female, she has added the mountain-bike title and, on Tuesday, the time-trial gold.

She has no team-mates to help her, so her main ally today is the course, with its two hills. "I'm definitely going to be marked, but this course is hard enough for the race to split up; hopefully it will, and a small group will be easier to deal with. Last year I won from a break, but the bunch could have pulled us back perhaps, but this course is so hard that a selection will be made of the best riders."

Her triple of medals across the three disciplines in the space of 12 months is already unprecedented, and today she is chasing another record: no junior man or woman has successfully defended a world road race title, simply because the titles usually go to a second-year junior and the following year he or she will be racing at senior level.

In the seven years since she began cycling, however, Cooke has acquired a taste for records because there is little satisfaction for her in beating junior opposition, according to her mentor, the former professional Shane Sutton, who is the Welsh national cycling coach.

Sutton was renowned for his hardness, but even he has been astounded at Cooke's competitive mentality. "She likes to kill off the opposition; that's the way she's always been. It doesn't matter who it is, who she is up against, her tenacity is unbelievable."

Born into a cycling family, coached by her father Tony, Cooke has dispensation to race against the men and is no shrinking violet: last year, in a local race in the Welsh town of Penarth, Julian Winn, a seasoned British international, watched in astonishment as she attacked for an early lap prize. "He couldn't believe what was going on," chuckles Sutton. "I told him it was just Nicole putting the boot in."

If Sutton admires Cooke's coolness under the pressure of a big occasion, he is astonished by her versatility. When she won her mountain-bike title in Vail in September, Cooke had not raced on a mountain bike for a year, since she won the bronze in the event the previous year. She finished seventh in the senior women's world cyclo-cross championship in February.

An articulate 18-year-old who has just passed A-levels in maths, geography and biology, Cooke would have been selected for Sydney last year, had she not fallen foul of a rule that keeps junior cyclists out of the games.

An Olympic gold is her big aim within cycling, but this is not a goal acquired recently: interviewed at the age of 12, she said that gold in Athens was her goal.

Whatever the outcome today, Cooke now has to choose a course for the next few years. Two professional teams are chasing her signature on a contract, including the Italians of Acca Due O, the leading women's team in the world, and she will also have the chance of a place in the British World Class Performance squad. In addition the Welsh see her as a potential Commonwealth Games women's champion in Manchester next year.

Sutton is a down-to-earth Australian, not given to hyperbole, but he is effusive. "I'm sure if she goes into the right system she can be Olympic champion in Athens. She obviously has the ability, but she needs the right pathway from here on in." In fact he goes further, far further: "She can be the best women's road racer of all time."

Cooke would, of course, go on to win that junior road race and would eventually take a unique double in 2008: Olympic and world road race gold medals. She was to be a fixture in the British team for the next 10 years and would inspire a generation of British women racers before retiring early in 2013. Like Queally, she was a hugely influential figure. Sutton was in the infancy of his coaching career at this stage, working within the Wales set-up with a view to the Manchester Commonwealth Games of 2002.

Riding the killer whale on wheels
6 September 2001

When Jason Queally sat for the first time in the Blueyonder Challenger at its unveiling in London yesterday he suddenly became aware of something which had not crossed his mind: in the quest for the world human powered land speed record it does not pay to be claustrophobic.

"It's like being in a racing car or a space pod," was the Olympic one-kilometre time-trial gold medallist's first impression of the £100,000 machine. "One of the great things on a normal bike is that you can see the whole world going past but with this one you're limited to what you can see out of the canopy."

Six months in the making, the Challenger vehicle bears as little resemblance to the "normal" bike on which Queally won his Olympic gold medal in Sydney last year as Michael Schumacher's Ferrari does to a Fiat Uno.

The formula one influence is key: the machine is born of a partnership between the bike designer Chris Field, who produced Queally's Olympic bike, and the motorsport constructors Reynard.

The front wheel, gears and pedals might not be out of place on Lance Armstrong's Tour de France machine but that is as far as it goes. The aerodynamic, computer-generated body, made of a space-age honeycomb of carbon fibre and kevlar looks part squashed Jaguar E-type, part torpedo.

Remove the body and the chassis bears an uncanny resemblance to a Hell's Angel cruiser: a vast seat – a formula one derivative – and upturned easy rider handlebars amid a Heath Robinsonian mix of struts, forks, cables and chains. Queally, who will sit in front of the vast back wheel, with a second set of gears under his bottom, says: "If you stuck two eyes on the front, when the light reflects off it, it looks like a killer whale."

From October 1–6 at Battle Mountain, a tiny gold mining village in the heart of the Nevada desert, 420 miles from Las Vegas, Queally and his 30-strong team will compete with four others in the World Human Powered Speed Challenge for the world speed record currently held by Sam Whittingham of Canada at 72.24mph. His team's initial target is 80mph, about twice the fastest speed Queally achieved in Sydney.

The course is on five miles of Highway 305, which runs across the Nevada desert "virtually flat for 90 miles apart from a small canyon", according to a local at yesterday's unveiling. The highway has a traffic count of about 30 vehicles per hour, so it can be closed for about half an hour a day, allowing the five contestants one run each, during which they will be timed over a 200-metre stretch.

Queally admits that he has trouble adapting to the recumbent position. "I got a recumbent bike for the road and in a quarter of a mile my legs were in bits. I need to spend time adapting to the position. It's been a lot harder than I thought. I just thought I could jump in, whack in the thigh power and break the record but the power you can produce is limited by the position."

The Blueyonder machine, he feels, will be less painful than his training machine, as his legs are elevated but time, he admits, is not on his side: the machine was due to be delivered in June and he will not be able to test it in its final form until next week, when he begins training on the disused USAF airfield at Elvington in Yorkshire.

There is a further complication. Queally will compete in the Olympic sprint in the world track championships on September 27 before he flies out to Nevada. He is trying to fit in at least one training session per week with his team mates Chris Hoy and Craig MacLean, with whom he will attempt to improve on last year's silver medal.

The quest for aerodynamics is not for the faint-hearted: once Queally's support team have shut him inside the Challenger, he cannot open the cover and will need two people to "catch" him when he stops, so he does not fall over. Racing enclosed in a cover, without the wind to cool him down, entails other problems: overheating and condensation. "I've heard stories of people passing out in the past because of lack of air and I don't fancy that," he says.

It could, perhaps, be worse. One of Queally's rivals, the American Matt Weaver, will race totally enclosed in his machine, lying on his back with only two television monitors linked to a television camera mounted on its nose to show him where he is going. It is more aerodynamic that way, apparently. Queally and his team considered the "blind" option but he prefers to see where he is going. In the next few weeks, however, he is heading into uncharted territory.

An amusing illustration of the things our Olympic gold medallists once had to do to earn a few quid. The attempt was not a success, but Queally was not the only one who struggled to capitalise on his medal. Bradley Wiggins had a similar experience after Athens: unlike those who followed them in Beijing, they had few opportunities.

Cooke discovers winning form at last in wheel-to-wheel battle
5 August 2002

A stunning *[Commonwealth Games]* gold medal, taken against the odds and the form book in the women's road race, confirmed in the most dramatic fashion that the South Wales wunderkind Nicole Cooke is successfully managing the transition into senior racing after her dominance at world junior level last year.

It was, however, a close call on Saturday morning for Wales's second cycling gold in the history of the games, as Cooke followed the track sprinter Louise Jones (1990) into the record books on the treacherous twisting roads of Rivington in the west Pennines, just north of the Manchester action.

Although it was dry when she raced, the 19-year-old came close to crashing on a tight left-hander two and a half miles from the finish which had earlier claimed Margaret Hemsley when the Australian looked a possible winner, and she had to chase to catch up with the lead group before unleashing her finish sprint.

In fact it was a wonder Cooke was in a winning position at all. After her disastrous ride in the time-trial the previous Saturday she had had to be put back together by the Welsh team staff, led by the team manager Shane Sutton.

"She was in bits, emotionally shattered; she was in tears in the back of the team van," Sutton revealed. "There had been massive pressure on her, with the press saying she was going to win three gold medals here. So we got her to come out and face them."

Afterwards, Cooke was found to be physically exhausted, after training too intensely before the games. "She was suffering from chronic fatigue and her carbohydrate stores were completely depleted," said Sutton. To counter this, in the six days leading to the road race she was placed on a regime of "virtually no training, apart from the odd potter with the team and her brother".

If Cooke, from Cowbridge, has a weakness it appears to be her massive willpower, which can lead to her training too hard, as happened in the run-up to the Games. Sutton would not say as much but Cooke's coaches must be concerned that she is overdoing it. Immediately after her gold medal ride she flew to the Netherlands for the women's Tour de France, which started yesterday and covers 1,000 miles in 15 days.

Hers was an unlikely victory in another way: when they escaped the peloton the lead group of a dozen included four Australians, and in the group of seven that fought out the finish she was without a team-mate whereas the defending champion Lyne Bessette of Canada had the support of Susan Palmer-Komar, the eventual silver medallist.

Dealing with the tactics would have been daunting for a seasoned racer, let alone a 19-year-old in her first senior season. "There was a lot more thinking to do," she said. Clearly she has an old head on her young shoulders. Sutton, who is also Cooke's personal coach, had the look of a man who could not believe what he had just seen, and he would only say "it was a triumph of guts and class".

He was not the only surprised party. Three hours after the finish Caroline Alexander of Scotland was still stunned. She had finished fifth after launching the finish sprint with Cooke latched on her rear wheel, and could not believe the Welshwoman had won after watching her in the race: "She was going like a bag of spanners."

After her sprint through the leafy grounds of Leverhulme Park, where vast crowds gathered in the sunshine before the giant television screen in an atmosphere more redolent of rock festival than road race, Cooke was asked how she had managed to pull the win out of the bag after the time-trial trauma.

"They are different kinds of event," she said. "With the tactics in the road race, and being able to see the other competitors, it brings out a different side of me. I thrive on face-to-face competition." In other words, once she sees the whites of the opposition's eyes she is transformed. In cycling, that is the mark of the greats.

This was a truly epic win, one of the best road race performances I can ever remember seeing. It set out Cooke's stall as a future great. It was also one of the highpoints of the Manchester Commonwealth Games, which were a harbinger of what was to come in London at the Olympics 10 years later: massive, passionate crowds, helpful, friendly volunteers and top-notch organisation.

UK Sport to consider Tour de France challenge
4 August 2003

Plans are under way to form a team to race the European professional calendar alongside the British world-class performance programme after the Athens Olympics as a stepping stone for aspiring British Tour de France riders.

The team would be part-funded by outside sponsorship and would be registered in Division Two, one level below the Tour de France and World Cup races. Its formation is likely to be part of the plan for the next Olympic cycle, from 2004–08, which will be presented to UK Sport by Britain's cycling performance director Dave Brailsford next year.

"We've got to the level we're at by being very tightly focused on track racing, but in the future we need to broaden our objectives," said Brailsford. "We need a dedicated road squad to bridge the gap between riding for Britain and riding for Division One professional teams. In the planning for the next Olympic cycle, we'll be looking at it very closely."

Since the arrival of lottery funding in 1998, there has been continual criticism from the grass roots of British cycling that the bulk of the cash and the management's focus has gone into track racing programmes. This has produced a steady flow of medals at world championships, and the healthy medal haul at the Sydney Olympics, but has done nothing to develop road cyclists to beef up the British presence at flagship professional events such as the World Cup series and Tour de France.

Some of the riders in the team – totalling no more than a dozen – would be funded by the lottery as part of their track training programmes. They would race the road for some of the year, as they do already, as stage races on the road are the best way of developing endurance for track distance events such as the individual and team pursuit.

"We already have a lot of the infrastructure such as vehicles, staff and equipment in place," says Brailsford. "The plan would be to bring riders up through the juniors, take them to Manchester for a year, drill track racing into them, then they would have the option of the track or the trade team."

The inspiration, as so often, is Australia, which began pumping state funding into track racing in the early 90s but also developed a road programme which led to this year's strong Australian showing in the Tour de France.

Brailsford believes Britain can emulate this. "If we can compete as we have on the track in the last couple of years, that means in the long term we are capable of matching what Australia did in the Tour. They had seven guys riding this year, and I don't see why we can't aspire to that."

Enter Dave B and his professional team built on the back of the Olympic track programme; seven years before Team Sky hit the road the germ of the idea was clearly there. This idea would, in the short term, morph into the road academy run by Rod Ellingworth. In the long term, however, Great Britain would realise Brailsford's vision of emulating Australia in the Tour de France.

Obree opens up on a story of speed, success and suicide
17 September 2003

Had it not been for a 15-year-old girl's decision to check up on her horse in a lonely barn in the Ayrshire hills one night just before Christmas 2001, Graeme Obree would be dead, and I would probably have written his obituary. Instead, we are sitting on a sofa in his house in Irvine, south-west Scotland, and he can explain why he wanted to die, to escape the depression that had followed him since childhood.

When Obree, twice a world champion and the man who revolutionised aerodynamics in cycling, was found hanging in the barn after his third attempt to commit suicide, he was a minute from death. The lungs that took him past a world record that the greatest names in cycling dared not tackle helped save him, as did the fact that the man who cut him down knew about resuscitation.

Suicide, Obree explains, is born of "a desperate need to not think, because thinking is so painful you can't carry on. Anything will do: substance abuse, sleep if you can get it, or death. It's why substance abuse is so common among depressives, because thinking is so painful. You will accept any substance to change your way of thinking, or not think, because it can't be any worse."

Now, diagnosed as manic depressive with a personality disorder, he is glad to be alive, and he feels he is winning the battle. "A lot of changes have come about through my psychologist, but it takes a long time. I have to protect myself, because if my mood starts going down it's like clawing myself out of a hole. I have to express my feelings, I can't let things fester. I used to just hide away."

Obree's attempts to take his own life and his fight against severe manic depression appear in his recently published autobiography, *Flying Scotsman*. His story, which must have taken considerable courage to write, is a harrowing but often entertaining reminder of how little we know of sportsmen, no matter how brightly the spotlight shines on them.

For three years, from 1993 to 1995, British cycling was mesmerised by Obree as he emerged from poverty and the obscurity of Scottish time-trialling to sudden celebrity. He came from nowhere to break in 1993 the hour track record, set by the Italian great Francesco Moser 11 years earlier and regarded as unbeatable. It was so intimidating that five-times Tour de France winners such as Bernard Hinault and Miguel Indurain had not dared stake their reputations against it.

There were numerous subplots. Obree competed for the record and the 1993 world track pursuit title with Chris Boardman; cold, clinical thinker with heavy financial backing versus spontaneous, unpredictable pauper. Obree broke the record, and won the title in an aerodynamic position of his own invention, on a bike built in his kitchen using, famously, a bearing from a washing machine. He subsisted on marmalade sandwiches and cornflakes. He was the two-wheeled Tough of the Track.

He was simply pigeonholed: genial, lovable British eccentric, the body of a world-class cyclist with the mind of Professor Branestawm. It was so easy to look no further. Yet a viciously painful childhood had left him badly damaged, bitterly isolated.

"I observed the world, but wasn't really part of it. I was dislocated from it. I never grew up."

As a schoolboy, Obree was attracted to cycling partly as a means of escape from bullies; eventually "the racing side was about feeling worthy", he says now. He was driven by "a need to win to feel worthwhile enough to operate, to go about the daily business of life. Winning the world championship in Colombia in 1995 against [the Italian] Andrea Collinelli, I was like a fox after a chicken. He had better form but I needed to win because of the fear of failure. All I could think was 'I can't lose the final, I'd rather die'."

Celebrity probably did not help. The reaction after he broke Moser's hour record was, he says, "a life shock. It has the same effect as having a good life which turns bad. One week I was on the dole, the next there were television crews from France, Belgium and Holland on the doorstep, 64 messages on the answerphone, and people saying: 'Come and race in Denmark, we'll pay you thousands'." A week before, he had been hunting down the back of the sofa for 20p to buy a loaf of bread.

"I was out of control, I didn't know what to do next; 'how about the world championship? OK, give it a go'. That would be unthinkable for someone like Chris Boardman. I think it did affect me. I didn't realise at the time, but I was just swept along. Sometimes I could have lain on a knife-edge and slept. Cycling was a front, a party trick, and I liked the reaction."

Flying Scotsman was begun in 1994, but it ended up being written as "a form of therapy", he explains. "You put it all down on paper, you try and get out the feelings that are trapped. It started with the psychologist saying it would do me good, and ended up as my life story. I had to make the decision either to write a 'pop' type book with lots of pictures but not saying much, or a real autobiography saying everything."

The book is far removed from the average sportsman's autobiography in its candour. There is much humour, in the tales of cycle touring and amateur racing, but without the mediation of a ghost writer the raw edges remain and the book is all the more striking for it. Obree describes trying to kill himself using acetylene gas in the same matter-of-fact tone as he does his successful attempt to beat Moser's hour record. His visits to mental institutions are related just as baldly.

The Obree story struck a chord with the British cycling public in the 1990s, and when the book was launched last week at the Manchester velodrome he signed 200 copies and was struck by the affection with which people regarded him. It is rare for any sportsman to lay himself this bare, but he knows why. "I want people to know the real person. I want people to understand what it's like, how it felt. I want my book to be the best I can be."

The Obree story remains one of the great sporting tales, but his telling of it is simply extraordinary. What shocked me about his suicide attempts and the background to them was that although I had followed his career in detail – albeit from far greater distance than that of Chris Boardman – I had no idea what was going on in his life. It was a salutary example of how, as sports writers, we tend to see the sportspeople we write about purely in the context of their sport, and it is one from which I hope I learnt a lesson.

Hoy pedals through the pressure to glorious gold
21 August 2004

The heat and the pressure in the Olympic velodrome could hardly have been more intense, but Chris Hoy rose above it all in the kilometre time-trial last night, emulating Jason Queally's triumph in the Sydney games and breaking his team-mate's Olympic record in the process to become the first Briton to be awarded a gold medal in this games, the Yngling trio not having been officially presented with theirs as yet.

As world champion, the 28-year-old Scot with the 66cm thighs started last of the 17 riders, and had to look on as the Olympic record fell three times in quick succession, first to the triple world champion, the Australian Shane Kelly, then to the 2003 world title holder, the German Stefan Nimke, and finally to the four-times world champion and world record holder Arnaud Tournant of France.

"It was pretty horrible," admitted Hoy. "I was more nervous than I've ever been in my life. In 2003 I lost my world title because I was put off by the times the other riders were doing, so today was all about thinking about my own ride. I had to get myself into my own world and shut off everything else. There's a lot of pressure going off last man; it's not an enviable position."

Hoy had sat in his chair by the start gate with an impassive face, apart from a brief handshake with Tournant, and seemed focused only on putting talcum powder on his sweaty palms, but then the pressure was ratcheted up.

For some reason, the starter began the countdown while Hoy was still in his chair by the trackside watching his bike being placed in the starting gate, rather than when he put his leg over the saddle as is the rule. "I had to run on to the track and I was pretty annoyed."

He was, however, fastest on each of the four laps, albeit never by more than a fifth of a second, and although he was "hurting a lot" as he slowed in the final metres, he was roared on by a sea of British fans and union flags in the back straight of this elegant velodrome.

The support included Queally, who screamed at him that the starter had begun the countdown and leapt in the air as his time was announced on the scoreboard, and 16 of Hoy's friends and family, led by his father David, his mother Carol and his sister Carrie.

"I saw the scoreboard and it was weird because when I won the Commonwealth Games and world championship I was so pumped I milked the crowd but tonight it was so hard to accept and believe it," said Hoy. "It's what I've been training for for all this time. I was so emotional I could not get my hands off the bars. I was in tears as I went round the track."

As Tournant and Hoy said, any one of the top four could have won, and the toughness of this discipline – too long for a sprint, too intense to count as true endurance – was underlined when Nimke almost had to be carried from the track.

Hoy was quick to pay tribute to Queally, "an inspiration", whose feat in Sydney led the former rower and Scottish BMX champion to move from specialising in the team sprint to this solo event.

The build-up had been almost as pressured as the evening itself, with hot competition for the two places between Hoy, Craig MacLean and Queally, who had been out of form since Sydney. The picture became more fraught when Queally's fitness began to build in the last two months, meaning that a final decision to field the British record holder MacLean was taken only a few days before the competition.

Hoy will lead MacLean, Queally and Jamie Staff in today's team sprint, where the British have not been out of the medals in a major championship since 1998, and he believes MacLean's seventh place yesterday should not affect the quartet. "Jason is on as good form as he's ever been and Craig will bounce back. We are capable of beating any team in the world."

Another British cycling medal is guaranteed today in the men's 4,000 metre individual pursuit. Last year's world champion Bradley Wiggins faces the 2002 Commonwealth and world champion Brad McGee in the ride off for gold and silver, while another Briton, Rob Hayles, bronze medallist in Sydney, has a chance of bronze against Spain's Sergi Escobar.

Wiggins set an Olympic record of 4min 15.165sec in qualifying, more than 3sec faster than the time held by Germany's Robert Bartko, and Hayles also beat the old record, finishing fourth.

The speed of the track was proved in the evening's first final, the women's 500m time-trial, where the world record fell to Australia's Anna Meares in 33.952sec. Great Britain's Victoria Pendleton has been focusing on the sprint, which starts tomorrow, and showed she is on fine form in setting a British record of 34.626sec for sixth.

Athens in a nutshell: the emergence of Hoy and Wiggins onto the national stage. Pendleton made a stuttering start to her Olympic career here. The story that I remember from this Games, however, was that of Queally: the British coaches were to make the wrong call in leaving him out of the team sprint line-up, when he was in the form of his life. He would miss out on a second Olympic medal and would never have the chance again. He took the disappointment in impressively stoical style: there was no public hissy fit, and he carried out his duties as team captain in exemplary style.

Third medal for Wiggins the history man
26 August 2004

Bemused, bewildered and blissful, Bradley Wiggins yesterday became the first Briton since 1964 to take three medals in a single Olympic games. He and his Madison relay partner Rob Hayles – bloodied and bruised as well as blissful – won bronze in a display of colossal guts and ice-cold composure.

All had seemed lost when Hayles fell off shortly after half-distance, and the duo's untrammelled joy as the race finished turned into an agonising wait after the German team put in an appeal over the distribution of points. The judges threw it out, and for once sporting justice was done.

Already the winner of the individual pursuit and a silver medallist – again with Hayles – in the team pursuit, the 24-year-old Londoner was overwhelmed to have matched Mary Rand's haul in Tokyo in 1964 of a gold in the long jump, silver in the pentathlon, and bronze in the 4x100 relay. For a British cyclist, it is a unique feat.

"I was told a few times that this was possible, but this sort of thing only happens to other people," said Wiggins. "I never, ever thought that anything like this could happen to me. It's terribly hard to take in. I'm still in a bubble here, and I'll have to wait and see what the response is when I get home, but it's mindblowing for me."

This 50-kilometre event is the longest Olympic track discipline, and is a curious cycling variant on tag wrestling, with one of each of the two-man teams circling the track slowly while his colleague races for a couple of laps before grabbing his hand and slinging him bodily into the fray. The object is to gain laps on the field, and score points which are awarded every 20 laps and are used to separate teams finishing on the same lap.

"The [individual] pursuit was incredible, the team pursuit was hard and a bit disappointing, but I had a day off yesterday, had some time away from the village and even managed to have a pint of beer, which must have done me more good than harm. I came here relaxed and ready for it."

He will find out soon enough how the British public responds when he rides next week's Tour of Britain as the leader of his Crédit Agricole team. His response since taking gold in the individual pursuit has been exemplary, however.

On Sunday and Monday he tried his damnedest to assist the team pursuiters in the latest episode in their lengthy, frustrating quest for victory over the Australians, and after that he could have been forgiven for relaxing a little as only the eighth Briton to take a gold and silver medal in one games in the post-war era.

This race was unfinished business, though. In Sydney, Hayles had crashed and broken his collarbone with two laps to go when the pair were in the silver-medal position, and they were relegated to fourth. "It haunts me," said Hayles before yesterday's start.

With 36 cyclists spread out over the 250 metres, travelling at up to 40mph, this is an adrenalin-fuelled, dazzling spectacle, but not easy on the nerves as cyclists weave past each other continually and throw their team-mates with gay abandon with inches to spare.

"I was about to attack, but a French guy swung up in front of me and I clipped his wheel," said Hayles. "If it had been a car accident it would have been my fault because I hit him from behind, but I'm blaming him. I had visions of Sydney and thought 'oh my God, the British public must think I'm an idiot'." He landed heavily on his left side, got up rapidly, with his hip and elbow skinned raw. "A few beefburgers," as their coach Simon Jones put it.

Riders are allowed four laps out for such an incident and Wiggins merely remained "in the race" while Hayles got back on a replacement bike but he quickly needed a second bike change. "It was the same one I fell off on in Sydney, so I wanted to get rid of it as quickly as possible. I knew I was OK, it was a question of getting my breath back and going for the lap near the end when everyone was tired."

They had made a superb start, taking an early sprint, and were well-placed in fourth but, with Hayles pedalling stiffly and painfully, they slipped to seventh. But Wiggins said: "I knew we had to wait for the right moment." It came with 32 laps remaining when Wiggins, who had looked the strongest and smoothest rider throughout, shot out of the string of riders in a last-ditch attempt to gain the lap that would put them back with the leaders.

It took 10 laps of all-out effort to achieve the lap gain but it brought the crowd to their feet. It took the duo into the silver-medal position, but the next sprint edged the Swiss past them. The finishing sprint was all that remained; Wiggins raced his heart out from five to go to keep the pair well placed, and it fell to Hayles to hold off Ukraine and New Zealand.

Cruel luck, and the implacable judges had already deprived the pair's team-mate Jamie Staff of a probable medal in the keirin.

The world champion had fought his way back into the final after going out in the first round of this event in which riders are paced for six laps by a small, puttering motorbike piloted by a grim-looking driver in a black catsuit.

Staff was judged to have obstructed another rider in the final two-lap dash for the line en route to winning the second round, and was disqualified. It seemed harsh, given that every round involved bumping, boring and jostling which led to two heavy crashes, and the former BMX world champion was devastated. At 31, this may have been his only chance for an Olympic medal, and for him, unlike Wiggins and Hayles, there may be no sweet revenge.

This was a simply outstanding race, inspiring more passion, I felt, than Wiggins's gold medal in the pursuit, with the drama and skill illustrating why the Madison deserves a place in the Olympics. Amusingly, Wiggins's reaction afterwards (fourth paragraph) is pretty much the kind of thing he said after winning the Tour de France. Jamie Staff was desperately unlucky here, but would go on to greater things in Beijing.

How science and self-belief took British riders to a higher plane
27 August 2004

While Britain's track cyclists came from nowhere to take four medals in Sydney, the Athens Olympics may well mark a sea change in their outlook and produce another great leap forward, according to the team's performance director Dave Brailsford.

"We've gone from just trying to get medals to being disappointed if we don't win. The performance in Sydney gave the riders and staff the self-belief. It was clear to everyone that we were going in the right direction and we've moved on from there."

Brailsford and his predecessor as performance director Peter Keen believe the team have developed in strength and depth and the results here bear them out. The four medals could easily have been six had the fates not intervened in the team sprint and keirin. In the 12 track events, top-10 placings were achieved in all but two.

The approach taken by Brailsford and Keen before him boils down to a quest for perfection which extends to unlikely areas. For example, in Sydney the team used largely off-the-peg cycles; now, looking to save fractions of a second, they have moved to making their own bikes, wheels and components.

The team also researched methods of keeping the riders cool in Athens' 30C-plus (87F) temperatures by linking up with the Naval Research Station in Gosport, who had looked at ways of treating servicemen in the Gulf. "They pointed us to the fact that the best way of cooling is by immersing the hands in water at 18C to 22C (65F to 72F)," said Brailsford.

"The question then was how to apply the science and we ended up with something simple: the riders have to sit in a chair when they are in the track centre waiting to race, so we have chairs with two bags of water at the right temperatures, so it doesn't matter if the weather is humid.

"Chris Hoy was sitting in the chair before his gold medal ride in the 1km, so that's an example of pure science being applied to this environment."

People management has also been given priority. "There have been big staff changes since Sydney when there was a lot of unrest in the camp. If you want to get the best from a rider on a given day, the people around him have to know what makes him give his best and they have to be inspired. We wanted to develop the best back-up team we could.

"It's not about happy families, that would mean we were in a comfort zone. I like the mood being a bit grizzly because everyone is pushing hard and is on edge."

Merely to employ a nutritional adviser might seem old hat, not so a forensic psychiatrist who has worked with prisoners at

Rampton mental hospital. More conventionally, Chris Boardman has also been brought in as "expert adviser" to the squad, largely to use his experience to brief riders on what to expect as potential medal winners.

The national lottery has pumped £6.7m into cycling since Sydney. That means more than £1.5m per medal here but the medals are only part of a bigger picture, says Brailsford. Brailsford points out that as acting chief executive of British Cycling, the national governing body, he has a responsibility to get people on their bikes. "What we're hoping is that Olympic success can be incorporated into helping cycling as a sport and recreation."

The ongoing success of the track cyclists, for example, is bound to have been a factor in the re-creation of the Tour of Britain which returns to the calendar next week.

But Brailsford's wider aim is to use the Olympic medals to draw major firms into pushing recreational cycling as part of the government's agenda of cutting obesity levels. He and his organisation are in advanced talks with "a major corporation" to back a high-profile campaign based around mass cycle events – a sort of "leisure cycling for all" – which is aimed at getting the nation back on its bike.

This follows from the Sydney piece (So where has this band of cyclists sprung from?) as an exposition of the methodology of the Great Britain track cycling teams and the marginal gains approach. Steve Peters – the psychiatrist from Rampton – makes his first appearance, although clearly I had agreed to keep his name under wraps for the time being. Chris Boardman reappears in the first of a variety of roles. The Tour of Britain was relaunched that September on the back of that successful Games; after a shaky start, it is now a massive event. Finally, Brailsford floats the idea of a leisure cycling sponsorship for the first time. Sky were to do this four years later.

8. INSIDE GB CYCLING

29 June 2008

This piece appeared in Observer Sport Monthly *in the aftermath of the record medal hauls at the world track championships in 2007 and 2008, by which time it was clear that the Beijing Olympics would be something special. I was given several days access to the team in the run-up to Beijing in order to compile this exposition of the team's philosophy of "aggregation of marginal gains."*

To be among the Great Britain cycling team at the world championships in Manchester in late March was to share a single feeling: can it really be this good? For once, the term gold rush was not overblown. This was a collective surge of emotion that mounted as each lump of the precious metal was hung around another Briton's neck, as each vignette of victory was stored in the memory. Rebecca Romero's yell of triumph on winning the women's pursuit; Chris Hoy's incredulous look on taking the men's sprint; Victoria Pendleton's burst around the final banking to defend her sprint title; Bradley Wiggins, three gold medals in the endurance disciplines to his name, showing his son, after the crowds had gone, how to raise his arms on the podium.

The bullet-headed performance director, Dave Brailsford, stood on that podium each evening – it was a handy vantage point in the track centre – and each evening his jig of triumph grew more animated. By day four, with nine gold medals won, Brailsford could rightly claim "we've crushed everybody", which is a rarity for any British team in any sport.

It could be added, without hyperbole, that the final tally of half the 18 titles on offer meant this was the best world championship for any British team, anywhere. It was achieved on home soil, when it truly mattered in an Olympic year, and as a result Britain's cyclists will travel to China in a few weeks with a realistic chance of taking between six and nine gold medals.

Yet 10 years earlier I had gone to the world track championships and returned after a few hours, because the team's sole hope, Chris Boardman, had bombed in his event. There was no one else worth watching, no true gold-medal hopes. Boardman had managed a gold at the Barcelona Olympics, but was past his best, while the Scot Graeme Obree was in retirement.

The British Cycling Federation were in meltdown, their members deserting in droves. The velodrome that hummed in March 2008 was, back in the 1990s, derided as a white elephant. Only Boardman flew the flag in the Tour de France and he had only a couple of years in him. The notion that 10 years later Great Britain would enjoy such dominance and such confidence for the future was laughable.

The turnaround, begun by Brailsford's visionary predecessor, Peter Keen, has been incremental and inexorable: a single gold in Sydney, two in Athens, four at the 2005 world championships, seven last year. Worryingly for the rest of the cycling world, Britain may be set to dominate Beijing, but the current flow of youngsters through their programme means their performance in London in 2012 could be even better. Under Brailsford, with his mantra "medal or nothing", a web of academies has been developed to identify and nurture talent, while his current goal is a professional road-racing team to compete in the Tour de France. It looks perfectly attainable: in 2007 five Britons rode the Tour, all connected in one way or another with the GB system.

It is a success story that is unique in a sporting country so attuned to failure that we shrug when all four football teams stay at home during Euro 2008 and merely purse our lips as our athletics stars fall by the wayside with the Olympics in view. British cycling is now where foreign coaches come to work with the best, and where professional cycling teams turn to learn how to create drug-free squads. *[This was a reference to the fact that in the wake of the Cofidis doping scandal in 2004, their management visited British Cycling to explore how to put a drug-free team together.]* While those on the inside are occasionally astonished by the momentum they have achieved, it has not happened by chance.

On those March evenings at the world championships, the GB cyclists were competing at home, in every sense. The Manchester velodrome is not merely on domestic soil; it has been the team's base since Keen turned up in September 1997 and nipped out to a second-hand shop to buy himself a desk. Now, the building, once seen as a waste of money, is home to the entire programme, with its 52 full-time staff, as well as the rejuvenated governing body, British Cycling. Spending a week in the neon-lit corridors, around the echoing oval of timber bankings, I discover that it has also become home to a peerless methodology that can be a benchmark for any British sport.

I start the week in a meeting room above the wooden boards of the velodrome, where the sprinter Jamie Staff is standing in his boxer shorts as his skin – and what little subcutaneous fat hangs on it – is palpated between a pair of callipers. "I'll be a miserable git if I cut out the biscuits," Staff says. Nutritionist Nigel Mitchell assesses Staff's considerable shoulders. "The gig to have in this game is to work with the Brazil volleyball team," he jokes.

In Beijing, Staff has a key role as starter in the team sprint relay, one of the few events where Great Britain will not be the favourites. He has a kilogram of body weight to lose and the responsibility seems to be hanging heavily upon him. "At the Olympics I don't want that kilo. I want to be that perfect," he says, and clicks his fingers at the avuncular figure of Mitchell. "I'm thinking about the weight I'll have to shift out of the start gate. I don't want to move a pound more than I have to. People talk about losing grams of weight off the bike or the helmet, but why do that when you can save it off the body?"

Fortunately for Staff's mood, he can have his biscuits, but their number has to be carefully considered, as well as the variety. Their joint conclusion is that thin oatmeal ones would be best, or perhaps a few squares of chocolate as a treat. It is not only the biscuits that have to be analysed. There is the recovery drink Staff imbibes during training sessions, his intake of amino acids, creatine and fish oils, the size and number of tortillas he had for dinner the night before. The pair are to meet every few weeks in the three-and-a-half months until the Games.

This meeting lasts an hour and is a telling little insight. Over the next few days at the velodrome, a strategy becomes clear: to seek small, incremental gains in every area where a cyclist can become as good as is humanly possible. When every small increase in performance is put together, over the decade since the lottery-funded team was founded, the result is today's healthy advantage over the opposition. Staff's 60 minutes with Mitchell is just one tiny part of this very large picture.

On Tuesday morning, Staff is one of a group of sprinters training in the velodrome's gym. As Staff waits for his digital alarm clock to tell him it is time for the next set of squat thrusts, Mark Simpson, a strength and conditioning coach from the English Institute of Sport – the sports-sciences organisation that supports elite athletes – is on hand, his computer monitoring each cyclist's progress against their personalised programme. It is a far cry from Staff's early days on homemade kit in a loft in Ashford, Kent, with only the book *Weight Training for Cyclists* to guide him.

Under Simpson's guidance, many of the sprinters are practising techniques common in powerlifting, to develop the explosive force needed for instant acceleration. "If the rider is a Formula One car, in the gym we are building raw horsepower," Simpson says. "The aims are to get the legs as powerful as possible, and at the same time make the cyclist's core strong."

The riders would, he explains, get by without his presence, but "I want a no-compromise service. In a lot of instances you need

254

to change the sessions because someone is injured, fatigued or even feeling extra good. I can encourage and motivate, and, as I write the programmes, I want to see how they respond."

After eating a sandwich that looks minute and sipping his protein drink, Staff gets on his bike. The group of sprinters circling the track includes Pendleton – double world champion a few weeks before – the up-and-coming Ross Edgar, and Jason Queally, who won the kilometre time-trial gold at the 2000 Olympics. All are doing subtly different training: Queally is doing top-speed work; Pendleton is working on her starting efforts; Staff is doing a medium-gear session, as he has the morning's gym work in his legs. Monitoring them is the sprint coach, Iain Dyer, and an EIS performance scientist, Scott Gardner.

After warming up behind Dyer's motorbike, the sprinters rest in the track centre and adjust their bikes for the next phase. "This is the glamour side," Pendleton says ironically, as she picks up an Allen key and changes her chainring, surrounded by scruffy plastic chairs, the velodrome echoing to the bounce, bounce of a basketball as a team of disabled players practise. Edgar has detected a rattle in his aerodynamic carbon-fibre frame. "It sounds funny," he worries. "That's the 50p you lost last week," Dyer says.

The scale of the British cycling operation becomes clear as you wander the never-ending windowless corridors, with their pictures of the team's medallists, and, outside the door of the offices, a map of Beijing. "People who work here call it the dungeon, because they never see the light," Staff says, pointing out the gym, the rows of changing rooms, the canteen that serves dodgy-looking pasta and sandwiches.

In one room, with soft sofas and a whiteboard, the team's psychiatrist, Steve Peters, takes each cyclist through their "foundation stones", a massive list of individual items that can affect performance: everything from diet to disc wheels to a dispute with a significant other. Peters estimates that 50 per cent of his work is with athletes, 50 per cent with "significant others", mainly the coaches.

That might seem a little obscure, but not in a system where every area is open to improvement: ironing out relationships between the athletes and the people who work with them is seen as critical. Peters is also behind the athlete-centred training system, where cyclists are given freedom to define their own programmes, the coaches playing the role of expert advisers rather than dictatorial father figures.

Then there are the more obscure corners. There is a hidden chaos of lathes, scales and drills where Tony Robinson, the team's engineer, spends his hours endlessly calibrating and recalibrating the team's Powercranks. *[These are the ubiquitous SRM cranks that measure power output and which are a core part of the team's data gathering.]* There is a room that contains a jig for measuring the rolling resistance of a tyre, perched on half a ton of solid steel that has to be recalibrated after half an hour's use.

And locked within the locked equipment room is the legendary "Beijing box-room", containing the items of aerodynamic kit that will not be brought out until August – and soon shut up again so the competition will not have time to look at them. They are the work of the "secret squirrel club" that has taken cycling technology to its furthest limits under the leadership of Boardman – or "Q", as Pendleton calls him.

Other members of the club include Scott Drawer, head of R&D at UK Sport, and Dimitris Katsanis, a Greek former team sprinter who has had a pivotal influence on their innovations. Katsanis heads a company that makes carbon-fibre mouldings for companies such as the McLaren Formula One team and produces items such as bulletproof seals for military helicopters.

Boardman has drawn on his experience as a professional when he and his trainer Keen utilized the radical, one-piece carbon-fibre "Lotus" bike with which he won Olympic gold in 1992. "I know what you can and can't do with a bike, and you have to go outside cycling [to advance]. Pete and I were ahead of our time, but when we hit the limits in cycling, what we did wrong was not to invite other people in." Now, with the help of his £500,000 budget from UK Sport, Boardman can, for example, call on a friction expert to look into the efficiency of the chain, or ask BAE Systems to assess axles.

He also has the use of a wind tunnel in Southampton, and "lab rats" among the riders – the pursuiter Rob Hayles and Queally being the most assiduous. He has even invested £10,000 in "Jason's brother", a life-size replica of Queally with movable limbs which, unlike the real thing, never tires.

"If you look at a square centimetre of the body or the machine, we've examined it," Boardman says. "Within the rules, we can't go further. We've polished and tweaked everything." Down to the nut that holds the front wheel in place? "Down to that nut." It all has to be done within cycling's peculiar rules on kit, which boil down to one principle: if the referees do not like an innovation, it can be banned on the spot. As a result, anything developed by the squirrels has to be subtle, with "an element of psychology", so that the men in blazers will not feel it is too radical.

As insurance against the officials, the equipment is quietly introduced in selected events and its use recorded so that a precedent has been established. Nor will Britain's cyclists be the only ones to benefit from the work of Boardman and his squirrels: his aerodynamic helmets will be used in Beijing by Team GB's triathletes, and the skeleton bobsleigh team will be using some of the technology at the next Winter Games, in Vancouver in 2010.

As a cyclist, Boardman's great passion was not the winning itself, but the quest for perfection. The same feeling can be felt everywhere within the velodrome. "I was passionate about understanding how things work," he says. "The beauty of it all is that it is measurable. You start off with what you are trying to achieve, set off down a path and measure your progress and that's what makes me passionate."

If every area has to be examined to the furthest limit, that includes training itself. Another day, back on the track, Pendleton does her quarter-lap standing-start efforts with a box under her saddle measuring the force she exerts each time she accelerates from the start line. "In the gym we know what stimulus a given weight will have on a muscle, but we have no knowledge in that area in track cycling," Gardner explains as he analyses her torque curve on the trackside computer. The results will enable the coaches to determine what gear choice will give the best outcome in training for a standing start. Given that in one world championship GB's team sprinters lost a medal by two-thousandths of a second, the attention to detail is understandable.

The riders circle every few seconds, hypnotising the onlooker: training consists of one warm-up after another, interspersed with a few brief spells of intense pain as they sprint at flat-out pace. "Make sure you lunch three hours before and eat plain food," Pendleton says with heavy irony. After an effort, she adds: "You feel like you are going to throw up, you lie in the foetal position. It's character building."

"You build the lactic acid in your legs, and it takes time to come out," Edgar says. "For 10 minutes afterwards, you just can't get comfortable." As the afternoon progresses, Staff and Queally grow visibly older, their faces greying and drawn as they complete their maximal efforts, warming up high on the banking and using the height to gain speed as they swoop down to the baseline for each 100 metres, with Gardner and Dyer yelling encouragement.

"People ask what we do – you say you are on the track for two-and-a-half hours and you did four efforts that lasted five seconds, and it's hard to grasp," Queally remarks. "I often lie when I'm asked, so it sounds like a bit more."

"With the power we produce, you do a lot of muscle damage, people can't understand that, because they can't put themselves in that situation," Staff says. And who, indeed, can empathise with a body that produces 2,000 watts of power, with rotational torque on the start line that is briefly almost twice that of a Formula One car, not to mention legs that can spin the pedals at four revolutions a second?

Busiest of all the rooms in the velodrome is the mechanics' lair, where the sprinters drop in to have their bikes serviced before each session. Ernie and Spike are two of the eight mechanics employed ('not enough by a long way", they reckon). The demands go well beyond the routine of servicing, preparing and washing bikes.

Of all the team, it is Bradley Wiggins, the triple world champion, who probably has the most machines (14, they estimate), and it is Edgar who requests the most tweaks: "Saddle down, saddle up a few mill, bar tape thickness here and there; his attention to detail is incredible." The women in the team are continually changing their saddle positions in search of greater comfort; the team pursuiters like to experiment with different arm rests and alter the position of their hand grips.

The handlebars that Wiggins used in the Tour de France's opening time-trial in London last year were built here, as his professional team's supplier could not come up with precisely what he needed. "We used this," Ernie says, brandishing a length of anonymous aluminium tubing.

Success comes at a price: the black carbon-fibre track machines are worth up to £10,000 each; the bars alone cost £1,700. Replacing the specially made, extra-stiff chainrings that have been in use at major events since Sydney will cost about £100,000. Some of the team use individually made shoes with soles custom-made from plaster of Paris moulds. [These are made by Bont, the make that Wiggins would put on the world stage in 2012.]

Beijing will be a colossal operation. "We move like an army," Ernie says, opening up the 18-page spreadsheet on his computer that lists every item for Beijing down to the gazebos that will keep the sun off the road time-triallists as they warm up. The containers of "dead goods" – sports drink, exercise bikes for warming up, those gazebos – left for China on 12 May. Two hundred items will be sent in by air freight.

The bikes will be individually checked on to the plane using bar codes held by the airline; merely getting the team truck into Heathrow requires special arrangements due to security. The petrol-based cement used to stick on the tyres rates as a dangerous substance and needs the same licence to enter China as the shooters' ammunition.

Later in the week, the sprint coaches meet the team's senior managers – Brailsford, head coach Shane Sutton, and Steve Peters (Boardman is absent, on a research trip to Italy) – to talk through the selection criteria for Beijing. For the male sprinters, the stakes are high. Only four will travel. While Hoy, Staff and Edgar are most probably assured of their places, having set the fastest time by a British team at this year's world championship, Queally is being pushed hard by the younger generation of sprinters such as Matt Crampton and Jason Kenny, who were within a gasp of winning medals in Manchester.

Queally has not ridden a world championship in two years and accepts his efforts this spring may be for nothing, although he will not leave racing without a fight for his place. "I'm clinging on, trying to make the most of it. But it's a good position to leave in. When I began, getting in the top 10 was something, now you don't get a mention unless you get two golds at the world championships."

The dilemmas the managers face are familiar to any selection panel: gut feelings or objective data; experience and history against youthful potential. There will be a trial, on 4 July, but even the data gathered on that day will be relative, because of the variables.

The ability to ride quickly around the track is not the only consideration. Can riders adapt to the other events? Can they "back up" over the four days of competition? Complicating the picture is the need for the sprinters to contest three drastically different events – the match sprint, man-to-man over three laps; the team event, in which three are timed over three laps; and the motor-paced keirin.

The specifics of the meeting remain behind closed doors, but, as so often within the velodrome, the process is what counts: letting the riders know precisely what they have to do and how they will be judged. Brailsford is open about the fact that every step forward creates fallout of some kind. "There are always glitches, we push so hard that there are always issues," he says. Many of those are raised fortnightly at rider-development meetings, essentially a forum where any athlete can get anything off his or her chest.

The four men complement each other well: Sutton, the passionate ex-pro with an instinctive feel for the riders; Boardman, the cold-headed technical visionary; Peters the non-judgmental human face from outside cycling; Brailsford drawing together the different strands, tweaking here and there. "I'm like a sculptor – you shave off a bit here and there," Brailsford says. "The danger would be if you took a mallet to the structure and the whole thing shattered."

They are already looking beyond Beijing: next winter's World Cups have to be planned and invites to post-Olympic celebrations are coming in. Between them, the group have created an approach to their sport that few others in this country have matched. "There is," Brailsford says, apologising for the jargon, "clarity of mission. Everyone is here because they understand we are here to win medals. Anyone, in any job, can sit down and pinpoint what they are doing towards the medal-winning process now or in the future."

The idea that every area can be perfected, without compromise, has been taken to its logical extreme. It is summed up in the appointment of Peters: to get mindsets right, do not just hire a psychologist, take on a forensic psychiatrist who worked at Rampton's high-security hospital. Experts such as Gardner,

Mitchell, Peters and Boardman have the freedom to innovate, but their skills are perfectly channelled by Brailsford. "What you have to do is give someone a budget, a programme to work to, delegate to them and make sure they are surrounded by a culture where everyone is striving for excellence," he says. It sounds simple. The reality is a complex chemistry.

A management consultant would say that process and outcome have been perfectly harmonised, but Boardman offers the best definition: "In Beijing, the athletes will get on their bikes and say to themselves, 'The guy over there has no advantage technically, I'm personally within 100g of the weight I want to be and mentally I'm prepared for an audience of millions of people.' What we are shooting for is that the cyclist sits on the start line and says, 'I'm as good as I can be, in every way.'"

Post-Beijing, the Senior Management team would be narrowed down to just Sutton and Brailsford; Peters remains involved with British Cycling to this day, although he is now working across other sports. Boardman ringfenced his position to that of head of R & D in the run-up to London and has recently given up the post.

9. BEIJING 2008

There were several strands to this Olympic Games: the personalities that emerged over the summer, the performances themselves and the background. The issue when selecting pieces on Beijing is a tough one: what to leave out, when there was so much going on?

The mechanic of the mind with an inside track on winning gold
8 May 2008

The sign on the door in the bowels of the Manchester velodrome reads simply "Steve Peters", but there is plenty else it could say. Abandon preconceptions, all those who enter here. Logic not emotion. "The voice of reason," as the Olympic champion Chris Hoy puts it. "The glue," to quote another athlete, referring to the unseen force that binds a complex unit into a coherent whole. If you ask Peters to describe himself, he uses these words: the mechanic of the mind.

The British cycling team's psychiatrist – silver-haired, breezy in manner and in his mid-50s – has been an unobtrusive yet powerful influence in a recent run of success that culminated in nine gold medals from a possible 18 in the recent world championships. He is one of the four-man core management team at the heart of the squad that is expected to provide a tidy pile of medals at the Olympic Games in Beijing this August and was a key element in the success of Hoy, an Athens gold medallist in 2004, and the six-times world champion Victoria Pendleton.

This week, more of his clients will be in action: the world champion BMXer Shanaze Reade begins her Olympic build-up with the Copenhagen World Cup event, while the triple world track champion Bradley Wiggins will start the Giro d'Italia. Next week it is the turn of Nicole Cooke, Britain's top woman road racer, in the arduous Tour de l'Aude.

It is not widely broadcast, but Peters' influence extends well beyond the world of two wheels. His clients include the quintuple junior swimming gold medallist Lizzie Simmonds, the UK's taekwondo No 1, Sarah Stevenson, an Olympic judo qualifier in Karina Bryant, and the Olympic bronze medallist pentathlete Georgina Harland. He also works in diving, netball, trampolining, cricket, sailing and Premier League football, and assisted Brian Ashton's England rugby team on their way to the final of last year's World Cup.

In cycling, Peters's brief is tailored to suit every individual. "He brings an understanding of how humans think and behave, way beyond anyone else that I've ever met," says cycling's performance director, Dave Brailsford. "More importantly, he can actually translate that understanding into clear and practical solutions. That permeates all aspects of what we do."

As well as the obvious roles his job title suggests, supporting the cyclists and their coaches, Peters also chairs selection meetings, as a neutral from outside cycling. "There are general things where he is of help," says Hoy. "If you are happy in your life, it generally shows in your sport. Before the races, he's a neutral, objective person you can speak to. He's there as a sounding board between the riders and the staff."

Peters' background is in forensic psychiatry; he once worked at Rampton Secure Hospital. He has no quick answers, "no recipe book" as he puts it.

"I don't come in and tell people what to do. I ask people to see in themselves what they need to be doing and help them get there. If you said 'I want to get fit' and you went to a gym, you could possibly go there and train yourself and do really well, but you would probably be better going there with a strength and conditioning coach who can work with you. It's exactly the same with the mind.

"You walk in with a belief system, ideas, behaviour that you apply to sport. Some people can do very well, but most of us aren't sure how to use the equipment. I say 'This is how your mind works, this is how you get strength in certain areas, this is how to build up on the weak points, this is the skills base you need'."

Peters' background has encompassed a maths degree – "Logic theory, which has a bearing on how I operate" – before a medical degree and psychiatry as well as, in his early 40s, running a 10.9sec 100 metres. At Rampton, he worked with men who had personality disorders.

"You try to contain their behaviour and see if you can adjust their belief systems," he explains. "What you do is help them change their personality or behaviour to what they want it to be. You have a spectrum of personalities, it's a completely individual thing. You use similar principles with a person off the street to an athlete – all you're doing is getting the optimal beneficial functioning for a human being. That's my job: to make people function as well as possible and in the way they want to."

Peters sees things differently. The prime example of this came during England's erratic campaign in the rugby World Cup last year, to which he came late in the day and in which he worked with certain players in areas such as controlling emotions and channelling aggression. In the psychiatrist's view, the team turned their campaign around in the 36–0 defeat to South Africa, precisely the point at which most judged they were heading for the exit.

"I saw that match with friends and they were saying 'They've had it' but I saw a mental strategy in place that could take them forward. As a result it was awful, but I had six parameters on whether they were working as a team. They weren't working as individuals trying to prove a point. There was courage and tenacity. They started going for every single ball. Everything counted. Did they control their emotions? These are basic things but they had pulled themselves together as a team."

Pared down to the basics, the Peters way involves three initial steps. First, the athlete is made to look at himself. "You get inside your head, see yourself as a machine. It's about how you interact with the world. It's quite complex and can take up to 12 months." The second step is where the athlete learns about how other people function, while the third involves communication skills. Peters underlines that 50 per cent of his work is with athletes themselves, while the other half is with "significant others", mainly their coaches.

He has an eclectic brief. "In my work with people, I look at them holistically, with everything on the table. It's the approach I would use in mental health work. It's vast." The result is the system of "foundation stones", in which the athlete and coach write down "everything they know which can make them succeed. You might have 150 points for one event, from physical skills and attributes, through nutrition and mental skills to personal life. The athlete decides which ones they would like to work on."

Peters' role extends to competition day, naturally, but here, again, the approach is comprehensive. "Some have natural coping strategies, some don't, so they have a strict mental warm-up plan. They will know what kind of things stop them performing, what goes through their head. We remove the negatives. They learn what part of their brain is giving them completely negative thoughts and they switch over, and that is a skill."

Where the British cycling team has broken new ground is in taking a bottom-up, athlete-centred approach, and here Peters has been key. "The athlete has to own their own programme," he says. "They formulate what they are doing." Rather than the coach telling the cyclist how he or she should be training, the athlete is strongly encouraged to take the coach's advice and take the final decision according to rules that have been previously agreed on, with the coach viewed more as an expert adviser. Commitment, ownership, responsibility and personal excellence are the watchwords, and again the nuance is important. "We

266

would like excellence. What we ask for is personal excellence, which is very different."

"The athlete agrees a benchmark to aim for and then the whole team gets pulled in – the strength and conditioning coach, the nutritionist, me – so you have what Victoria Pendleton will call 'Team Pendleton', where Vicky selects who her team are. When I first arrived, it felt like the benchmark was set by the coaches [and] the coaches said to the athletes 'You do the following.' Sometimes the athlete didn't make it and we had a problem. Now, there is no guilt or blame, we're all trying to get them to that benchmark, and if they don't get there, it's sad. It's a whole philosophy – we call it the carrot with no stick."

This was one of the first times Steve Peters broke cover. Like the rest of the British cycling team he went from zero to national hero overnight.

Pooley determined to outsmart Cooke
28 June 2008

In a fortnight the British Olympic Association will announce a cycling team for Beijing boasting unprecedented strength and depth. Many factors account for that but among them is sheer serendipity. The right athletes have emerged at the right time and a prime example will be found on roads around Helmsley, North Yorkshire today, where Emma Pooley will attempt to give Nicole Cooke a run for her money in the race for the women's national title.

Three years ago Pooley travelled to this course as an unknown with three road races behind her and was a surprise fourth. Now she is ranked ahead of Cooke at 12th in the world – 13 months ago she did not have a single ranking point to her name – and she became the only British woman besides Cooke to have won a round of the World Cup when she took the Binda Trophy in late March. Selection for Beijing is discretionary, based on results, so she should be a shoo-in to join the Welsh woman in Beijing. Today, naturally, she would like to break Cooke's iron grip on the national title.

"I'm not going to race for second. It really annoyed me last year that everyone treated the race as if it was a foregone conclusion, as if they were assuming that Nicole is going to win. It's frustrating but I think it's worse for her in a way because she has to win or everyone will ask what is wrong. She has been overwhelming at the nationals. She's very strong and very smart, so I'll need to be smarter."

When Pooley managed two top-10 placings at last year's world road race championships in Stuttgart British officials could not hide their excitement. Suddenly the Beijing equation had changed. Cooke's ability to challenge for a medal has never been in doubt but in Athens, as in world road championships over the years, she lacked a team-mate who could back her up at key moments. Pooley's spectacular rise could be part of the answer, as she explained at her base in Zurich recently.

"In a race like the Olympics, where there are only three riders in a team, you need riders who are a danger, because otherwise if they attack the teams know it is a pointless move and won't tire themselves out in reacting. It's crucial to have people in the team who are not just able to help but who are a threat in their own right because it makes teams work a lot harder." Next week, when the pair ride a Welsh men's stage race, the Ras de Cymru, they will be trying to hone those team skills.

With an 11km ascent in each lap, the Beijing road-race circuit will suit a climber such as the 25-year-old Pooley. When she visited last December, the steepness of the climb, and recent snow, meant that at one point she and other athletes had to push their bus. "The view is stunning and there were peasants there digging away the snow, brushing the road. It's awesome the way it winds up the hill. The only problem for me is that the race finishes at the bottom of the hill not the top."

Having taken up road racing relatively recently, Pooley admits her achilles heel is the tactical and technical side, summed up by last year's women's Tour de France, where she attacked Cooke on the Col du Tourmalet, gained two minutes by the top of the mountain, yet could not hang on. "I was only two and a half minutes behind overall and, if I'd been a better descender, it might have been a different story. I almost looked dangerous for a while. It's a slow learning process: most racers start when they are juniors and they are naturals at it."

Pooley was a runner as a schoolgirl and made the transition from triathlon to road racing purely by chance while a student at Cambridge after going out training with the local cycling club. She now combines full-time racing with a PhD in soil engineering at Zurich. If the occasional need for a little flexibility with the demands of her studies is accepted, that is not surprising: her tutor is Sarah Springman, president of the British Triathlon Association.

Whereas most elite British cyclists are full-time athletes, many of them having come through the system from junior level, Pooley is a throwback to the days when bike riders worked or studied alongside their racing. "I have bad races and think I could be in a job that pays a pension but I couldn't quit now. The problem is, I do have an option and that's dangerous because you have a get-out clause."

"There was a time [in 2006] when I wanted to quit and I was persuaded to go on. People tell you your potential and give you a dream of greatness. I can see the potential. I can see races where I do something wrong, a technical thing, but I do OK, so if I can learn those things I will go well. I'm 12th in the world rankings, which is not to be sniffed at but from nowhere to there in a few months is pretty exciting."

Pooley has yet to discover where her new-found ambition will take her, because her rise has been so rapid. "Until I won the Binda Trophy, every race was a bonus. I should have been happy to come sixth in La Flèche Wallonne, for example, but when you've won one World Cup race, you want to keep improving at the same rate." As the French say, the more you eat, the bigger your appetite, or as she puts it: "The better I do, the more driven I get."

Pooley is one of the athletes I most like to write about: sparky, driven and fun to interview. At Beijing she was one of the "bolters", coming from nowhere to take a silver medal in the time-trial, backing that up a couple of years later with a world title at the discipline. She deserves a world road title some time in the next few years.

Romero changes seats in pursuit of history and independence
29 July 2008

When Steve Peters describes the characters of his charges as the Great Britain cycling team's psychiatrist he likes dog analogies: Chris Hoy the German shepherd, Victoria Pendleton the golden retriever, and so on. Rebecca Romero, double world champion and potential Olympic gold medallist in the 3,000m individual pursuit, would probably be a greyhound – fleet of foot and a bundle of pent-up nervous energy.

Romero does not do yes and no. A question to her is met by a lengthy answer that hints at intense self-analysis. But there is no debate about what is beckoning her this August: a unique place in British sporting history. Already a silver medallist in the quadruple sculls in Athens, Romero could become only the second British athlete to win medals in two different sports at the Games – more significantly, perhaps, the first woman to do so.

The feat has not been achieved since the 1920s, when Paul Radmilovic took medals in swimming and water polo – disciplines which are arguably far more closely related than sitting in a boat and sitting on a bike. There are few doubts that Romero can win gold, particularly among those who watched her take her first 3,000m individual pursuit world cycling title in Manchester in March, when her comprehensive demolition of the American Sarah Hammer in the final was followed by a yell of ecstasy.

Romero says of that title, and her British record of 3min 29.593sec for the distance, that it was "so unexpected, unthinkable, that I wonder if there was an element of luck; I can't understand how I could possibly achieve this". It has fallen to her coach, Dan Hunt – a massive influence since she joined the cycling team in 2006 – to remove the doubts, reminding her that "becoming a world champion doesn't just involve luck".

With Hunt's assistance, her progress since moving across from rowing has been way beyond expectations: initially the plan was to spend two years trying merely to qualify for Beijing. By this January the target had been revised: gold or silver. Now only gold will do. For a novice who joined cycling in June 2006, it is amazing progress. Romero did have a cycling background, of sorts, but it was at Pearson Cycles in Sutton. She helped out after school – making tea, taking bikes out of boxes and helping shut up shop. Even then she was a self-starter: the job was taken so that she could buy a bike on account, setting her earnings against the cost.

Had someone been there to channel her talent and drive she might well have been a cyclist from her teens. Instead she entered rowing – again on her own initiative – having looked up the south-west London clubs in the *Yellow Pages* (she ended up at Kingston rather than Twickenham because the latter was locked up when she paid a visit). Eleven months after starting as a novice in September 1997, she was at the junior world championships.

She describes her experience at the Athens Olympics, where the quad were favourites but managed silver, as "traumatic" and by the time they took the world title in 2005 she wanted out. "I'd been unhappy for the last few years of my rowing career, with the squad system and the way I had to go about being an athlete. Yes, it's a hard life, there are sacrifices, hard work, but at the end of the day the medal you get should outweigh them. It didn't." She sums up: "How are you supposed to eke out the last half a per cent to win a gold medal when you are unhappy and it affects the rest of your life?"

Those who ponder what alchemy it is that should bring a raft of medals to Britain's Olympic cyclists – if the formbook is anything to go by – need only reflect on Romero's experience once cycling came calling. "I describe it as moving from school to university. In rowing you were told what to do, you didn't have independence. When you move to university you're self-sufficient, you have tutors to guide you, you use their skills and do your own research. Within cycling you are part of the team but also an individual. It's supportive, you are on equal terms, you have a voice. The athlete is at the top of the hierarchy, a whole structure, a whole staff and support team are there as services for you as an athlete. I'm trusted as an athlete."

The essential point is that cycling was able to embrace Romero, even though, by her own admission, she is not a person who fits easily into a system. "I'm definitely the person who moves aside from the company where they are working to set up their own business. I'm independent, self-reliant, I aspire to stand on the podium by myself, not diluting my talent. I'd always have preferred to do single sculls rather than a team event. It comes with my personality, wanting to take the different route. Your destiny is in your hands. If you screw up you've screwed up for yourself, and if you do it right you get the credit."

The adaptation was not simple. As a rower she knew how to work hard but that was it. She had to learn to pedal a fixed-wheel bike, how to ride around the vertiginous banking of the Manchester velodrome. "When I was trying to do an effort on the track, I wasn't only trying to give it 100 per cent, it was in a position I wasn't used to, plus the bike handling. I didn't have the technique to get it all out. I'd finish an effort saying, 'That was all I could do but it's not as fast as I could go'. It was about getting the power out through two little pedals and a muscle-firing speed I wasn't used to.

"Both are straight endurance sports, so there is a similarity there. You need a big VO2; power. If you take a standard 2km rowing race, it would be six to eight minutes; compared to a pursuit you would sit for the majority of the race just below the red line. With the pursuit you get to speed, get above the red line and hold that. Both hurt in different ways. With a pursuit it's lungs, breathing; I'm ripped to shreds. In rowing your whole body is affected more. The difference is that in rowing you only have to do what you need to win; the pursuit is a time-trial, so you are racing yourself."

If others take it for granted that Romero can win a gold medal in Beijing, she is the first to counsel caution. In Manchester she says "all the focus was on the ride-off for a medal and what everyone saw was the final, where Sarah Hammer blew a gasket and I beat her by a long way. But if you take the qualifying times, I was ahead but not by a massive margin". She believes that the fact that she so dominated the final "skews what people think about my standard compared to the rest of the world. I don't think I'm in front by a considerable margin. It's a distance small enough to be clawed back and for someone else to overtake me".

She is also keen to point out that the race may be changed by the different format of the Olympic Games, where the pursuit takes place over three days, compared with the world championships, where it is over in a single day. "You can look back at the worlds and say historically this person always backs up really well or they die off in the second race. But with three races in three days if you get to the final, someone who might not back up the same day might get better over three days' racing."

In Beijing Romero will double up with the women's points race, largely because there is no one else in the team who is in a position to do it. Her endurance strength will count in her favour – if she can escape the field she will take some catching – but, as she herself admits, she has yet to acquire the tactical sixth sense shown by experts in bunched racing. "I have nothing to lose and that could work in my favour" is her verdict.

If she makes history this August, Romero is unlikely to be satisfied with that. There may already be a faint hint that she can see the limitations of the pursuit when she says "your life is dictated by figures, data, stopwatches. You have magic numbers you work to". Adding a third sport to her list has certainly crossed her mind.

"I'd definitely be tempted. I want to get to Beijing first but, if I can manage one unique achievement there, I might think about raising the bar a bit more. If the same opportunity happened, as happened in cycling, I could jump at it as a personal challenge. It might have to be a winter sport as I might not be able to wait for another Olympic cycle." Nordic biathletes and cross-country skiers have been warned.

Romero got her gold medal in the pursuit and made her piece of history, yet another of British Cycling's breakthrough athletes of 2008. But Beijing was the end of her brief international cycling career. She was unable to find a discipline that suited her when the individual pursuit was dropped and retired at the end of 2010.

Cooke does her homework and gives Britain first gold of Games
11 August 2008

Road racing has never been an exact science and never will be, but the British cycling performance director Dave Brailsford and his team have been working on it and it showed yesterday. When Nicole Cooke sprinted across the line to claim Britain's first medal of these Olympic Games, it not only marked the pinnacle of the Welsh woman's eight-year international career but was also the culmination of a meticulous planning process going back more than a year.

That planning went to one extreme that few cyclists have contemplated: a dress rehearsal on the road of the most likely scenario for a sprint finish, so that when Cooke arrived within sight of the line yesterday, she had in effect been through the sprint before. "We were trying to cover all options and we were hoping that exactly that would happen," said the women's road-team manager, Julian Winn.

What happened leading to that sprint was the dream scenario evoked in team meetings: a relatively calm race until the field arrived at the two circuits up to the Badaling fortress and down the hill again, a strong attack from Cooke's team-mate Emma Pooley at the bell to sow confusion in the field and tire out the opposition, and Cooke using her strength and extensive single-day racing experience to execute the coup de grace. That is straight out of most tactical manuals; not so the dress rehearsal of the finish, which was another example of the British cycling team's determination to leave no stone unturned.

"We did a lead-out on the hill on Thursday, the training day," said Winn, who was racing himself until only recently. "I led them out, then Emma picked up the tempo, Sharon Laws was on her wheel, so we had already rehearsed that finish. We knew the point, at 200 metres to go, where we wanted Nicole to go. We knew at what point the legs would be getting heavy."

The only moment of doubt – among those watching at least – came when Cooke emerged from the final corner a few lengths behind her four companions. Like the other British riders she had started the race using lightweight tyres, which they opted not to change when the rain started. The downside was that she could not lean her bike as far as usual on the last bend.

"We wanted to make sure she laid off coming into the final corner, but perhaps not that far," said Winn. "We were afraid someone might come down in front of her, so we told her to keep to the left. We knew she would chew them up after that."

There was equal precision in the attack from Pooley that proved the springboard to Cooke's race-winning move. "The plan was Emma would go three kilometres from the turnstiles on the last lap," said Winn. "As soon as she came into the road she was to attack as hard as she could to put the Germans on the defensive. It worked. Emma's attack was fully committed.

"Nicole could watch and wait because the other riders know what Emma can do on her own, so they were thinking, would she ride away or was she bluffing? We felt the Germans were the most dangerous and they were put on the defensive. One was using up all her energy chasing and Trixi Worrack, their best rider, was flapping."

Critically, the searing chase when the Germans responded to Pooley's attack left the big favourite, Marianne Vos of the Netherlands, without a team-mate to assist her once Cooke had escaped just over the top of the climb.

In every road race, there is a key moment when the winner has to make an instant commitment or opt to wait, and for Cooke that instant came when she joined the three women – Emma Johansson, Christiane Soeder and Linda Villumsen – who had just begun chasing the Italian Tatiana Guderzo after she escaped at the top of the climb. "I thought, 'Yes, we can stay away, these girls want to catch Guderzo so whatever happens we'll be going fast.' There was no decision, it was just, 'Yes, this is the time.'"

This first Olympic gold in a road race for the national lottery-funded cycling squad vindicates the creation in May 2007 of "Team Cooke", an informal group including Brailsford, the psychologist Steve Peters, Winn, the performance manager Shane Sutton, the women's endurance coach Dan Hunt and the cyclist's father Tony. "It was like a working group trying to find out the best-case scenarios for getting me to the Olympics," she explained. "It's a team effort but it's not just the riders, the staff and back-up as well."

One aim was to ensure Cooke had the necessary support on the road, and here the team were helped by the rise of Pooley in 2007 and the discovery earlier this year of Sharon Laws, who was unlucky to crash twice here. Hence her glowing tributes afterwards to both team-mates.

Another crucial element was Cooke's willingness to adopt a new structure to her season, over-riding her competitive instincts and opting out of short-term success in lesser races to save her mental and physical energy for this single day. "I had tried the other route, racing all season, but got to major championships without full energy in the tank so why do the same thing if it had been proven not to work?" she said. "But it was a high-risk strategy because I was trying it for the first time. I stuck to the plan and I believed in it."

Chris Boardman, an individual pursuit gold medallist in 1992, once compared road racing to a lottery, in which a cyclist has only a few chances of taking a winning ticket. The ultimate accolades will rightly go to the gold medallist herself, who showed incisiveness – in itself a sign that physically she was completely on top of matters – and courage exactly when it mattered. However, as she would be the first to admit, "Team Cooke" made the Welsh rider's chances of pulling out that ticket as good as was humanly possible.

This was one of the key moments in Beijing: the uplifting beginning in the first cycling event of the Games which put GB on a roll. The critical thing, as this report shows, is that nothing was left to chance, either by the team in the immediate build-up, or by the wider "Team Cooke" in the months before the race. Cooke would go on to win the world title in Varese that September, but after that she would struggle to regain the heights of 2008. Winn, for his part, left the GB squad at the end of 2008 and subsequently worked as a directeur sportif at British squad Endura.

Four brush world aside after blood, sweat and tears

19 August 2008

Amid the talk of aerodynamic skinsuits, superbikes and performance analysts, the human dimension in Britain's triumph on the velodrome should never be overlooked. "They have bled for this for two years," said the 4,000m pursuit coach, Matt Parker, after his proteges Bradley Wiggins, Geraint Thomas, Paul Manning and Ed Clancy had pulverised their own world-record time to take the British cyclists' gold medal total to six.

Parker revealed the work in January in Mallorca that led to these results: six months out from the Games the team pursuit riders were already training over the island's mountains for seven hours a day at a blistering pace, including a combination of the standing starts that begin a pursuit and lung-bursting extended efforts at huge intensity up the toughest Mallorquin mountain pass, Sa Calobra.

Back then it was sobering to find out that they were training in a way that would daunt Tour de France professionals. Yesterday it made perfect sense when they gained the high point of all the peaks attained in the 10 days since Nicole Cooke sprinted across the line to win the women's road race. It surpassed, by a whisker, the team sprinters' demolition of the world fastest time for three 250m laps that opened Britain's track medal-fest.

Forty-eight hours earlier their 3min 55sec ride in the first round had opened a dramatic prospect but the ensuing British time of 3:53.314 took this event into a new dimension in the same way that Michael Johnson shattered the 200m and 400m times in Atlanta or Bob Beamon took long jumping to a new level in 1968.

This was perfection: rarely more than a few inches between the wheels, each change impeccably timed and in the final kilometre the prospect of catching the Danes to spur the quartet on. They ended up ignoring the schedule and deciding to blast for the record, on the strength of a few barely audible shouted instructions as they rode. As they took their gold medals, there was a moment of reflection for Wiggins and Manning, both bronze medallists in the discipline in Sydney and silver medallists in Athens.

"We were saying what an eight years it's been," said Wiggins. "We spent a few years going nowhere, cruising about the 4min barrier, then Shane Sutton came along and gave us a bit of a kick up the arse, the two kids [Clancy and Thomas] came along and added impetus. They don't seem to know what fear is. They will lap it up until Christmas."

Those who wonder why the British are so successful should ponder this: the quartet's training programme began in October 2006. According to Parker, the turning point came at the World Cup in Manchester in February 2007 when Wiggins, Clancy, Manning and Rob Hayles broke the 4min barrier once and would have done so twice had they not been impeded in the final as they caught the Russians. "We deliberately tried to go under 4min twice on the same day which had never been done before and that instilled confidence in the youngsters like Ed and Gee."

Beijing was a Games of defining cycling performances and this was one of the highlights among those, taking the team pursuit into a new dimension and opening the prospect of a sub-3min50sec ride. In January I had spent a day with Parker following Wiggins and company in the team car as they prepared in Majorca: it sounds simplistic but I was stunned by how hard they trained, given that the main event was seven months away. Clancy and Thomas repeated their gold medal and world record four years later in London. Manning retired after Beijing and went on to train the women's trio to the world record and gold medal at the 2012 world championships and Olympics. Parker's next move was to mastermind Wiggins's transformation into a Tour de France star, before becoming "head of marginal gains" in the run up to London. After those Games he joined the Rugby Football Union as No 2 to the England coach Stuart Lancaster.

Impenetrable Hoy joins greats after sprinting to third gold
20 August 2008

For the second time in three days, Great Britain's track cycling coaches had to deal with a conundrum thrown up by their team's dominance: two riders in a major final. This was the most prestigious title on the track, the men's sprint, the blue riband of track cycling because of its tradition going back to the 1896 Games, in which Chris Hoy was bidding to become one of Britain's greatest Olympians by winning a third gold medal in a single Games.

Hoy's victory ahead of his own team-mate, Jason Kenny, crowned an unmatched day for British sprinting with the women's title going to Victoria Pendleton, but behind the win was an intriguing piece of man-management. In the one corner an athlete at the peak of his powers, on the brink of making history, in the other a thrusting youngster in Kenny, one of the surprise packages of the five days racing here. A delicate situation, which might have had lengthy ramifications had it been wrongly handled, if one man felt he had been favoured over the other.

"From now on, they are not allowed to talk to any of the coaches, they can give them time checks in the countdown to when they are ready to roll, and that's it," said the team's performance manager, Shane Sutton, after the two men had won into the final, Hoy by beating the Frenchman Mickael Bourgain, Kenny with a straight-rides win in his semi-final against the German Maximilian Levy.

"We'll let them race. There will be a handshake before they start and we will let them go. There will be no camps, no sides," said the sprint coach Ian Dyer. When the time came to choose who pushed off which rider in the final, Dyer and the tactics coach Jan Van Eijden changed over between the two rides so there could be no accusation of favouritism.

"That was the fairest way to do it, because one of them could have said to me, 'oh Jason's riding this gear' or something," said Hoy. "It was very clear they wanted to be level and fair. It was difficult because normally you have a chat about how are you going to beat this guy and we were on our own this time."

Kenny said: "It was exactly the same in one way. You have a plan and a plan B. But you get used to being told what this guy is going to do, so about 10 minutes before the race it was like 'what I am going to do?' So you have to think about it, and you think 'I have ridden a couple of these races in the past.' You just try to do the basic things right."

The youngster was British under-16 champion four years ago this week and is a product of the SportCity Velo cycling club, based at the Manchester velodrome. He proved Hoy's doughtiest opponent after showing astonishing bike handling ability during his first semi-final round against Levy.

His first-round gambit was an early jump which forced Hoy to respond with a lap and a half remaining, while in the second round he attacked at the bell and they raced shoulder to shoulder into the finish straight. Hoy was a clear winner, and he subsided in tears in the arms of his father before he joined Kenny and Pendleton in a clinch in the track centre.

Hoy seems impenetrable, as solid as the Mount in his native Edinburgh, but the emotion finally got to him. "From the outside, it looks as if you are all calm and everything is great but there's always doubts you have. You try to push them out and focus on the job you have to do. I didn't think about three gold medals, not even today. I wasn't thinking about that. I was thinking purely about the sprint itself, the technical elements because if you break it down, it takes care of itself."

Of all the British track cyclists, only Hoy and Bradley Wiggins had competed on all five days and the Scot had come through with a perfect performance, unbeaten in every round. For a man in only his second major sprint championship – the first earned him a world title in Manchester – it was a supreme effort.

"You're drained mentally but we prepared ourselves for this," said Hoy. "We knew it was a five-day event not just two or three like a World Cup. I've trained hard on my recovery, a lot of hard efforts with short recovery time. It's paid off. Psychologically you know you have it when you come to the tough bits."

Hoy's motivation and his ability to think forward can appear superhuman at times. Within an hour of the national anthem playing, with three gold medals hanging around his neck from one Games, he declared he was already thinking of the next, in London.

Kenny, and others, will push him all the way. He says he may, if all goes smoothly, finish his career at the Commonwealth Games in Glasgow in 2014 and if there is any justice in the world by then he will be at the head of a train of young Scottish sprinters who see him as a role model.

But the key to this win may be in his thoughts on the one key factor that made the difference between him and the others here. "The Olympics. The gold medal, that's the factor. If it wasn't for the Olympics, probably after the kilometre was dropped I'd have thought that's it. It's the desire to rekindle that feeling of what it is to be Olympic champion, it wouldn't matter if it was in the team sprint, or the keirin, table tennis, volleyball. I'd do any sport for that."

Another day, another defining moment, another national hero breaks through. My prediction that Kenny would push Hoy all the way to London was prescient if not exactly the toughest call ever.

Pendleton masters the waiting game of nerves and will

20 August 2008

There are hidden depths to Victoria Pendleton's bubbly girl-next-door persona. After she crossed the line in the second leg of her final against Anna Meares, taking the title that has been her sole goal since 2004, she said something to herself while whizzing round the banking, before lifting her arms in triumph. She could not recall what the words were, "and I don't think I could repeat them if I did remember".

The Queen of British track racing might have said something not totally regal but that was understandable. Pendleton is an utterly driven athlete who had this one single chance to take a gold medal – unlike Chris Hoy, who at least had two back-up events if he slipped up in one – and she had to keep her patience until the final hour of the final day before her moment came. Not surprisingly, later on, she was overwhelmed, to the extent that she could not distinguish one ride from another when looking back.

That barely mattered: they were all perfect. She was never truly threatened, not because the opposition were not up to the task but because she was in total control of each round from the moment on Sunday when she qualified in an Olympic record time. A cast-iron will to dominate is the key element in a successful match sprinter and Pendleton has developed that since her inglorious exit in Athens when by her own admission her mind simply was not strong enough.

What is astonishing with Pendleton is the difference between her clinical racing style and her regular admissions that she is a bag of nerves. The man who has enabled her to master her emotions at the times that matter is the team psychiatrist, Steve Peters, the key to her success she said yesterday: "The psychology of what drives me as a person has been essential, getting everything in perspective, getting me in the right mind-frame. My expectations were too high. I was beating myself up psychologically at every moment. It was knocking me back."

"Just one more ride," whispered Peters to Pendleton before she set off to face Anna Meares of Australia in the second of the two rounds. It was straightforward: a jump down the penultimate banking to take the lead going down the back straight, the definitive acceleration down the straight, a narrow lead on the final banking and a chasm between the two of them by the line. A few laps warm down and she collapsed into the arms of the tactics coach, Jan van Eijden, the man who takes her round the velodrome in Manchester with an elbow in the ribs here and a shoulder barge there to get her used to the physical stuff.

The emotion was understandable. Pendleton had to endure a nerve-jangling two days before she even took to the track. No wonder she said that once she had the gold medal around her neck, she felt "like I've been waiting for ever". Asked how she spent the wait, she replied: "I painted my nails a few times, watched the TV, struggled to find something to eat because obviously you haven't much of an appetite, went on the rollers, just biding my time. It was very tough, harder than I anticipated, especially with the success of the team. On some days I was very emotional in a good way because it's good to see your team win and it was awesome to see my team-mates win.

"The pressure was mounting because I wanted to do what they've done and win a medal. It was important to be part of that. This week, watching the guys perform gave me some experience of what it must be like being a parent. I was a mess watching them and there was nothing I could do because they were on TV. I was like 'woh, is that how my mum and dad feel, because that is awful' and I felt quite guilty. How dare I inflict that on someone else?"

Afterwards Pendleton thanked her coaches, including one man who is not here, the English Institute of Sport weight training coach, Mark Simpson, "for kicking my arse" during the process that has put muscle on her slender shoulders. Her sessions under Simpson's watchful eye in the gym in the Manchester velodrome are so intense they can be almost painful to watch but the punishment paid off last night.

On the day that her team-mate and "hero" Hoy became a triple gold medal-winning legend, it should be pointed out that no one will ever know whether or not Pendleton might have been capable of something similar because the cycling powers that be and the International Olympic Committee has deprived her and her fellow women of the chance to do so. The disparity between women's and men's track events – seven to three – is grotesque in what passes for an age of equality. Pendleton will still be racing in London assuming the younger generation have not elbowed her out and it is to be hoped that by then she will have more than a single medal to go for.

Just over a year later the UCI and IOC brought in wide-ranging changes to the track programme for London which while getting rid of the bulk of the endurance races – Madison, points, individual pursuit – did at least achieve parity.

10. THE ACADEMY

The academy: Blood, sweat & gears

Cycling in Tuscany may sound fun, but for a new generation of British road racers it is the ultimate boot camp. Can the GB academy produce a Tour de France winner?

Observer Sport Monthly
20 September 2009

If a single image is worth a thousand words, Peter Kennaugh's mural of cycling photos speaks volumes: picture on picture on picture, all lovingly snipped from magazines and Blu-Tacked on the wall of a bedroom in a modest villa in the Tuscan town of Quarrata. The mural is higher than Kennaugh's head, extending most of the way up the wall opposite the single beds belonging to the Manx 20-year-old and his room-mate Luke Rowe, both aspiring professionals in the Great Britain under-23 academy.

The message is obvious. On waking every morning, Kennaugh and Rowe lift their heads and see Mark Cavendish, Eddy Merckx, Roger de Vlaeminck, Mario Cipollini and other greats, arms spread in victory at the finish lines of one-day classics, world championships and Tour de France stages, faces grimacing in pain or grinning in triumph. It is a constant reminder of their mission and that of the six other young cyclists in this house: to join the biggest names in road racing and match them if possible.

Britain has no tradition of road racing: until the prolific sprinter Cavendish came along, it was incredibly rare for a Briton to win a professional event. There had been talented individuals – Tom Simpson, Robert Millar, Chris Boardman and Dave Millar – but there was no consistency and no recognised pathway to follow. The academy aimed to change that by using the philosophy that has led GB to Olympic domination in track cycling. Cavendish (2004–6) is the most successful alumnus, with 10 stage wins in the past two editions of the Tour de France and victory in the Milan–San Remo one-day Classic in March.

The house in Via Madonna is the interface between the no-stone-unturned philosophy that guided Britain's track cyclists to seven gold medals in Beijing and the professional road cycling world. The young riders here race for Great Britain on the track, focusing on endurance events such as the individual and team pursuits and Madison, with the European under-23 championship as their main goal. In summer, they race the international under-23 road calendar, which is largely based in Italy, and culminates in the world championship next weekend in Switzerland.

Each year, the best under-23s in the world are snapped up by pro teams. Of the 13 Britons who have been through the academy since its foundation in January 2004, six are now professionals. It is a remarkable hit rate. The academy's success has also inspired Britain's Olympic coaches, led by performance director Dave Brailsford, to persuade Sky to sponsor a British-based professional team aiming at the Tour de France. Announcing the TV company's five-year backing of 25–30 cyclists, at an estimated £35m – probably the richest deal in pro cycling in these straitened times – Brailsford said: "I'm convinced we have a core group [of Britons] who can perform at the highest level. You look at the academy, some of the guys coming through, and the youngsters behind them, and you can be confident they will develop into world-class road cyclists."

One of the first riders to be signed up for Team Sky was Kennaugh, a dark-haired, intense youth, winner of two major Italian under-23 events in 2008. Other riders in the first intake included academy graduates Geraint Thomas and Ian Stannard.

A racer since he was 10, Kennaugh says: "This is all I know. My aim has always been to turn pro, but I have to repeat what I did last year, and that's the tough thing." It may seem curious to have a lottery-funded programme to produce young cyclists who can race in the Tour de France for commercial sponsors but it is not without patriotic benefits. The toughest professional races just happen to be the best way for a pursuiter – team or individual – to gain the fitness needed to win an Olympic gold, as Giro and Tour regulars Bradley Wiggins and Geraint Thomas showed in Beijing.

"The academy is key to the future success of British cyclists on the professional road scene," says Rod Ellingworth, the coach behind the concept and still Cavendish's mentor. "It means that the British riders turning pro are of a certain quality. The feedback from teams who take our riders is that the British new pros aren't having to learn basics, which matters, because as pros, they are left on their own." Brailsford is certain British cycling can produce a potential Tour de France winner in the next five years.

That seems astonishingly ambitious given the history: before Bradley Wiggins's fourth place this year, only two Britons, Robert Millar and Tom Simpson, had finished in the top six overall, and only four years ago not even one Briton started the event. But if there is a British contender out there, the chances are he will have been through the Quarrata house, or will pass through in the next couple of years. As well as current pros such as Wiggins and David Millar, former academy riders Jonny Bellis, Ed Clancy and Ben Swift may also be on Brailsford's target list for Sky, while Cavendish will remain the team's big target, although he is not keen to leave his current squad, Team Columbia-HTC.

It's a measure of the way the alumni see the academy that Thomas, Stannard and Swift all live nearby, and Cavendish has just bought a house there. They can train with their old mates and support such as a mechanic or massage is still available.

Cavendish devotes a large section of his recent book, *Boy Racer*, to his time with the academy, which he says played a key part in his rise, and he is echoed by last year's graduate, Swift, a soft-voiced, diminutive Yorkshire lad who is in his first pro year with the Russian team Katusha. "I wouldn't be what I am today without it. I definitely wouldn't have gone pro as early, or have been as well prepared." This year, Swift won his spurs rapidly by taking the points jersey in the Tour of the Basque Country, one of the toughest races on the ProTour circuit, and came close to a stage win in the Giro d'Italia.

Although the academy is not formally a feeder team for Sky, it is a natural next step for Kennaugh and the others, even though Brailsford is adamant that places must be earned on merit. "They made it clear we won't get on just because we are British, but you hear little things about what's going on and it's all quite exciting, what names they are signing, all the speculation," says Kennaugh. "A lot of people are going to want to be part of it because it's going to be one of the best teams on the block; everything will be done in super-detail. For years GB has just been a track team, so it's a massive step to do it on the road. It's never been done before so they have to go and prove their critics wrong. It will be awesome."

From the outside, life in Tuscany seems to meet the aspirations of most racing cyclists. On the day I visit, Kennaugh, Rowe and the little group, including Olympic bronze medallist Steven Burke, ride through the cypress trees and olive groves of Chiantishire for 90 miles, race up the scenic Monte Serra, carry out sprint training on a marshland road with not a Fiat or Vespa in sight, and simulate riding in a race group, reaching 35mph in the slipstream of the car driven by their trainer, former professional Max Sciandri. Later they have a massage, then rest, then dinner.

The two-storey house in a quiet backstreet looks anonymous apart from a flagstaff in the front garden, where a union flag is flown after a GB win. A full-sized workshop for the 30 bikes and a massage room take up most of the basement, along with the line of specially fitted showers which ensures no one has to wait after training. The eight riders live here from March to September, with only a couple of short breaks, and are expected to be largely self-sufficient: the masseur and mechanic live elsewhere in the town, as does Sciandri. There is a rota for cooking and cleaning, and on occasion – after hard training days, before big race days – they can call in a local woman to cook, for a few euros apiece. Every need has been catered for, as might be expected of the GB cycling programme.

But it's "not just coming to Italy to ride bikes", as Swift asserts. In a way this is British Cycling's equivalent of the Big Brother house: all the inmates want the same thing, and they won't all get it. Some drop out along the way, because it does not work for them. There is pressure to be selected for races, where a six-rider team is the norm; eight into six doesn't quite go. And there are the inevitable personality clashes – "little things that build up, which might not be big in the outside world but which grate on you", as Kennaugh puts it. "It's hard living with the same people for seven months. A lot of guys would crack in the first week."

That's intentional. The first phase in the road academy is now notorious for the six-week "Manchester boot camp", which opens the winter for the academy's new intake. This is the brainchild of the set-up's founder, former pro Ellingworth, plain-speaking, ginger-haired and with a firm belief in tough love, who dreamed up an army-style induction to weed out any dead wood and bond his proteges into a close-knit unit. The drop-out rate is relatively low: of the 11 who joined in 2004–5, only six are now outside the GB system.

Swift enthuses: "The boot camp was like a military initiation, to see who really wanted it. You'd be up at 6am, ride to the track in Manchester for an 8am session, then learn Italian, then back on the track; sometimes road riding, Italian, road, then racing in the track league. It was dead good for team building, because everyone got tired at the same time, the second-year guys who'd been through it would help the new lads get through."

As well as 8am sessions on the track in Manchester, the teenagers have up to eight hours education a day – French lessons, physiotherapy, diet, bike maintenance. "I had them working from 7am to 7pm, because what makes them special is that they don't have to go to a normal job," says Ellingworth. "I was ruthless, because I knew that the best teachers were super hard at first, then backed off." Through the year, any lack of discipline – lateness, poor behaviour – was countered by a penalty: washing cars and bikes, hard training in the rain, on one occasion three hours riding non-stop around the velodrome.

After the Olympic cycling programme made its breakthrough in Sydney in 2000, there were concerns about where the next generation of track cyclists would come from. Looking after young cyclists in the run-up to Athens, Ellingworth had felt his charges were not being pushed hard enough, and that the grant system – a flat allocation of £10,000, tax free – did not give them sufficient incentive to work hard, given that most were still living at home. So he went back to square one and spent a winter devising the academy concept. "What I wanted was driven riders, a crack squad like in the army, well drilled and willing to give everything for their country."

Ellingworth wanted to bring the youngsters to a point where they could move into either a professional team or the Olympic squad – or both – having had the basics of how to train and race instilled in them. His list included basic knowledge of mechanics such as stripping a bike, race skills such as using the convoy of team cars to catch the bunch after a puncture and leading out a team sprinter, and an understanding of the full range of track endurance events such as the pursuits, Madison, points race and scratch.

"The idea was to have more than just a mini professional team. The goal was to get them away from their families and create a halfway house before they moved on: teach them how to look after themselves, cook, clean, speak a foreign language, everything you need if you race abroad on your own. I wanted to put them in lots of races and make them learn. And I didn't want them sitting on their fat backsides with a PlayStation or drinking coffee, because this is a job."

To make the riders "hungrier" for success, the grant was cut to £6,000 per annum, and half was retained to pay for accommodation. "They would have to live on £58 per week, so they had to learn to budget, and it would mean if they won a lap prize in a race or sprinted for 20th place, it might be only a fiver or a tenner, but they could buy a CD or treat the lads to a coffee." To keep them aware of their status, they were given a less prestigious racing category – first, one below the top, Elite – and bikes with a spec one down from the very best: Shimano's second-line Ultegra rather than the top-range Dura-Ace.

In 2004, when the academy was founded, all this was a complete contrast to the sports science which dominated the track team's approach and which remains integral in preparing for Olympic events. Sports science judges cyclists primarily on their physical potential through lab tests; the academy opened up the Olympic system to supreme competitors who might not show their ability sitting on a simulator. Cavendish is the best example; Swift another.

Ellingworth is now in charge of training up those British professional cyclists for the world road championship team; he also still looks after four academy graduates in Cavendish, Swift, Stannard and Thomas. When Brailsford's Team Sky squad officially gets rolling in 2010 he is likely to be a team manager and trainer. His successor in charge of the under-23s is Max Sciandri, who has been involved since the academy moved from Manchester to Tuscany in 2006.

Sciandri has a less direct approach, seen in a little moment at the top of Monte Serra when the Manxman Mark Christian, who set a searing pace up the climb, says three words to him:

"72.5 kilos this morning." "We talked about losing weight and I picked up two bottles of washing liquid weighing 1.5 kilos each, and said to him 'you imagine riding with those in your pocket,'" says Sciandri later. "He's watched his diet, lost the weight, and he's just experienced what it feels like to ride without that 3kg on his body, and that's important. This whole experience is about learning simple things."

Kennaugh agrees that the academy is about more than just bike racing. "It's matured me a lot. Before I was less sensible, but it's taught me life skills, how to look after myself, deal with other people. I was argumentative, mood swings left, right and centre, but you're going to be no one's friend if you are in a mood, so I keep my problems to myself now or talk to Max or Rod. Before I relied on people, wanted everything done for me, expected my parents to do it all. I was disorganised, messy, clothes everywhere in total disarray. But if you look in my room now, everything's organised, because it saves energy for racing."

It's not just about tidy bedrooms. The academy has produced the goods: the proof is there in the sight of Swift coming close behind Cavendish in Giro stage finishes, Jonny Bellis sprinting to Britain's first medal in the under-23 world championship in 2007, and Thomas, Clancy and Burke brandishing their medals in Beijing. There are now similar set-ups across the Olympic cycling disciplines: sprint, women's endurance, mountain bike – and the effect has been inspirational. Across the country, talented teenagers are competing to get into the academy's feeder system, the Olympic Development Programme. The competition is intense, but they can see a clear progression from pre-teen competition to Olympic golds or the Tour de France's yellow jersey.

It would be unreasonable to expect Britons to dominate road racing as they did track cycling in Beijing but worldwide only Australia has a structure that nurtures young talent in a similar way. The example is telling: from almost nothing, Australians are now everywhere in the Tour, outnumbering traditional nations such as Belgium and Holland, winning stages and jerseys and going for the overall win. If the conveyor belt runs smoothly, Britain might just be next.

This article appeared in Observer Sport Monthly *in September 2009. Much has changed since then. Cavendish went to Sky for 2012 and left after a single season. Thomas and Kennaugh remained at Sky and went on to take gold medals in the team pursuit at London 2012, as did non-Sky member Burke, one of those riders I met at the academy that spring. Rowe signed for Sky at the end of 2010. Stannard remains at Sky and became British national champion in 2012. Mark Christian went on to ride for the An Post-Sean Kelly team, one run below the highest level, and has yet to make the breakthrough to World Tour. Sciandri ceased to head up the academy at the end of 2010 and has been replaced by Beijing medallist Chris Newton, who moved the set-up back to Manchester.*

11. BEIJING TO LONDON

Charting the progress of the Great Britain Olympic squad over the few years before the London Games was a radically changed affair. The high profile of the sport and the transformation of the key riders into national stars meant access was harder as they were now protected by agents. On the other hand, the writer no longer had to explain what a keirin or team pursuit was because this was now a sport which reached every household. And there were stories aplenty: the rise of the women's team pursuit squad, Hoy and Pendleton's battle with anno domini, *and the emergence of Team Sky. This old warrior's resurgence gave me particular pleasure.*

Queally still roaring at 40 but British sprint trio go cold in chilly Poland
6 November 2010

While Great Britain were guaranteed at least three medals in last night's finals at the European championships after qualifying fastest in the men's and women's team pursuit and the women's team sprint, in the morning there was a triumphant return to international competition for Jason Queally, an Olympic gold medallist in 2000 in the kilometre time-trial.

The Lancastrian has managed the seemingly impossible in the past 18 months to transform himself from a sprinter to an endurance athlete to race the 4,000 metres team pursuit, and to do it at the age of 40 is still more remarkable. He lined up yesterday with the 2008 Olympic gold medallist Ed Clancy, Steven Burke and Andy Tennant – all his juniors by between 14 and 17 years – and in the evening's gold–silver ride-off the quartet was set to face Russia, who were almost two seconds slower than Great Britain's 4min 01.935sec in qualifying.

Queally was a bundle of nerves before the qualifying round and swung off the pace with three of the four kilometres covered, but was set for what should be his first international medal since he took silver in the kilometre and in the team sprint in the 2006 Commonwealth Games. Great Britain's time was not particularly fast – the standard these days is sub-four minutes – but conditions in the BGZ Arena were surprisingly chilly, slowing everyone down.

"I found it tough, but I'm delighted," Queally said. "You always pray it's going to be easy. I ended up doing three kilometres, I was hoping to do another turn at the end but if I had gone back into the line I would have slowed the guys up. It was my first team pursuit in competition and it doesn't feel any easier. I'm just pleased to be 40 years old and still riding my bike. It keeps me away from the real world. I want to stay and play for as long as possible."

The two disciplines, sprint and team pursuit make radically different demands, as Queally explained. "Today I gave it all in 12 laps, but there's more management in a team pursuit. A team sprint is full on, like a kilometre, but in a team pursuit you are managing your effort, because if you go too hard it impacts on the other guys."

Queally insists that he is only in the team "because other guys aren't here," but Clancy for one would like to see him switch to a starting role, using his sprint talent to get the team up to speed faster. "If that means he only lasts eight or nine laps that's still better for us, because we have plenty of guys who can ride third or fourth in the line. He's still learning, but it's impressive what he's done in such a short space of time."

This was one of the most heart-warming performances I can remember in recent years, partly because of the sheer romance in the notion of Queally reinventing himself as a team pursuiter at the age of 40, partly because as I have said earlier he never received the acclaim he deserved for his breakthrough gold in 2000, and he was unlucky to fall foul of the selectors in 2004. He switched again the following winter, back to the team sprint, but failed to make the cut. Ironically, Clancy told me in October 2012 that had Queally stuck to it, he might have made London as a team pursuiter due to his sheer speed.

Pendleton's legacy blooms
20 Feb 2011

Victoria Pendleton is set to end her racing career after the London Olympics, but on the evidence of the past two days her succession is assured. The young pretenders Jessica Varnish and Becky James, 20 and 19 years old respectively, finished sixth and eighth in the sprint, having teamed up to finish fourth in Friday evening's team sprint, making it clear they will push Pendleton all the way to August 2012.

Neither joined Pendleton in the last four but that was no disgrace in a field that was not far off world championship level. They qualified comfortably in the top 16, looked equally assured in the opening rounds before the reality check in round two where Varnish was outclassed by the fastest qualifier, Anna Meares of Australia, while James had the equally daunting task of taking on Pendleton.

They are talented, confident young women but that is not enough against the top two in the world, even though Pendleton is not firing on all cylinders this weekend. But their time is bound to come, and the Great Britain coaches are quietly excited at the prospect.

"Jess is more explosive and has outstanding ability for the standing start lap, while Becky has a longer turn of speed, for either the team sprint or the match sprint," explained the Great

Britain coach, Jan van Eijden. "Jess put in a personal best for the standing-start lap on Friday, it was her first time below 19 seconds, which is a really big step physically and mentally, like for the boys going below 10 seconds for the flying 200."

"Becky has a bit more of a sprint head on her, she is able to make the best of what she has physically, although Jess is currently ahead on speed. Both have progressed incredibly fast in the last six to 12 months since they became full-time cyclists. I will never say never but it will be incredibly hard for them to overtake Vicky before London, because to do that they would have to be the best in the world. That's a massive task."

Varnish, who began her racing career at the Halesowen Cycling Club in the West Midlands, is currently the favourite to put in the opening lap for Pendleton in the team sprint in the London Games, depending on how Shanaze Reade's return to the track progresses. James, a product of the Abergavenny Cycling Club, is a year behind, but has already raced to bronze in last year's Commonwealth Games. Both are from cycling families: Varnish's father, Jim, is a master's sprint champion while James's sisters, Ffion and Megan, compete at under-14 level.

When Pendleton retires, the legacy of her long period of dominance will not be limited to her Olympic gold medal and eight world titles. The tracks of Britain are currently swarming with young women who want to emulate her success, who have no qualms about taking on the men and who sport her pioneering look of Ugg boots worn with Lycra leggings.

The women's youth omnium events, which act as a feeder into the lower levels of the British Cycling development pyramid, are hotly contested. That has fed through to senior level: women's races across the country are oversubscribed even before the season has got under way.

Another striking product of that system is Laura Trott, still only 18, a competitor for England in the Commonwealth Games last year and a definite contender for a place in London in either the women's team pursuit or the omnium or both. "The future of the omnium," was the verdict of one British coach yesterday, and her fourth place in the European championships last November was more than promising.

In the afternoon, she qualified comfortably in the women's scratch and was one of three British under-23 women who rode 3min 23sec in qualifying in the 3,000m team pursuit on Friday, together with Dani King and Katie Colclough. All three will join their seniors in the mix for the world championships.

At the start of this year, British Cycling was given £1million to fund a programme to get 80,000 more women riding their bikes. They have no shortage of role models.

This was an important piece, I felt, because every time I visited a velodrome in Britain I seemed to see dozens of ambitious young riders, male and female, but the significance of Pendleton as a role model was obvious. Varnish went on to partner Pendleton in the team sprint in London, being unlucky to miss out on a medal. James suffered ill-health in the build-up, but was named as reserve for the home games. Trott, of course, was to become one of the stars of London, having risen rapidly together with King, who was also a gold-medallist. Colclough switched her attention to the road with Team Specialized.

Hoy goes up a gear with focus on perfection
20 October 2011

The issue facing Sir Chris Hoy and the managers of the British track team over the next nine months is simple: how do you replicate perfection? In winning three gold medals in the Beijing Olympic Games – in the sprint, keirin and team sprint – Hoy could have done no better; in taking seven on the track, the cyclists could barely have done more. In London next August Hoy will have the chance to do the same but it is a huge task to contemplate. He is philosophical about it, which seems surprising until you figure out this is probably the only way you can be in the face of a challenge of this magnitude.

"I could repeat it, but it's an unlikely thing to achieve. It would be amazing if I could do it again. The way I'm looking at it at this stage is that London is an opportunity to win a gold medal in front of my home crowd, to win two would be better, to win three would be better still. I don't feel as if … certain riders in the team talk about the Games as if it's this huge pressure, a horrendous thing to worry about, I can see why you might think that, but for me it's a chance to do something I've not done before. If I do everything I can and don't make it, I can accept the result."

So how do you go about tackling it? You go back to the basic British cycling principle: process rather than outcome. You don't think about the bigger picture, but focus on getting the details right. That principle is what pervades the conversation with Hoy during the break between rounds in the national keirin championship, as he munches on a frugal lunch – sandwich, malt loaf, protein shake – in the gym in the Manchester velodrome.

"I started thinking beyond London this summer and realised there is no point thinking that far ahead. I don't know what the next 10 months is going to bring. It's not about the big picture, it's about saying you will hit every day the best you can within what you can control." Hoy makes no bones about the fact that since the Olympic countdown started for real, after March's world championships in Holland, he has gone up another gear.

"I've compromised a bit the last couple of years, there were things I chose to do, certain events, communication things, media, charity things. You have to have a balance in your life and if I put the foot to the floor for four years the chances of being able to keep it going to London would be slimmer. But I've kept at a level where I've been in touch with the best guys in the world, still had some good performances," – of the opposition, he accepts merely that the Frenchman Gregory

Bauge has moved on in the past couple of years – "but now we are within striking distance of the Games I'm not holding anything back."

That means setting personal bests in the gym, which Hoy has been "hitting hard, which I didn't the last two years for fear of injury. You still lift heavy, but not pushing it." This year, he has lifted more than before Beijing – "It doesn't make you fast but it increases your potential" – and there are other items such as "nasty lactic intervals". "You look at every area, there's no reason not to be 100 per cent. I've had a good five months."

He ponders, for a moment, when he may have a drink this side of London. "I've not had a glass of wine or beer for quite a while. I'll have a bottle of wine after the Kazakhstan World Cup [in early November], that'll be the first for ages, then it's New Year, then hopefully a celebration after the world championships in Melbourne. That's three bottles between now and the Olympic Games. It's not like I'm craving alcohol, but the need to relax, let your hair down, do something different.

"You think: 'What difference will a bottle of wine make?' but it's not about the Games, it's about next week's training. I will race the best I can and if I don't win I'll shake the other guy's hand, he's a better man than me. But I don't want to not win and start thinking: 'I did that appearance, the week after the training wasn't great, it had a knock-on effect to the week after,' or: 'I went out for two beers and had six because a mate was back in town.'

"That doesn't affect London directly, but the whole process. If you look at a good season you can find a certain point when it kicks off, a good week in a month away, it becomes three weeks, then four. The whole thing is about morale, momentum, and it can go the opposite way. You have a bad session, you feel a bit crap, and go downhill."

The point that has to be made here is that, although Hoy races relatively rarely compared with a road cyclist such as Mark

Cavendish, every training session is competitive: times have to be matched or beaten, team-mates monitored, certain weights surpassed. He is, he says, "racing every day", with a constant succession of targets.

There is a glorious emotional twist in what Hoy is trying to achieve in the next nine months. It is more than 15 years since the Scot and the Lancastrian Jason Queally first teamed up for a major international championship in the team sprint, but on Friday the partnership is set to be reforged in Holland. It was 1996 when Queally dislodged a foot from his pedal in his starting effort alongside Hoy at the world championships, in the hoary days before lottery funding transformed the Great Britain team; both men will be hoping for better fortunes in the European championships in Apeldoorn, the Netherlands, this weekend.

"To think of him coming back in and potentially being part of a team that has the potential to win a gold medal is incredible," Hoy says. "I remember when Jason stepped up to get his gold in 2000, thinking that he could retire now: "It doesn't matter what he does, he will always be an Olympic gold medallist." It was what set the whole cycling programme rolling. It set us on our way for the next 10 years."

At 41, Queally is six years older than Hoy, who says, having once contemplated retiring in his early 30s, he may – just may – follow his example and continue at the highest level as his 40s approach. "There's no reason why I shouldn't go on as long. Illness and injury can conspire against you the older you get, but as long as you are healthy and have motivation ... It will depend on whether there are other things I want to do in my life after London and Glasgow. You can't plan too far ahead. At my age you don't even buy green bananas."

CEREAL ACHIEVER

Hoy's life has changed dramatically since his golden exploits in Beijing:

2008: Becomes first Briton in a century to win three golds at a single Olympics. Follows this with BBC sports personality of the year title, has Scotland's Commonwealth Games velodrome named in his honour – and becomes brand ambassador for Kellogg's Bran Flakes

2009: Knighted in the new year honours, rustles up an autobiography and receives a second honorary doctorate, but on the track crashes at a World Cup event in Copenhagen and misses the world championships

2010: Gets married in April. Wins keirin gold – again – at the worlds, but is beaten in the quarter-finals of the sprint. He then suffers a humiliating defeat to little-known Irish rider Felix English at the Europeans, though he takes two golds at the Melbourne World Cup

2011: Reminds his rivals who's boss by taking keirin gold at the Manchester World Cup, left, and cleans up in the sprints at the nationals

The box shows that Hoy's progress towards London was not seamless by any means. The Scot would, however, go on to take a brace of gold medals in London, in the team sprint and keirin, having been left out of the match sprint, where Jason Kenny was given the place. Queally's hopes of making London ended in that World Cup; he suffered a loss of form, and the search began for alternatives, with the team eventually opting for the young Philip Hindes at starter in the final weeks before the Games.

"I wait until your face gets red, then squeeze the throttle harder"
15 December 2011

Ben Swift is squeezing the sweat out of the pad in his crash hat. It is a dark midwinter morning in the Manchester velodrome and about the time much of the country is setting off for work or school. "This shouldn't be happening," he mutters grimly. Around him are seven pairs of bleary eyes in drawn faces. It is close to the end of the Great Britain 4,000m team pursuit squad's boot camp, a key part of their Olympic title defence next year on home turf in London.

The pace this morning is between 52 and 58 kilometres per hour for 20 minutes or so at a time, lap after lap, round and round the velodrome, which is devoid of human life apart from a workman clearing up beer barrels. Swift, Ed Clancy, Andy Tennant, Peter Kennaugh, Sam Harrison and Steven Burke – all potential starters in London – line out behind a motorbike driven by the coach, Dan Hunt, who is wearing a thick ski jacket against the morning chill.

They are joined for the morning only by two road professionals with track backgrounds, Andy Fenn and Ian Stannard, who view this as a convenient alternative to their usual training. The eight form a neat string, one rider swinging up from behind the padded back bumper each lap. On a toot of the horn the eight split into groups and begin racing the motorbike, upping the speed to gain a lap on Hunt. Another toot and they are racing each other in pairs, each pair trying to catch the other and then take a lap on the motorbike. Then they do it again in fours, half a lap apart, chasing each other in an imitation of a team pursuit.

The technical term for this is "interval training with inhibited recovery". For the layman, it means the riders blast like crazy for a little while, then rest, but never quite as much as they need to get rid of the lactic acid pain. In the five-minute intervals between sessions, they gulp down energy gels, stretch aching legs, and grumble, in a good-humoured way. As they rest, one of the eight asks Hunt how he gauges the pace. "I wait until your face gets all red, then squeeze the throttle harder," he replies. He is joking. Perhaps.

Every now and then during the day, the performance director, Dave Brailsford, nips out of his office to watch Hunt and his charges. It is a little indication of how much this particular title matters. No disrespect to Sir Chris Hoy or Victoria Pendleton, but if the coaching team in Manchester were asked which gold medal would count for most next August, it might well be this one. The reasons are a blend of history, tradition, and circumstance.

The team pursuit is seen as a key indicator of a nation's cycling strength, because, unlike the match sprint – the two-wheeled equivalent of the 100m – there is direct crossover with the road racing pyramid topped by the Tour de France. Bradley Wiggins, lest we forget, began his career here. The British tradition in this event goes back to the previous London Games in 1948. Since the Olympic track disciplines were controversially rejigged post-Beijing, this is the only endurance medal left with any real tradition or history.

The thinking behind the boot camp is simple. The team pursuit has become more competitive since the British quartet of Clancy, Wiggins, Geraint Thomas – absent from the camp on our visit due to illness – and Paul Manning smashed their own world record en route to the gold medal in Beijing. The Australians are still as competitive as ever, but the Russians and New Zealanders are posting ominously fast times.

"As yet no one has gone faster but other teams are going as fast as us," says Hunt. "It's a four-horse race now. Right now the Australians are probably favourites because they are double world champions. It's difficult to think about it eight months away, but the four [British] guys on the line will be expected to win. It's about small margins now – we won Beijing by six seconds, caught the other team, but this time there is going to be about a tenth of a second in it."

The camp is a chance to put the riders through a massive block of intense base training under the supervision of the team's support staff in Manchester. The nutritionist, Nigel Mitchell, can be seen ferrying little flasks of urine around the hotel first thing in the morning – the samples are taken partly to assess the riders' hydration levels, but more as a reminder to them to keep getting fluids down them.

Mitchell ensures they get the calories they need each day, up to 7,000, cooks their lunches of basmati rice, quinoa, sweetcorn, chicken and ham, mashes up the anti-acid broccoli juice known inevitably as "green shit" and cooks rice cakes for the lengthy road rides over the Pennines. The physiotherapist, Phil Burt, has scanned each rider for flexibility before the camp, and is on constant hand to fix injuries before they even occur.

Getting the riders into the velodrome for several weeks has another purpose, as Hunt explains. "I've got seven riders training at a time when they traditionally wouldn't be. It's eat, sleep, ride, go home at the weekends. There is a physical element and a teamship one. They are going through things together, helping each other. The gold medal will be won by guys who have unity, who have spent so much time sitting on each other's back wheels that they know a flick of the heel here or there means they are good or bad. Twenty-four hours before the race, these are the sessions you remind the lads about."

The morning session is about pure endurance, foundation work, and is followed by massage, lunch, rest in the team room in the velodrome. The speed comes in the afternoon. The current world record is 3min 53.314sec; Hunt and his team of sports scientists believe in London it could well go down close to 3min 50sec or below that barrier. "It's not something we say flippantly. It's a whole new area." Such speeds take massive efforts for tiny returns, to go just a few decimal points faster.

Apart from a break when a downpour sends rain cascading through a hole in the roof on to the track, the afternoon consists of a series of "flying" five-kilometre runs starting from race speed, "like riding a team pursuit uphill but fast", as one rider puts it. The aim is to ride for longer than in a four-minute pursuit, with the legs churning a larger gear than usual, to build the strength necessary for riding at approaching 70kph in formation, when adapting to the minutest variation in pace makes huge demands on the leg muscles.

It looks like high-intensity weight training, and seems about as pleasant. Each is a brutal five-minute effort with four of the riders riding in team pursuit formation, the other two hanging off the back.

By the fourth one, the faces are showing the strain. By the end of the day, the riders have covered close on 70 miles on the track. So much for Tuesday; they repeat the double dose on Thursday, the other "day of doom" – Clancy's term – while the other days see long road rides or speed work on the boards.

The day ends with a stretching session overseen by Burt in the velodrome gym. The big-gear efforts are damaging for the muscles, making the riders predisposed to injury; flexibility is vital. "I'm absolutely wrecked, my arms are hurting, everything is hurting," says Kennaugh, who is one of a group of riders jostling for selection behind the two shoo-ins, Thomas and Clancy.

"You try to recover at the weekends, but the track is that intense that your legs are just battered. It's definitely working for me. Try getting me out of bed at six back home to go training, I'd just turn the alarm off. The bottom line is, it's hard mentally and physically, but if it was easy, everyone would do it. If we can't do this once every four years, what are we here for?"

The best bit of access I enjoyed before the Games for which thanks to Dan Hunt in particular. What impressed here was the level of effort involved, nine months out from the main goal – as I'd seen with

Matt Parker in Majorca the January before Beijing. Harrison and Swift didn't make the cut for the Games; Tennant was if anything more unlucky. He was selected as one of the final five and assisted them to a world title ahead of Australia the following April, then had to look on as Clancy, Burke, Kennaugh and Thomas rode to gold in London. Hunt moved to Team Sky as a directeur sportif *in January 2013.*

Cavendish's landmark of glory on long road to 2012
18 December 2011

If the bookies are correct and Mark Cavendish is crowned BBC Sports Personality of the Year on Thursday, it will be due recognition for a towering achievement. Cavendish's world elite road race title was an event of elusive rarity, and it crowned a team performance of consummate perfection which merits a place alongside the 1966 and 2003 World Cups.

Like Sir Clive Woodward's long march to Sydney in 2003, the 2011 world road title owed much to one coach and his obsessive hunt for a single goal over several years, with immense attention to every last detail. Cavendish's mentor, Rod Ellingworth, was the man in the Woodward role, but with a twist. The target is actually more long-term: the London Olympics.

In September 2008, Ellingworth, a no-nonsense 36-year-old from Lincolnshire, had forged a reputation by building the Great Britain cycling academy when he was asked to come up with a plan to win the road race title in the London Games. Working back from August 2012, he identified the key landmark along the way as Copenhagen, September 2011. It was clear in 2008, after Cavendish had won four stages of the Tour de France, that he would be the leader. "I felt we had the riders, so the question was: how do we do it?" Ellingworth recalls.

The world road race championship is unique in the cycling calendar in being contested by national selections of riders from trade teams. Cyclists who race against each other all year come together for one day in pursuit of a single goal, which may bring them no immediate benefit: the winner within a national team may be a rider from a different trade squad. Ellingworth identified one key issue from day one: getting the riders to buy in.

To start with, Ellingworth made a point of getting to know each of the 15 potential team members. "Over dinner or something, I talked through the project, told them what I wanted." At their first get-together in June 2009, he played them archive footage of Tom Simpson's road race victory in 1965 then asked the riders: "How are we going to win the rainbow jersey again? What does it take? How are we going to come together as a team?".

Famously, Simpson's rainbow jersey was unveiled in front of the team, with a video clip of each of the riders. The message was: you can be part of this. As well as training camps, newsletters kept the riders in touch with each other, outlining performances in the races that decided Great Britain's place in the world rankings. This in turn dictated how many riders eventually made up the team. In the end, a last-gasp push in the final qualifying event secured an extra two rider places for the team. Those numbers mattered on the day.

In June this year, at the last training camp, the riders were split into groups and asked to detail what tactics they would use to ensure a bunch sprint would happen for Cavendish. "When I put up the tactical plan on the Friday before the race, it wasn't my tactic, it was theirs," Ellingworth says. "That drove the selection: they said they needed these riders, to do this job."

The riders were given a DVD of the route in June, and a guide to the entire world championship was issued in August, "in massive detail. The idea was that there should be no excuse for them not to know anything."

The experienced David Millar was appointed road captain, with the job of deciding when the team had to begin chasing the day's escape; another veteran, Jeremy Hunt, was made Cavendish's personal minder. On each of the 21 laps, when the race hit the one climb, Cavendish would change to a low gear and slip back through the bunch rather than using energy fighting to keep his place; Hunt then guided him back to the head of affairs.

To keep the riders informed during the race, two boards were displayed in a spot on the course that had been carefully selected. "It was about seven or eight kilometres to go, so that if something was happening on the last lap, they would have time to act if need be. It had to be on a quiet bit of the course, where they could see it from a distance." One board had information about the race situation, the other a brief instruction.

Three days before the race, the riders looked over the course as a group, accompanied by Ellingworth on a motorbike, which enabled the coach to discuss the final details with them: lines to take through each corner, which side of traffic islands to ride, narrow sections in the road. "On that Thursday evening Cav said he was super-confident, that he would have to be eighth or 10th out of the last corner, he knew he would have to be let loose from behind the leaders at the end."

But if there was one key moment when Ellingworth knew he had succeeded in his mission to pull the team together, it came at the pre-race briefing, when he asked the riders to go through various worst case scenarios. Cavendish said he would be in trouble if he punctured late on, at which Bradley Wiggins replied: "if you puncture at 600m to go, we are all waiting for you." The message was simple: no one would be racing for himself.

What of London? Cavendish will again be the team leader, the challenge an even sterner one. "It will be harder to control because the course is so difficult, teams smaller, communication will be harder because the roads on the circuit are narrow, and we don't know how easy it will be to support the riders.

"Copenhagen was a box to tick going to London, but a huge box. You wonder if anything can be as big again, but once you're in that Olympic bubble, it will be huge. It's a matter of doing it again. We can do it again, I'm sure."

Cavendish's world title was the towering cycling achievement of 2011 and he was justly awarded that Sports Personality *trophy. What intrigued here was the way that Ellingworth looked to cover every detail; this was probably his finest hour as a coach after playing that key role setting up the GB academy, and this was certainly the best example of the marginal gains approach being brought to road racing. Note that David Millar makes an appearance; he raced for Great Britain as soon as his ban was finished in 2006 and went on to be an integral part of the team for Copenhagen and the London Olympics. Hunt retired at the end of 2012.*

Kenny and Hoy step up their "beautiful" battle for single Olympic sprint spot
16 February 2012

The contest between Jason Kenny and Sir Chris Hoy for the single slot available in the match sprint at the London Olympics is pure sporting soap opera, one subplot following another as each of them pursues the ultimate prize. It is, however, getting increasingly serious as the final goal approaches: this weekend's World Cup at the Olympic velodrome promises yet more twists in the tale.

Having the defending Olympic champion and silver medallist competing for one slot "is a beautiful situation to be in", said the GB head coach, Shane Sutton. The fact that – since the Frenchman Gregory Bauge's demotion for a doping offence – Kenny is the defending world champion and Hoy the silver medallist merely adds to the lustre.

It is a rivalry built on a backdrop of co-operation: they are usually room-mates – and are again this week in their Docklands hotel – which is another neat subplot. They are also the key elements in Great Britain's team sprint, both gold medallists in the discipline in Beijing and now the two men around whom the GB lineup for the three-man, three-lap time-trial is being built.

Sunday's sprint tournament on the London velodrome is another chance for the pair to match up: Kenny, after his defeat of Hoy at the Revolution meeting, has reversed the advantage the older man gained in the autumn when the Lancastrian admitted he was "just going rubbish". Both cyclists are adamant that they try not to pay too much attention to their personal battle.

"It's like racing anyone else," says Kenny, "no different from racing the French boys or the Aussies." "There are so many riders out there you can't afford to think about anyone else, that would be detrimental," says Hoy. Such pressures are actually nothing new to the triple Beijing gold medallist, who has had to fight for his place since his early days in the squad in the 1990s.

"Power versus speed" is Sutton's summary. The Great Britain sprint coach, Iain Dyer, describes a battle between a young man with sharper instincts and speed out of the blocks and a more powerful, older athlete. Hoy needs to dominate his opponent through the power and sustained speed he acquired over years of riding the kilometre time-trial; Kenny relies more on tactical awareness, looking for an opening where he can use his ability to change speed in a split-second.

"Jason has the edge in acceleration," says Dyer. "The lower the speed they accelerate from, the greater Jason's advantage – if they are rolling from a higher speed that advantage is annulled. You see a slightly higher top speed from Chris if he runs his own race which is a good weapon. They are both "long" riders – it's a question of whether Jason's acceleration can tell in the race or if Chris can get to the top speed he wants to."

The added twist is that Kenny – who is exactly 12 years younger than Hoy – is more experienced as a sprinter, having begun as a teenager while Hoy did not begin match sprinting until he was over 30. It might not have looked that way but, as Hoy points out, when he dominated Kenny in the final in Beijing, he was "more of a novice than Jason".

"Chris has only recently focused on match sprinting so he has had to do all his learning in a public place at 75km per hour," says Dyer. "When you are racing at a younger age it all happens more slowly so it's a different learning environment."

Hoy himself has spoken of the need to sharpen up his tactics but the variety of strategies opponents adopt to beat him – notably the attack in the opening yards from the German Robert Förstemann that lost him the second round in the 2010 world championships – is testament to the fact that his skill set is so complete.

"He is a very strong, dominant physical presence, opponents know that he is fast, "long" and strong in the saddle, they can't sprint against him as they would against a "normal" sprinter, so they have got to look for a chink in his armour, and so he is on the receiving end of some out-of-the-ordinary tactics," says Dyer.

Which of the pair races the sprint in London will be decided by a board of selectors chaired by the performance director, Dave Brailsford, with Sutton and a third party – probably the former professional Keith Reynolds – assisting, in July. "We will probably leave the final selection as late as possible," said Sutton, conceding, however, that "whoever performs best at the world championships will have his foot in the door. It comes down to evidence. You remove the person from it. You don't look at the person, you look at the numbers." Whatever the evidence, it will be a huge call and will go down to the wire.

KENNY V HOY

Aug 2008: Hoy beats Kenny in the Olympic final

Oct 2009: Hoy wins national sprint title in Manchester; Kenny takes bronze

Mar 2010: Both eliminated in the quarter-finals at the world championships

Sept 2010: Kenny beats Hoy in the semi-finals at the national championships

Nov 2010: Hoy loses in the first round at European championships; Kenny takes the bronze medal

Feb 2011: Kenny beats Hoy in two races at the semi-final at World Cup in Manchester; loses final to Kevin Sireau of France

Mar 2011: Kenny beats Hoy in semi-final at the world championships in the Netherlands

Sept 2011: Hoy overcomes Kenny in a semi-final, then beats David Daniell to win national title

Jan 2012: Kenny beats Hoy in the semi-final at the Revolution meeting in Manchester

This piece was written in the build-up to the London World Cup in February 2012, which acted as a test event for the Olympic track cycling the following August. The contest between Hoy and Kenny for the single place was a fascinating piece of soap opera, but it also underlined the craziness of having one rider per nation for the sprint and keirin in London. At least one other Frenchman, Briton, German and Australian would have been worthy of a place, meaning that the highest level of competition in sprinting in 2012 was in the world championships in April, which saw the fastest ever qualifying session for any match sprint ever.

Pride comes after the fall for Pendleton
7 April 2012

Sporting rivalries occasionally move beyond the realms of hype into the domain of the sublime and surreal. This was the territory explored in the penultimate episode of the Victoria Pendleton versus Anna Meares saga *[in Melbourne]*, which ended with the Briton taking her sixth world title, regaining the crown she surrendered to the Australian in Holland last year. For once, the pre-race polemic was upstaged by the main event, although among the war of words came this prescient comment from Meares: "All sportspeople push the limits. Sometimes the lines get crossed and the people who make the judgment on that are the *commissaires*."

As a summary of one evening's race, it is hard to better. Limits were pushed by the Briton, the Australian and the eventual defeated finalist Simona Krupeckaite of Lithuania. Lines were crossed – rarely has the red sprinters lane played such a key role – and the *commissaires* tried to make sense of it all. Pendleton and Meares have three dates this year: in February in London they turned each other inside out in a three-round epic, round two here left honours even, with the prospect of a grand finale at the "Pringle" in London in August.

At the start of the evening session, few would have given Pendleton a chance of regaining the title. She had been way behind in qualifying, looked sluggish in her first two rounds but appeared sharper in the quarter-final. History was against her as well: since taking the world title in 2010, Meares had taken their every encounter. In desperation, the coaches opted to increase Pendleton's gear, hoping she could run Meares long and hard and wear her out. As she sat by the track beforehand, she had the look of a woman waiting for the gallows, lip atremble.

The first match appeared to be going the way of Meares, who was overhauling Pendleton in the finish straight as the Briton veered to her right, losing control as she made contact with the Australian. Down she went on her right shoulder. "She hit hard, I saw it, I heard it, I felt it," said Meares.

Once the Briton had been dusted off and her trackrash seen to, it was on to round two. Again Meares looked in control but as she held off Pendleton on the final banking, she jinked her back wheel upwards, going above the red line that decides whether a sprint is straight or not. Pendleton had to switch upwards to avoid her front wheel colliding with Meares's rear wheel, and the relegation came. That made it one-all, Meares having thrown away a victory that looked assured.

Round three was where Pendleton showed sheer bloody-minded grit. Meares had been rattled and showed it with a little kick of the back wheel as she dived at the bell; the Australian attacked, but left just enough of a gap for Pendleton to use her slipstream to inch her way past in the finish straight. "Anna panicked and went for home," was the summary of the GB head coach, Shane Sutton.

In the final, Pendleton was up against Krupeckaite, a seasoned campaigner with two world titles to her name but none of the psychological baggage Meares brings with her. She is no bogeywoman and match one went Pendleton's way. Then came the final twist: a seemingly straightforward victory for Krupeckaite in match two, in which, having swung all the way up the track on the penultimate banking, she was disqualified for veering a little way outside the red on the back straight. Pendleton was warming up for the decider when she was told: the news took a good 10 seconds to register. Cue a sea of tears and a flood of hugs in the British pits.

Her reward was massive: a sixth match sprint title putting her level with the recordholder, the Russian Galina Tsareva, an amateur of the Brezhnev era. Critically Pendleton goes on to

London with what, for this most tortured of riders, might be dangerously close to peace of mind. "It's the most significant of my titles," she said. "It's the last time I will do this, it means as much as my first [title] when I didn't think I had the ability. It feels weird and iffy to win when you don't cross the line first, but those are the rules."

While Ed Clancy followed up his team pursuit gold of Wednesday with an agonising near-miss – fourth, level on points, decided through countback – in the men's omnium, and Laura Trott stands a good chance of winning a medal today in the women's race, that was mere Mills and Boon compared with the blockbuster penned by Pendleton and Meares. The latter summed up: "It is a book that hasn't finished being written." Roll on the final chapter. Whatever its conclusion, one thing is certain: Pendleton will leave cycling as a world champion.

This was one of the most extraordinary sprint contests I've ever witnessed, more interesting in my view than the Olympic final in London. It was fantastic theatre, a reminder of the sheer brilliance of track cycling as a spectator sport. And in its bonkersness – the crash, the disqualifications – it was the perfect curtain-raiser for London.

Meares braced to snatch the crown from Queen Victoria
27 July 2012

Be careful what you wish for. Anna Meares is "really sick" of meeting her perennial rival Victoria Pendleton at the semi-final stage of major competitions and would like to meet her in the Olympic final. That would be the only fitting conclusion to their nine years of shared personal history but it can only happen if Pendleton, usually a slow qualifier, finds the early speed that will guarantee her top seeding. There were indications from the team's holding camp in Newport that "Queen Victoria" was setting personal best times, pointing to a possible repeat of the Olympic final of 2008.

The national focus in the run-up to the pair's last meeting will all be on "Our Vicky", the British heroine who can bare all for a photoshoot or bare her soul for a television documentary or interview. She has kept little hidden from us in recent years: we know all there is to know of Pendleton, and mostly the British media and fans seem to like it. But what of her great rival? You would have to be a blinkered chauvinist not to appreciate Meares's qualities as well: professionalism, an epic level of motivation, levelheadedness, and a very definite sense that there is life outside her sport. Pendleton speaks of her longing to discover a world outside cycling; Meares, you sense, has a fair idea of it already.

The pair's careers have run in parallel since 2002, when they met in the Commonwealth Games in Manchester and "it hasn't changed too much since then". Meares is 28 and took her first major title in 2004, Pendleton is 31 and made her breakthrough a year later. They could, perhaps should, have been friends: at the Stuttgart world championships in 2003, they were sharing a beer when someone spilled a drink on Meares's jacket. Meares recalls warmly how Pendleton took her downstairs to the lavatory and helped to clean her up "so I could get back up there and have a good night". Fate has decreed otherwise.

Meares's take on her relationship with Pendleton is nuanced. She feels it has been hyped up – "There's a rivalry, but not to the extent that the media want" – acknowledges it is good for the fans, and recognises that having the British woman to aim at has been key in her career. "She went down the sprint path, I went for the [500m] time-trial. When that was axed she was well down the pathway and it took me time to deviate back towards that event. She's been a huge motivating factor for me in that event, she's been a huge motivator for every woman.

"To be the best you've got to beat Vicky, for me to have the belief that I could contend in London I had to beat her at her own game.

It took me until last year to do it. It was so emotional for me, I'd spent so long getting beaten at that event, you get frustrated with it after a while. There are times when I've gone, "how on earth am I going to beat her?" The British sprinters had so much speed, they didn't need to work on tactics." One route Meares chose was to work on her qualifying, aware that getting an easier run through would increase her chances. Pendleton tends to be a slower qualifier, top seven or eight rather than top three, which is why the pair so often have met in semi-finals over the years.

The pair's relationship is the more important because the personal element counts for so much in sprinting. Before Beijing Pendleton had the whip hand; since then, the momentum has swung Meares's way but the world championships in April made it unclear who is on top. That uncertainty is what makes the tournament in London seem so enticing.

"The sprint is a battle for control," says Meares. "Each rider is setting the other one up to fall into a trap, whoever can set it up and capitalise on it will be the one who wins. Speed is only one aspect, decision making another. You need to be on top of your game, understand, relax, not be too tense otherwise you start thinking. If you think it takes time to make the decision and that means opening the door for your opponent. Both parties are trying to manipulate the race to suit your strength and not that of your opponent, and with Vicky that's extra rewarding."

After losing the world title to Pendleton, Meares paid tribute to her rival: "For her to pick herself up after hitting the deck as hard as she did and come away with the win speaks volumes of the level of character she has. I know a lot has been said about her being fragile but I know she will bring her A-game to London for the home crowd. I know I need to work harder if I want to get that title off her. She goes to the Games as defending Olympic champion, world champion, and I want it."

Meares was a slow starter at bike racing, the youngest of four children, and forced to play second fiddle to her elder sister Kerry, who would snaffle the bigger bed in shared hotel rooms and grab the front seat in the car for the two hour drives to the nearest track to their Queensland home. Eventually the pair became rivals for the single sprint slot available to Australia, with the younger sister overtaking her elder sibling. It was clearly complicated.

She speaks also of the accident in Los Angeles in early 2008 that could have left her permanently disabled. It was seven months from Beijing when she clipped a wheel in a keirin, fell at 65kph and hit the banking, with the force pushing her head back and causing her to crack a vertebrae. It was 2mm away from being a clean break which would have left her at best quadriplegic. To come back, amid massive attention from the Australian media, and gain silver to Pendleton in Beijing – Australia's only cycling medal of that Games – was a victory in itself.

Where Meares is most refreshing, however, is in her sense of herself as a role model in the thorny area of female body image. She speaks passionately about an adolescence in which she was not happy with her body, and how she came to terms with it, and feels strongly that her experience can help others. "I understand the position I'm in. I've realised how much effect I can have on people, how many kids want to contact me.

"I love being involved in sport because it shows kids a different image of what it is to be a strong woman, a different stereotype. It's not always about being skinny, being under pressure in your image, it's about presentation and confidence in yourself.

"I love the fact that the women I compete against in my sport are big, strong, powerful – they've got curves, muscles, confidence, courage. If that's something I can give to young kids out there I'd be pleased. It's difficult when you are a young girl, you see beautiful girls and women in magazines in bikinis. You don't have that confidence. I wasn't happy in the body I had, as I've grown up and matured I've realised I don't have that model body physiology." She sums up in the pithiest of terms: "I got teased a bit as a kid because I had a big butt, but I've put it to good use."

While Pendleton has told the world she is quitting after London, Meares may be on the way out too. She initially contemplated teaching or coaching as a career and has combined training with university studies, but is now moving more towards a possible career in radio journalism. She will decide after the Games, not wanting to distract herself in the run-up. Whatever the outcome, she acknowledges that together she and Pendleton have created a story of their own, "what we have brought to the table for our sport, is something which has drawn people in." And might they have a drink after it's all over? "I'll have a rum, Vicky can have a beer."

MEARES V PENDLETON: AN ACCELERATING RIVALRY

World Championships
Melbourne, April 2012

A crash, a disqualification – possibly the most extraordinary round of the women's sprint ever. In the first match of the semi Meares won as Pendleton fell; then the Briton pushed the Australian into error and Meares was ruled to have left her line, costing her the race. Pendleton then won in the final

Olympic test event
London, February 2012

First time out on the London velodrome, the intensity built. The pair destroyed each other in their semi-final, won 2-1 by Meares in one of the fastest women's sprint rounds in history

World Championships
Apeldoorn, Holland, March 2011

Meares rocks Pendleton's confidence with a semi-final defeat on her way to the world title. It is the first time the Briton has lost her crown since 2006

The Pendleton v Meares rivalry was one of the great stories of London 2012. Owen Slot of The Times *and I interviewed Meares in Melbourne that April and we both left deeply impressed with her drive, her vision of life outside cycling – her views on body image were particularly arresting – and her sense of humour. I think when they met in the final that August, and Meares won, Owen and I were the only Britons in the velodrome who would have been happy to see either woman take the gold.*

Cavendish left looking grim by Vinokourov's winning finale
29 July 2012

After the euphoria of the past nine months, *[the men's Olympic road race]* was the reality check. We have become so used to success by British cyclists, success that is flagged up months in advance, that it is easy to forget that cycling is a sport where the random element can never be eliminated. That, after all, is the essence of the sport: man's attempt to make sense of the unpredictable stuff thrown up by the road and the opposition.

Mark Cavendish and his team finished this race completely spent after their attempts to control events were thwarted by concerted attacks from almost every other team in the race, with the Swiss, the Italians and the Belgians to the fore. There should be no complaints, however, although the British might perhaps regret the lack of a plan B.

The gold medal for Alexander Vinokourov will provide the perfect retirement gift for a cyclist who has taken the sport to the heights in his native Kazakhstan while plunging it into the grimmest depths elsewhere. Vinokourov brings with him enough baggage to keep Pickfords busy for a month, and he remains unrepentant about the blood doping that cost him two years of his career. Superb bike rider as he is in terms of tactical nous and aggression, he was not a winner who can shed any light on the sport's past, or give it optimism for its future unless your eyes light up at the prospect of a further influx of oil cash from the Wild East.

Cavendish crossed the line in 29th place, displaying the same grim set face he had shown in Beijing after he and Bradley Wiggins had flopped in the Madison. His quest for an Olympic gold medal will have to wait another four years. In the end – and there was no discredit in this – his four team-mates proved unable to square the tactical conundrum that came in appointing "the fastest man in the world" as their leader: they knew they would have to hold back on the Box Hill climb to keep their leader in touch, that this would allow escapees to disappear up the road, putting them on the back foot. Cavendish finished the race with a half-flat front tyre after a puncture sustained in the run-in.

What did for British hopes was a spectacular, perfectly timed move from Fabian Cancellara on the last of the nine ascents of Box Hill, just as it looked as if the race was coming together to the final run into central London. The hulking Swiss took with him a bevy of other strongmen who had bided their time on the circuits: his team-mate Michael Albasini, the Colombian Rigoberto Uran, who would eventually take the silver medal, Vinokourov, and the Spaniards Alejandro Valverde and Luis León Sánchez.

"It went on legs, we were always racing at Mark's pace on the climb so we couldn't react to those sort of things, it was never our plan," said David Millar. "A lot of teams were launching their strongest riders up the road to tire us out, and it worked. But it backfired for a lot of those teams as well. There were a lot of good sprinters with us who had a chance of getting medals. It was coming back nicely, we'd been racing for five hours, didn't have that extra bit.

"All we needed was a couple of extra guys but most were exhausted or had guys up the road. It was a slim chance, but with every team racing to thrash our race up it was going to be hard to do it." "Other teams were content that if they didn't win, we wouldn't win," said Cavendish, somewhat unfairly singling out the Australian team for "negative" tactics. "We expected it. If you want to win you've got to take it to them. We controlled it with four guys for 250km and we couldn't do more."

Cancellara and company rapidly caught up with a lead group of about 20, some survivors of a move that had gone clear before the race reached Box Hill, a group that included the veteran Australian Stuart O'Grady, who would finish sixth. They were a small peloton in their own right, 32 men united by a single goal: to evade Cavendish and avoid a sprint. The gap to the field was never more than a minute, hovering about 50sec, but that was too much, with three Spaniards and three Swiss to set the pace.

The British worker bees – Wiggins, Chris Froome, Millar and Ian Stannard – had been at the front controlling matters since the race entered the leafy suburbs with O'Grady and 11 companions in the lead and, not surprisingly, they did not have quite enough in the tank. The only other team without a rider in the massive lead group was Germany, and they were slow to commit more than one rider to the chase. The breeze that blew on the riders' backs as they sped at 40mph through Oxshott, Esher and Kingston upon Thames meant that the speed needed if the bunch were to close the gap was simply not sustainable.

As, one by one, Froome, Millar and Wiggins dropped back from the front of the field, completely spent, the Swiss plan went awry on Star and Garter corner in Richmond Park when Cancellara locked his back wheel and ploughed into the barriers. He appeared to have damaged his collarbone, which will not help his chances in Wednesday's time-trial. As the big Swiss struggled, Uran jumped clear in Upper Richmond Road, and Vino went with him, clearly determined to improve on the silver medal he took in Sydney to Jan Ullrich. His experience was always going to tell and he duly dumped Uran 250m from the line.

This was, suggested the president of the International Cycling Union, Pat McQuaid, the biggest crowd ever seen for any Olympics, with a million people estimated to be lining the roadsides of Surrey. Apart from the strangely empty lower slopes of Box Hill – closed to crowds to conserve the natural habitat – and a handily empty stretch of wall outside the Priory where the peloton took an early natural break, the crowds exceeded those on a Tour de France stage, lining the verges and pavements four, five and six deep.

The union flags waved in their thousands, one sign along the way read "Mod is God", Prince Charles and Camilla turned out on the Mall to meet the riders before they left – but the swell of national optimism that had built since Cavendish won last year's world championship, and had surged during Wiggins's Tour de France win, was not enough to ensure the race went the way of Great Britain.

This was the opening to the London Games, and it was the event that Cavendish was widely expected to win, following his triumph at the Worlds in 2011 and Wiggins's Tour victory the week before. What mattered in this piece was to explain precisely how and why he and his team mates had been thwarted, and why they should not be criticised.

Glory keeps on coming for Wiggins with his fourth gold

2 August 2012

The kit on his back changes but Bradley Wiggins marches on and he may keep marching on until Rio. With the yellow jersey swapped for Stella McCartney's blue and red creation, the human machine inside remained the same, dominating the Olympic time-trial as he had done both the long contre la montre stages at the Tour de France to continue his *annus mirabilis*. The 32-year-old is now Britain's most prolific Olympian, his gold medal taking his personal tally to seven, one ahead of Sir Steve Redgrave.

"To be mentioned in the same breath as Sir Steve Redgrave or Sir Chris Hoy is an honour as it is," Wiggins said. "It's all about the gold medals. There's only one colour really. It's No 4 for me, not No 7. So I have got to carry on to Rio now and make it five." To date, this is his fourth gold, to go with a brace in the individual pursuit, from Athens and Beijing, and the Beijing team pursuit. To that he adds a pair of bronzes, the team pursuit in Sydney – at the age of 20 – and the Madison in Athens, where he also won the silver medal in the team pursuit.

As for what comes next, the Tour de France winner is undecided. He mentioned a vodka and tonic or two in celebration, a brief stay in London to watch his old team-mates in the team pursuit and Hoy going for gold in the keirin. After that, he has talked of riding the Tour of Britain, the world championship team time-trial, but in reality he has yet to decide. His season began on 1 November last year, when he launched into full training for the Tour, and most likely he needs a break to take in the scale of his achievements this year and to reflect on what might come next.

Continuing his unbeaten run in full-distance time-trials this season – as opposed to briefer stage-race prologues – Wiggins finished 42sec ahead of the world champion Tony Martin of Germany, a healthy margin of almost a second per kilometre for the 44km distance, with the Tour de France runner-up, Chris Froome, taking bronze. As at the Tour, where he won one stage to Wiggins's two, and finished second to his Sky team-mate, the Kenya-born Briton again performed above expectations but went under the radar. Between them they took the home cyclists' tally to three medals in four events and in terms of momentum that can only bode well for the track races which start today.

Fabian Cancellara, the defending champion, whose participation had been in doubt following a heavy crash in the road race which had left him with a heavily bruised shoulder, was far from his usual imperious self. So often Wiggins's nemesis in the past, the Swiss was out of the picture before half the 44km had been covered. His deficit on Wiggins at the 18km mark was 31sec, which sounds minimal but represents a mountain in these circumstances. At the finish he had slumped to seventh, and he collapsed briefly afterwards clutching his shoulder.

"Spartacus" had been made to look very human, but he has been Wiggins's target for years; of late it has been Martin in the sights of the Londoner and his coaching team. Vitally, last September Wiggins took Cancellara's scalp at the world championships; this February, it was Martin's hanging from his belt, by an infinitesimal margin – less than a second – at the Tour of Algarve. Since then, he has not looked back. Now, as he pointed out afterwards, he will be the one to aim at.

After winning the Tour de France, Wiggins showed a healthy disregard for protocol by addressing the British fans; here, he did something similar by freewheeling from the finish area for a mini lap of honour among the crowds, who were unable to enter the Hampton Court Palace precinct where the medals were handed out. "The great thing about cycling is its accessibility, we all know about Olympic ticketing. All the real fans are out there, in here it's a bit of a prawn sandwich fest."

"Wiggo, spin to win", proclaimed the banner close to the start, along with the mod roundel that has become synonymous with

329

the first British winner of the Tour de France, and the sideburned national hero's legs spun smoothly enough, his back barely moving despite the effort, in contrast to Froome's "busier" style and the fourth-placed Taylor Phinney's imitation of a nodding dog. He lay only second to Martin at the first checkpoint but pulled ahead by the second, 18.4km into the race.

The rest resembled his Tour de France: a seamless road to victory, with the difference that here he was cheered on by a vast crowd of mainly British support. The men's course was based on the same loop through Cobham and Esher as the women, but two additional circuits were added: one at the start, westwards towards Walton on Thames, turning at the Queen Elizabeth II reservoir, and a second at the end north through Teddington and Strawberry Hill. The picture was the same as for the women's event earlier in the afternoon: massive crowds thronging town centres and leafy lanes alike.

The metronomic progress of most of the participants belies the tension in time-trialling. It looks smooth on the surface, but plenty can go wrong. Luis León Sánchez, a stage winner in the Tour de France, had his progress halted within metres of descending the start ramp when his chain snapped, and then had a puncture; the New Zealander Jack Bauer misjudged a bend and came close to crashing.

The initial running was made by Martin. After just under 8km he led Wiggins and Cancellara by six seconds, with Phinney at 9sec and Froome a further 1sec behind. The battle for medals looked tight, but the gaps opened inexorably as the duel between Wiggins and Martin gained in intensity. Ten kilometres later, the picture had become clearer: Wiggins led, 11sec ahead of Martin, the gold medal battle clearly between the world champion and the Tour winner. The final time check, in Esher High Street, with 15km to run, reflected the Tour champion's dominance. Martin had slipped away again, 23sec back; Froome was now at 42sec and clearly heading for bronze.

Shortly after passing through the town, belting down Portsmouth Road, Wiggins overtook Sanchez, who had started four and a half minutes ahead, and disappeared into the distance, a Ferrari to a horse and cart. That was an image to place alongside the punch in the air as he crossed the finish line in the Tour time-trial at Chartres, and it summed up the day: Wiggins dominant in a final triumphant lap of honour at the end of the greatest summer of his sporting life.

As Wiggins and I wrote in his account of 2012, My Time, *there was a magical quality to this day. It felt that way to me. For the journalist, there is a curious sense of anti-climax at the end of a Tour de France, because usually the final key stage is on the Saturday, and Sunday's stage on the Champs-Elysées is where the main actors tend to rush off to do this and that, while Sunday deadlines loom large. Since the Greg LeMond Tour of 1989, there has been no sense of the Tour actually being won on the final Sunday.*

So this had a very different feel to it as the defining moment of the Wiggins summer. It was also the moment when "Sir Wiggo" was born in the minds of the British public. The support for their man was massive and if his Tour triumph had felt a little remote perhaps, this was on the doorstep. It was also that rare thing: a British star heavily tipped to win at home and then delivering. Hence his elevation to the pantheon of celebrity where for the British public he needs no introduction.

Goodbye to the greats
7 August 2012

Super Tuesday was everything it was expected to be, as the final session at the velodrome produced high drama, bucketfuls of tears and two gold medals and a silver for Great Britain, who continued their dominance to end the track programme with nine medals from 10 events. Had the referees not intervened in the women's team sprint on day one, the squad would have achieved 10 out of 10. As it was, their domination is unprecedented in British sport.

The Great Britain squad bade farewell to two figureheads, Sir Chris Hoy – in his last Olympic Games – and Victoria Pendleton, racing her final laps of the track. Both their events were a microcosm of their distinguished careers. Hoy's domination in the keirin was spectacular, his ability to pull a victory out when defeat threatened typical of the man. Pendleton's emotional rollercoaster in the match sprint, apparent victory then defeat by Anna Meares after a relegation, reflecting the supreme competitiveness and emotional vulnerability which have been her hallmark through three Olympic campaigns.

The next wave of British cycling stars is here already, the baton passed by Hoy as Laura Trott prepared for her moment in the limelight, the victory in the 500m time-trial that clinched her solo gold in the omnium after her team pursuit triumph. "Just before the 500m, Chris Hoy said to me, 'You can do this,'" she revealed. At only 20, she has time to overtake the greatest track cyclist these shores have produced.

Hoy may continue to the Commonwealth Games in Glasgow in 2014 but his Olympic career has underpinned the success of British cyclists over four Games. His intervention with Trott exemplified his senior role as an iconic model and target for youngsters such as Jason Kenny and Philip Hindes. He exits Olympic sport as Britain's most-decorated medallist, with six golds to his name, surpassing Sir Steve Redgrave and drawing level with Bradley Wiggins on a career total of seven, although the cycling Modfather has "only" four golds to his name.

It was a last-gasp victory, snatched from impending defeat in the most theatrical style after Hoy forced himself to the front of the string two laps out as he had done twice before. On this occasion, leading out nearly cost him a medal, as the German

Maximilian Levy closed then came briefly past him entering the final banking.

Levy was coming the long way round, and Hoy kicked again as the straight beckoned to cross the line two-thirds of a bike length ahead of the German. "I saw the front wheel come past and thought I couldn't let his back wheel come past, so I drove harder than I've driven before and his wheel came back." Afterwards, he was applauded off the track by a guard of honour formed by the British team personnel, and then the tears flowed, inevitably.

They flowed as copiously for Pendleton: after more than 20 years, two Olympic gold medals, nine world titles and a Commonwealth gold her career is over. The 31-year-old from Stotfold, Bedfordshire, left cycling to rapturous, deafening applause but it was left to her old rival Meares to play the part of pantomime villain, defeating her in the final in two straight rounds and leaving her with a silver medal in her final race.

Pendleton and Meares lined up in the final for their last encounter. It was as tense and venomous as might have been expected. In the first match Pendleton made her effort up the back straight after the bell, and the Australian came at her strongly. Meares put an elbow into Pendleton's thigh as the British woman briefly moved off her line as they sped through the final banking.

Pendleton held on by barely half a tyre to take the match, with the crowd initially delirious with delight at what appeared a clear win in the face of Australian skulduggery, before the *commissaires'* ruling turned the cheers into a chorus of boos.

The British woman had to win the second match to stay in the hunt but the Australian won the match on the second banking, when she slowed to a virtual standstill at the top of the slope, forcing Pendleton to jump into the lead. It was a pre-planned move, "my chance to get the psychological advantage" she said, and meant she could run at Pendleton, who looked mentally rattled and stalled coming out of the penultimate banking.

333

Her acceleration down the back straight was matched by Meares, who overtook her coming into the final banking, punching the air with delight. She broke down in her press conference afterwards, and said that merely getting here felt like a victory in itself. "I won't don a skin suit ever again. I'm looking forward to all the stuff I've denied myself for the last 10 years. I'm looking forward to having a life."

As Queen Victoria prepared to take her final bow, Princess Laura stepped up, adding a gold medal in the six-event omnium to the gold she had won in the team pursuit. The 20-year-old from Cheshunt, Hertfordshire, won three of her six disciplines to clinch gold from the USA's Sarah Hammer. Trott went into the final event, the 500m time-trial, in second place, needing to beat Hammer by a clear three places. The pair were last up on the track, in which the riders race two laps against the clock, with Trott starting in the back straight to the sound of the Rolling Stones' Satisfaction. She needed to win if possible, and in some style. She produced the fastest first lap and was quickest at every timing point, crossing the line in 35.110sec with Hammer in fourth, giving her the overall title by a single point.

Trott had begun her omnium campaign by gaining maximum points for being fastest in the flying lap time-trial. She slumped to 10th in the points race but that was followed by an exhilarating ride in the elimination race, the dramatic high speed event which has become her party piece. She displayed superlative bike-handling skills and speed to win, and then added second place to Hammer in the 3,000m individual pursuit. Much depended on keeping tabs on Hammer in the 10km scratch race, where she finished third, one place behind the American, setting up the final confrontation.

The status cycling in Britain enjoyed by August 2012 could be measured in various ways, but one was the number of journalists present for "Super Tuesday". The Guardian *had around a dozen hacks in the press box, not all along merely to spectate, as this was one of a wide range of pieces in the paper the following day, marking one of the high points of the London Games. In the space of 12 years, the transformation from Sydney – when I had to explain, all of a sudden, where these cyclists had sprung from – was immense. Hoy's future remains uncertain as this book goes to press – he may, or may not, go through to Glasgow – while Pendleton quit on this day and was most notably seen on Strictly Come Dancing that autumn. Trott added a golden romance to her brace of gold medals, with her relationship with Jason Kenny going public a few days after this. She and her partner will march on to Rio, but they owe a massive debt to all the pioneers, Hoy, Queally, Wiggins and Pendleton in particular.*

12. IN MEMORIAM

It cannot be said that writing obituaries is a pleasure, but for a specialist writer on a daily newspaper the exercise is satisfying to say the least, offering as it does the chance to present to the readers some of the individuals who simply don't get into the pages, as the examples which follow should show. Beryl Burton was a classic example of a sports star of immense talent who never received the national acclaim she deserved. This at least was a step towards redressing the balance.

Beryl Burton
7 May 1996

Beryl Burton, who was found dead beside her bike on a Yorkshire roadside on Sunday, was more than just a great cycling champion: for more than a quarter of a century "BB", as she was popularly known, was an institution, the dominant figure in British women's bike racing. "Beryl was not just one of the greatest cyclists, but in my opinion she was one of the greatest athletes of all time," said Peter McGrath, chairman of the Road Time-trials Council.

That this coming Saturday, a day before her 59th birthday, she was to have taken part in the women's national 10 mile time-trial championship which after several years of ill health she stood no chance of winning, underlines the fact that her love of competition – beginning in the days of truly amateur sport – went beyond even her hundreds of world and national championship medals.

Burton was in the finest tradition of a line of British cycling greats, currently represented by Chris Boardman: she was a specialist in the solitary skill of racing against the watch on road and track who gained national and international stardom largely

337

by working outside the system with little or no help from the sport's governing bodies.

Typical of this was the fact that when she took her first world title in the track pursuit in Liège in 1959, she paid her own way to the start. She won a further five world pursuit titles, and took two world road championships, both in the only style she knew – using her strength against the watch to win alone, with the rest of the field chasing her.

The Yorkshire lass's domination of British women's time-trialing began in 1958 and will never be repeated. For 25 consecutive years Burton was crowned British Best All Rounder, a title awarded for the fastest woman over the set distances of 25, 50 and 100 miles. She won the national 25-miles title 26 times, the 50-mile title 24 times, the 100-mile title 18 times, landing her final gold medals in 1986 at the age of 49. Her national records at 25, 50 and 100 miles – some set in 1976 at the age of 39 – still stand, while it took 20 years for her 10-mile record to fall.

More impressive, however, were her performances against the men of the time, who were regularly beaten by the dimple-cheeked curly-haired "slip of a lass". The legend was born when she topped the men's record for the 12-hour event, covering 277.25 miles in the set time. On her way, she caught and passed Mike McNamara, who although beaten on the day by Burton, was on his way to a British men's record for the distance – a record which was actually lower [for a time] than the women's distance set by Burton.

Burton recalled in her autobiography *Personal Best* that after 223 miles she caught and passed McNamara, who had started two minutes before her. "I thought some gesture was required on my part. I was carrying a bag of Liquorice Allsorts in the pocket of my jersey. I pulled one out. 'Liquorice Allsort, Mac?' I shouted. He gave a wan smile. 'Ta love.'"

There were other feats against the men a year later when she set a women's 100-mile record in a time of three hours and 55 minutes. Burton was also the fourth fastest cyclist of either sex in Britain over the distance and again beat the best man comfortably. A cycling writer at the time compared the achievement to a woman breaking the four-minute mile by "a substantial margin".

Burton's solitarily competitive streak can be traced to her schooldays, when she set herself increasingly tough standards for the playground game of bouncing a ball against a wall After a brief excursion into swimming, her ability on two wheels became obvious when she met her future husband, Charlie Burton, an amateur cyclist from her home town of Leeds.

Charlie was to provide support for the next 40 years as Burton juggled the family commitments which followed the birth of her daughter Denise in 1955 with full-time jobs and punishing training schedules.

She was a truly amateur cyclist: some employers, such as the GPO, were less than helpful when it came to fitting in world championship trips, while in the mid-1960s she was putting in punishing shifts in a market garden run by a local rival. She remained loyal to the amateur Morley Cycling Club for the whole of her career.

Apart from occasional sporting failures – notably several frustrated bids at the world one-hour record and a disastrous attempt on the men and women's 24-hour title and record, when her knees gave out after she had taken a commanding lead – there were to be two other major sources of frustration in Burton's life.

One was that, in spite of her MBE in 1964 and OBE in 1968, the British press never recognised her feats. She complained that her British 12-hour record for both sexes made the bottom of page seven of the Yorkshire Evening Post. "If she had achieved comparable feats in a more popular sport such as tennis, often beating the top male competition of the day, she would have been a household name around the world," commented a lifelong associate.

Burton's other regret involved her relationship with her daughter Denise, who built a good international career in her mother's shadow, but could not avoid becoming her rival in the early 1970s.

The bitterness between the two women was such that after they had both sprinted neck and neck for the gold medal in the 1975 British road race title, Burton would not shake her daughter's hand. In spite of a tearful reconciliation after meeting head to head in the British track championships later that year, relations could never be the same again.

It remains one of my great regrets that I never managed to interview Burton, largely because my speciality was European racing at the time when I might have had the chance to meet her; I have similar regrets about Percy Stallard, another of the sport's great characters.

Percy Stallard
15 August 2001

Percy Stallard, who has died aged 92, was the father of cycle racing on public roads in Britain. His act of rebellion in organising a massed-start race from Llangollen to Wolverhampton on June 7 1942, in the teeth of vicious opposition from national governing bodies, revolutionised the sport and paved the way for events such as the Tour of Britain.

"The ideology of one man, Stallard, gave this country road racing as we know it today," wrote Charles Messenger in his history of the British League of Racing Cyclists (BLRC). "That ideology set the pattern whereby government legislation was introduced on March 1 1960, which made it legal for racing to take place on the road."

Cycling was in Stallard's blood: he was born in his father's bike shop, close to Wolverhampton station, which he was to take over until his retirement in the 1990s, and which is still run, in a different location, by his son Michael, twice British cyclo-cross champion. As a talented racing cyclist, he faced the same restrictions that his fellows had encountered since racing on the public highway was stopped by the police in 1894.

Time-trials – where the riders raced alone and unpaced against the watch – were permitted in Britain if run well out of the public eye, and if riders were "inconspicuously clothed" in black alpaca jersey and tights. In contrast, massed-start races were immensely popular in Europe, led by the great multi-stage races such as the Tour de France and the Tour of Italy. Since 1897, however, they had been banned on open roads in Britain by the governing body, the National Cyclists Union (NCU).

Stallard was selected for the world road-race championship in Monthléry, France, in 1933, and Leipzig, Germany, in 1934, finishing 12th and 7th respectively, and was inspired by the experience to train his own team of Wolverhampton cyclists – one of whom, Ray Jones, won the silver medal in the 1938 Empire Games – and campaign for the adoption of massed-start races on British roads. His point was that massed start was not unlawful in this country, but his repeated pleas fell on deaf ears.

"This is the only country in Europe where this form of sport is not permitted," he wrote in 1941, adding, "there seems to be the mistaken idea that it would be necessary to close the roads. This, of course, is entirely wrong."

The lack of road traffic during the second world war gave Stallard his chance to gain approval from the police to put massed start on the open road. He announced the running of the Llangollen-Wolverhampton race in April 1942 – "proceeds in aid of Express and Star comforts fund" – and was promptly banned by the NCU.

The event went ahead, none the less; it was won by one Albert Price, and all those involved in it were suspended. What became known as "the revolt" led to the foundation, 18 months later, of the British League of Racing Cyclists, and to a bitter 17-year conflict with the NCU, during which cycling clubs across the country were split by the need to declare their allegiance to one body or the other.

Stallard, ironically, was expelled from the league soon after its foundation for criticising its standard of race organisation, although he returned and organised the first London–Holyhead, the longest race in Europe, in 1951. His influence was vital: in the 1950s, under the impetus of the league and its calendar of races, the Milk Race, later the Tour of Britain, was founded, subsequently running for more than 30 years; in 1955, the first British team took part in the Tour de France; and British cyclists, such as Brian Robinson and Tom Simpson, became the first Britons to compete successfully at the highest level of the sport since the 1890s.

The BLRC and the NCU merged in 1959, and Stallard quit the sport in a state of disillusionment. Feelings ran high at the time; his assistant in the cycle shop, Ralph Jones, was the BLRC delegate at the international meeting in Spain which recognised the merged body, the British Cycling Federation. On his return to Wolverhampton, Stallard sacked him.

Stallard made a return to cycle race organisation in the 1980s, running events for veterans, but his chief love, by then, was hillwalking. He visited Australia and the Grand Canyon, and ran more than 100 coach tours to Snowdonia and the Lake District, on which, as one participant put it, "he would try to burn everyone off".

He never lost his cantankerousness or gained any respect for authority. While walking up Scafell Pike one day, he and his group were told by a warden to turn back due to thick mist; the group returned, and later met Stallard at the bus, only to be told, "I came to climb the bloody mountain, so I went to the top."

Ironically, since Stallard's great days, cycle racing on Britain's roads has again come under threat, this time from the increase in motor traffic and the cost of policing major public events. The result has been a reduction in the calendar, and, two years ago, the demise of the Tour of Britain itself.

Percy Thornley Stallard, racing cyclist and organiser, born July 19 1909; died August 11 2001.

The Tour of Britain was relaunched three years after Stallard's death, and has since gone from strength to strength. British Cycling have finally seemed to resolve the issue of protecting races on British roads but this has required parliamentary involvement. The threat now, alongside police costs and traffic, is now principally from a lack of willing organisers ready to raise the money to meet those expenses. As a result, the events between the Tour of Britain and the grassroots are withering away.

Pantani dies broken and alone
16 February 2004

Marco Pantani's death on Saturday in a rented apartment in Rimini was a pathetic, lonely end for one of the sport's larger-than-life heroes, but there was an implacable logic about his final descent that was redolent of Greek tragedy.

Initially it was thought that Pantani had died from an overdose of anti-depressants: "There were medicines of a tranquilliser nature [found with Pantani] that could have had a role in the cause of death," said the state prosecutor Paolo Gengarelli, adding: "No one has mentioned suicide and I am excluding it."

However, late yesterday the news agency Ansa suggested that the cause was a heart attack. Citing investigative sources, Ansa said the coroner who examined Pantani had concluded he had died of a "cardio-circulatory arrest", but that the cause was not known. An autopsy is scheduled for today. It is believed that he died at about 4pm on Saturday.

Italian cycling was in a state of turmoil at the death of its most charismatic champion since the heyday of the *campionissimo* Fausto Coppi in the early 50s, winning the Tour de France and Giro d'Italia in 1998. "I am devastated. This is a tragedy of enormous proportions," said the 2003 world champion Mario Cipollini.

Pantani checked into the Roses apartment-hotel, 20 miles down the Adriatic coast from his Cesenatico home, on February 9 and spent his last five days alone, making no phone calls, with meals being delivered to his room.

He was apparently engaged in writing his reflections on cycling, but the pages he left behind did not offer any indications of suicide. Apparently Pantani, who was unmarried, had become estranged from his family, having lost contact with his father, his most passionate supporter, and the last person he spoke to appears to have been the hotel porter.

Staff apparently found him "strange and vacant", and when he did not order dinner on Saturday night they checked his room and found him half-naked near the bed, with an empty box of anti-depressants nearby. Other boxes, some empty, were found elsewhere in the room containing four different kinds of anti-depressant.

The 34-year-old last raced in the 2003 Giro d'Italia, finishing 14th. He was refused entry to the centenary Tour de France because the organisers did not consider him good enough, and he spent much of June at a clinic that specialises in depression and drug addiction.

By the start of this year, it appeared that his competitive career was at an end: he had apparently put on two stone and told a local newspaper that he was "disgusted" with cycling after almost five years spent fighting a series of court cases and bans amid continual allegations of drug use.

These were the final episodes in a fall from grace of epic scale and suddenness precipitated on June 5 1999 at the ski resort of Madonna del Campiglio, where he was expelled for failing a blood test from the Tour of Italy 36 hours before the finish, when well on course for victory.

By then Pantani had risen to be Italy's most popular sportsman – on a par with the motorcyclist Valentino Rossi and the skier

344

Alberto Tomba. He had fought back from a compound fracture of his left shin in 1995 to win the Giro d'Italia and Tour de France in 1998, the first Italian to win the Tour for 33 years and only the seventh cyclist to achieve the double.

Pantani had already achieved vast popularity because of his unique style, wholly reliant upon do-or-die attacks in the mountains, and engaging personality – he used to take a guitar into the bars of Rimini and serenade local girls – as well as the capacity to fight back from a spate of crashes.

His Tour de France victory in 1998 came as the Tour descended into chaos after the withdrawal of the Festina team and police raids in search of drugs. On a bone-chillingly wet day in the Alps, he demolished the 1997 Tour winner Jan Ullrich in the style of greats such as Fausto Coppi.

It was widely believed that, because of the police raids, he was riding clean and that his epic victory had restored some of the race's credibility. That made next year's events the more shocking: he failed a test intended to restrict the use of the blood-booster erythropoietin (EPO) by a margin that clearly indicated use of the drug. EPO increases the quantity of oxygen-carrying red blood cells, enhancing stamina.

Pantani was not banned after the blood test, but prosecutors opened investigations on the basis that he had fixed results by taking drugs, committing "sporting fraud".

By 2000 he was racing again, staging a surprise comeback to ride that year's Giro after a blessing from the Pope at the start. In the 2000 Tour de France, he managed two mountain-stage wins before quitting the event in secret amid rumours that he was trying to avoid the drug testers.

The 2001 "San Remo blitz", when two police forces raided the Giro in search of drugs, destroyed what remained of his credibility. The *carabinieri* found a syringe in his room containing traces of insulin, and he was banned for six months. The wildest rumours followed – from a cocaine habit to anaemia

345

due to damage to the bone marrow from years of boosting his blood cells artificially.

Pantani spent his final years convinced that cycling had permitted him to become the scapegoat for a sport in which, by the mid-90s, drug-taking was the rule and from which, inevitably, he received little support when he was exposed.

This Pantani piece was not a formal obituary – I did write one as well, in a more condensed version – but this piece seemed to have its place here. The Italian's death was a horrendous event. He had been exposed as a drugs cheat, and was in massive denial, but it was impossible to forget the charismatic cyclist and the engaging, eccentric character that he was. It was also impossible to avoid the feeling that collectively the entire sport bore a measure of responsibility for his death. "We all killed him," were my first words on hearing of his death; this is how I still feel today.

Charly Gaul
8 December 2005

Cycling has always regarded mountain climbers as a race apart, performing incredible feats in the Tour de France and Giro d'Italia, but slightly out of kilter with the rest of the world, and those contradictions were epitomised by the life of Charly Gaul, the original Angel of the Mountains, who has died aged 73.

"A sad, timid look on his face, marked with an unfathomable melancholy, he gives the impression that an evil deity has forced him into a cursed profession amidst powerful, implacable rivals," was one writer's view of Gaul. Cursed or not, cycling was probably better than working as a slaughterman in the abattoir at Bettembourg, as he did before turning professional at the age of 20.

One of only two Luxembourgeois ever to win the Tour, the "prince of the Grandy Duchy" was last seen at the reunion of former Tour de France winners, when the centenary race was presented in October 2002. He cut a curious figure – plump, shambling, confused – his eyes hidden behind thick spectacles above a wispy beard, a far cry from his heyday in the 1950s, when he won the Tour once and the Giro twice.

According to one of his great rivals, the Frenchman Raphael Geminiani, the diminutive Gaul was "a murderous climber, always the same sustained rhythm, a little machine with a slightly higher gear than the rest, turning his legs at a speed that would break your heart, tick tock, tick tock, tick tock". "Mozart on two wheels," was how the French writer Antoine Blondin saw him.

Gaul won 10 stages in the Tour and was twice crowned King of the Mountains, but he forged his reputation in just two days in the Tour and Giro, both in the foul weather which adds a nightmare quality to the toughness of climbing and descending mountains, but which seemed to suit him.

His victory in the 1956 Giro d'Italia was won in a single stage through the Dolomites, finishing up the eight-mile climb to the summit of Monte Bondone, when he leapt from 11th place to first place overall, ending the stage blue with cold, barely able to stand, wrapped up in a blanket. Many of the field simply retired. "This day surpassed anything seen before in terms of pain, suffering and difficulty," wrote the former Tour organiser Jacques Goddet.

A year later, Gaul lost the Giro by making the elementary mistake of stopping to urinate in a hedge. His rivals attacked, he never regained contact, and earned the nickname *Cheri-Pipi*, which roughly translates as "Dear little wee-wee". Afterwards, Gaul reminded Geminiani and his team-mate Louison Bobet that he was a former butcher. "I'll make sausagemeat of you." In the sporting sense, he managed just that at the end of the 1958 Tour, on a rainsoaked stage through the Chartreuse Massif.

Geminiani was expected to win the Tour, and Gaul was more than 16 minutes behind – then, as now, a margin considered insurmountable. The little man pointed out to Bobet where he would attack, and did so, racing alone over five mountain passes in rain that washed the painted finish line off the road, "a curtain of water, a deluge without an ark," as *l'Equipe*'s reporter described the conditions. Geminiani finished 14 minutes behind, and the Tour was in Gaul's pocket.

He took the Giro again in 1959, and could well have won the Tour more than just the once – in 1955 and 1961 he came third – had he not been handicapped by the 1950s system of national teams. Luxembourg was unable to field a squad strong enough to support him against France and Italy, and after his 1956 win he was shunted off into an "international" team with Danes, Dutchmen and Britons, including this country's Tour pioneer Brian Robinson.

Gaul retired from cycling in 1963, made an abortive comeback in 1965, then spent six months running a cafe near the main station in the centre of Luxembourg city, before slipping out of public view as effectively as he had slipped away from the pack in the Alps and Dolomites. For a quarter of a century, his whereabouts was a mystery, before he was discovered in the middle of an Ardennes forest, following a hermitic lifestyle in a small hut.

He was invited to the Tour's start in Luxembourg in 1989, and returned to the world. Five years later, cycling found a new angel, the Italian Marco Pantani, the only cyclist Gaul would recognise as a possible heir in terms of climbing skill, and a man with an equally troubled life, who died last year. By then, Gaul was following cycling with a fan's enthusiasm, supported by his third wife and their daughter, who survive him.

Charly Gaul, cyclist, born December 8 1932; died December 6 2005

Gaul's death was a reminder that in the early years of the 21st century there were few stars left from what I view as cycling's golden age – the two decades following the second world war. The knowledge that the men who had born witness to that era were rapidly disappearing was what inspired me to write Fallen Angel, *my biography of Fausto Coppi. I realised that it was now or never.*

Felix Levitan
3 April 2007

Felix Levitan, who has died aged 95, began his working life running errands at a Paris cycling magazine and rose to become an organiser of the Tour de France for 40 years. He laid the foundations for the event's rapid growth in the late 1980s and invented two integral parts of the Tour's make-up: the grand finale on the Champs-Élysées and the polka-dot "redpeas" jersey awarded to the race's King of the Mountains.

Levitan was born into a family of Jewish shoemakers in Paris's 15th arrondissement. His brother was an amateur cycle racer, and together they tried to hang on to the best professionals of the day as they trained in the Bois de Boulogne or the Longchamp racetrack, before, at the age of 16, he began working as a telephonist on *Le Pedale* magazine.

His first published piece was entitled *"Vouloir, c'est pouvoir"* – "if you want to, you can" – which he said was "not very good". But more accurately, he described the title as his personal credo. Subsequently Levitan worked for the newspapers *l'Intransigeant* – first thing in the morning – and, in the evening, its rival *l'Auto*.

Even though Levitan described himself as "appallingly irreligious", he did not escape the round-ups of Jews during the Nazi occupation of 1940–44, and he was interned in the Cherche-Midi military prison in Paris. His wife Genevieve managed to arrange his transfer to Dijon, without which he was certain he would have ended up in a concentration camp.

When the Paris press was restructured after the liberation, he was appointed head of sport at the *Parisien Libéré* newspaper, and when a joint team was appointed by the *Parisien* and its sister newspaper *l'Equipe* to run the first postwar Tour in 1947, Levitan found his true vocation. While *l'Equipe*'s head Jacques Goddet concentrated on the sporting side – devising the course and the entry criteria, tweaking the rules to liven up the event – Levitan made the race pay.

The Tour had originally been devised as a means of creating exclusive copy for the newspaper that ran it, but Levitan turned it into a commercial enterprise in its own right by expanding the garish cavalcade of advertising vehicles and making stage towns pay heavily for the privilege of hosting starts and finishes. The race's prologue time-trial was instigated in 1967 as a way of getting more cash out of the town hosting the *Grand Départ*. Most importantly, he understood the significance of selling television rights, which are now what pays the race's way.

Small and dapper, with a frosty smile, Levitan was formally appointed joint organiser in 1962, and he copied the dictatorial style of his and Goddet's predecessor, Henri Desgrange. The eight-times stage winner from Yorkshire Barry Hoban recalled one occasion on which he had won an intermediate prize: it was confirmed by the judge, only for Levitan to reverse the verdict. "You can't do that," expostulated the cyclist. "My dear Barry, I have every right," came the implacable reply.

In 1975 came Levitan's two masterstrokes. One was the decision to make the best mountain climber wear a red spotted jersey, the *maillot à pois*, or the "measled vest" as one English writer termed it: the jersey is now one of the race's three major prizes together with the yellow jersey of overall leader and the green jersey worn by the points leader. For that same year's Tour, Levitan devised the ambitious plan of running the closing stage through the heart of Paris, along the Rue de Rivoli and the banks of the Seine, with the finish on the Champs-Elysées. The French president Giscard d'Estaing welcomed the idea – and attended the finish – but his police chief restricted the race to a loop up and down the great boulevard, with the riders performing a U-turn before the Arc de

Triomphe. The circuit is now the most distinctive feature of the whole event.

Levitan did not stop there. He began a shortlived women's event alongside the men's Tour, and was the driving force behind the arrival of Colombian cyclists in the event in 1983. His dream was to export the Tour to America, with the race starting in New York and the riders flown across the Atlantic to complete the event in France.

His vision of cycling as a world sport, if not that of a tour of the world, was eventually realised, but an abortive event in the US, the Tour of the Americas, proved his undoing: he was sacked suddenly in 1987 on the grounds that he could not account for the money spent on the event, but later a court ruled the Tour's parent company had no case against him. The recipient of three grades of the *legion d'honneur*, he returned to the race on occasion, but he and his event were never truly reconciled.

Felix Levitan, cycle race organiser, born October 12 1911; died February 17 2007

Levitan was a character who had intrigued me since I had first begun reading about cycling in the late 1970s. I spoke to him while researching a book a year or two before his death. It was clear that he did not wish to speak about the event which had meant so much to him.

Harry Hall
9 November 2007

Cycling team mechanics are an unsung group, who work into the night repairing their charges' machines, then spend the day in the back of a team car waiting to change a wheel or fix a loose spoke. Harry Hall, who has died aged 78, was perhaps British cycling's most famous spannerman, and the man who heard the last words of the world champion Tom Simpson when Britain's greatest ever cyclist wobbled up Mont Ventoux to one of sport's most famous deaths in the 1967 Tour de France.

Simpson keeled over as his heart began to give out in the intense heat, and as the mechanic, Hall was first to him, along with the manager Alec Taylor. "Me straps Harry, me straps," Simpson said, referring to the leather cords with which his feet were attached to the pedals. Hall strapped him back into his bike and pushed him off. A hundred yards or so higher up, he fell again, and this time he did not get up.

The experience was traumatic for Hall, a punctilious mechanic who still had detailed records of all his charges' gear ratios and tyre changes when I visited him in 2000, and who still had the frame number he had taken off Simpson's bike that evening. He had also shot cine film footage of the champion earlier on the climb, for home movies that would be shown to his clubmates that winter.

Born in Manchester and originally a printer, Hall founded his cycle shop in Manchester in 1957 on Hyde Road in Gorton and subsequently moved to the city centre, in Cathedral Road and later Hanging Ditch, where it remains a Mecca for northern bike riders. The shop was famous for providing race service to Britain's biggest amateur events through the 1970s and 80s, assisted by a converted Mini van, a ubiquitous feature of British racing at the time.

The shop also sponsored some of Britain's strongest cyclists, including some who would go on to ride the Tour de France, such as Paul Sherwen and Graham Jones. The sponsorship deal was uniquely incentivised; cyclists were given a bike, for which they would have to pay at the end of the season. If, however, they managed to get photographs in a cycling magazine during the season of them and the bike, they would get credits to spend on kit at Hall's shop.

Hall had been a racing cyclist himself before acquiring the shop. He would convey himself, his mates and their bikes to races in a converted flatbed truck which was used in the week for delivering coal. From the late 1980s, he took a back seat in the shop to return to racing as a veteran, winning the British and world championships in his age category in 1989. He leaves his wife Jean and sons Graham and Robert.

Harry Hall was instrumental in the help he gave me when writing the biography of Tom Simpson – Put Me Back on My Bike – *and it was his testimony that lent strength to the idea that perhaps "Major Tom's" last words were not what they had been held to be for over 30 years. That visit to his "den" in 2000 to be shown Simpson's race number in its original plastic bag, and his notebook from the race was simply unforgettable. And like most British cyclists from the 1970s and 1980s, I always smile when thinking of the Mini.*

Laurent Fignon
2 September 2010

Laurent Fignon, who has died of cancer aged 50, won the Tour de France twice, but was also widely celebrated for losing it, in the narrowest defeat in Tour history. He was a charismatic cycling champion with trenchant views on his sport, the last Frenchman who seemed capable of living up to national expectations in the Tour, which he dominated with such insouciant ease in 1984 that the cycling magazine *Vélo* published his photograph that July along with a one-word caption: *l'Ogre.*

Nicknamed "the professor" after an abortive attempt at university studies, and with distinctive looks – long blond hair, thick-lensed spectacles and a John McEnroe-style headband – the Paris-born Fignon had the cycling world briefly at his feet after winning five stages in his Renault team's total of 10 (out of a possible 23), at the age of 23. His fellow Frenchman Bernard Hinault, who had dominated cycling for six years, finished more than 10 minutes behind, and had never looked Fignon's physical equal. On one occasion, Fignon was asked how he felt when

Hinault attacked. His answer was: "When I saw him going up the road, I had to laugh."

The dominance was brief, although the expectations survived a little longer. Fignon's place in cycling history is based on the celebrated role he played as the runner-up in the greatest Tour ever, in 1989. By then he had spent four years trying to regain his best level after two achilles tendon operations in 1985. His battle with the American Greg LeMond was a tense affair, with the two men swapping the lead for the three-week duration of the race until Fignon carved out a 50-second lead before the final stage, a time-trial into Paris.

Fignon felt his advantage was sufficient, but he was suffering from an abscess which made it virtually impossible for him to sit on his bike, and LeMond was using radical new aerodynamic handlebars. Fignon crossed the line on the Champs-Élysées and subsided in tears on the cobbles, having lost by just eight seconds after almost 88 hours of racing – still the narrowest margin in Tour history. It was a brutal defeat, a magnificent comeback for LeMond – who had come close to death in a shooting accident the previous year – and its impact turned the Tour into a truly global sports event.

Fignon won other major races – the Milan–San Remo Classic in 1988 and 1989, the Giro d'Italia in 1989 – and suffered a controversial defeat in the Giro in 1984, when the organisers pulled out all the stops to ensure a home victory. But his impact extended beyond his victories and his great defeat. In 1985, when Renault pulled out of sponsorship, he and his manager, Cyrille Guimard, came up with a novel system of managing team finances. Previously, teams had tended to belong to the sponsor, and were vulnerable when a backer lost interest. Instead, Guimard and Fignon set up their own company to run the team and own its assets, selling advertising space on the team's jerseys and cars to a main sponsor. Most professional cycling teams are run in this way today.

He was also one of few cyclists to reinvest their winnings in their sport. After retirement in 1993, he set up a promotions company to run events for cycle tourists, and he bought the second-biggest race in French cycling, the Paris-Nice "race to the sun", in 2000. As an organiser, he was unable to compete with the Amaury Sport Organisation, which has a virtual monopoly on major races in France, including the Tour, and he eventually sold Paris-Nice to them in 2002.

Subsequently he scaled down his promotional ventures and put his energy into developing a training centre in the Pyrenees. He also published his memoirs, *Nous Etions Jeunes et Insouciants* (2009), which I translated into English this summer under the title *We Were Young and Carefree*. The book was painfully honest about his attempts to get back to full fitness after his operations, spoke mercilessly about former rivals and described an epic drinking session with Hinault and an occasion on which Fignon lied to his manager to enable a team-mate to use his hotel room for a romantic assignation with "an unofficial Miss France".

Fignon's main premise was that cycling was "a living, breathing art", a world that created "complete men rather than just sportsmen", and that it had been robbed of much of its magic by the demands of sponsors and the widespread use of the blood-boosting drug erythropoietin, which he contrasted with his own amateurish use of cortisone and amphetamine.

He worked as a television commentator on the 2009 and 2010 Tours, in spite of his illness – the harsh croak of his voice will remain my enduring memory of this year's race – and in one of his last interviews, in January, he was typically forthright about his health: "I don't want to die at 50, but if there is no cure, what can I do? I'm not afraid of dying. I just don't want it to happen."

Fignon's death was another I felt deeply. As with Pantani, there had been several memorable interviews during his racing career and he had been a joy to watch racing; I had also followed his second Tour win while living and racing in France in 1984, and I had been impressed by his attempt to reinvest in cycling after he stopped racing. He would have made a great Tour de France organiser. Knowing that he would be unlikely to survive his cancer, I was determined to see his autobiography translated into English and I am proud we managed it.

INDEX